All the b

Business Applications of Repertory Grid

Business Applications of Repertory Grid

Valerie Stewart
Andrew Stewart
with Nickie Fonda

McGRAW-HILL Book Company (UK) Limited

London · New York · St Louis · San Francisco · Auckland · Bogotá · Guatemala
Hamburg · Johannesburg · Lisbon · Madrid · Mexico · Montreal · New Delhi
Panama · Paris · San Juan · São Paulo · Singapore · Sydney · Tokyo · Toronto

Published by
McGRAW-HILL BOOK COMPANY (UK) LIMITED
MAIDENHEAD · BERKSHIRE · ENGLAND

British Library Cataloguing in Publication Data

Stewart, Valerie
    Business Applications of Repertory Grid
    1. Repertory grid technique
    I. Title   II. Stewart, Andrew
    III. Fonda, Nickie
    155.2   BF698.8.R38   80–41916

    ISBN 0–07–084549–2

1234 MB8321

Typeset by STYLESET LIMITED · Salisbury · Wiltshire

Printed and bound in Great Britain by
Mansell (Bookbinders) Ltd., Witham, Essex

Contents

Preface

This is a book about a technique called Repertory Grid. Grid technique was devised and nurtured by academic psychologists, but in recent years there has been an enormous upsurge of interest in Grid on the part of industrial users. At its simplest, Grid provides a way of doing research into problems — almost *any* problems — in a more precise, less biased, way than any other research method. More subtle uses of Grid have made it possible to evaluate training, facilitate negotiations, resolve conflicts, assemble teams, coach and counsel people with problems. The speed at which the news about Grid has got around British industry is astonishing; demand for seminars and articles on the subject grows apace. Yet hitherto there has been no coordinated account of the use of Grid written for the industrial user. This book attempts to fill the gap.

Anyone who earns his living in whole or part by asking questions is a potential user of this book. Grid can help you if you are engaged in market research, quality control, design, attitude surveys, training-needs analysis, negotiation, counselling, team building and a host of other applications. If you have no experience of the Grid technique, then we suggest you begin with the first part of the book, which is a teach-yourself guide to becoming a Grid practitioner. If you follow the chapters and examples you should become a fairly proficient interviewer and able to use much of the technique, though it would still be useful to try to get some live practice in with a more experienced person. If you are already skilled in Grid technique you may want to pass straight to the second part of the book, which deals with individual applications of Grid technique. In the second part there are chapters on many industrial subjects; each chapter is meant to stand in its own right, which means there is a certain amount of duplication across chapters. We hope this does not annoy you too much; it seems easier on most readers than cross-referencing to other chapters. And if you are partly skilled in Grid technique you may want to browse through the first part to brush up your technique before going on to the second part. The sequence of chapters, and the exercises, is useful in classroom teaching of Grid if you deal with students.

A great many people have contributed to the ideas in this book. Countless seminars and discussion groups, many clients with whom we worked on various assignments, fellow practitioners, sceptics — all have taught us something. Special mention must be given, however, to Barry Peel and Marjorie Knight, of the Imperial Group, who conducted a large and difficult Grid study and then were kind enough to reflect over it in depth for us; and to Peter Bouch of the British Printing Corporation, and Dick Cooper of Fisons, who as well as letting us work with them on Grid were generous enough to give their time to look over the manuscript. Needless to say, responsibility for errors and omissions remains with us.

A final word to the reader. Grid is a developing technique. We are constantly hearing about new applications of Grid, or new developments. It is not a static body of custom and practice, but a growing one. We hope that the reader who finds this book useful will go on to develop his or her own new applications, and thereby help bring a new standard of excellence to research and performance improvement in industry.

Valerie Stewart
Andrew Stewart

Part One
Teach Yourself Repertory Grid Technique

1. Finding out about people

Once there was a psychologist called George Kelly. In his job — he was a clinician — he had to get to know many people, classify them, get to understand their points of view, help them understand themselves better. He was worried that the science of psychology as it had then developed was standing in the way of his meeting these objectives. In particular, he had three problems, which are discussed below.

Today's researchers in industry often share Kelly's problems. In fields as diverse as personnel and quality control, marketing and safety, there are people who need to do research — who need to get to know other people, to classify them, to understand their points of view, to help them understand themselves better. And often the research methods available to industry stand in the way of meeting these objectives. So let us begin by looking at Kelly's problems, as he saw them from his clinician's office in the American 1930s, and see how much they have in common with the problems of today's industrial researcher. Then we can see how easily the tool Kelly invented to overcome these problems — the Repertory Grid — can be transferred to industrial use.

1.1 Kelly's problems

The numbers game

In the 1930s, psychology was a very young science and many of its practitioners wanted it to have the respectability and the methodology of the physical sciences. They wanted to be able to utter laws about human behaviour — *if A*, *then B* — with the same degree of confidence that a physicist, engineer or chemist can. The textbooks and research papers of the time bear bulky testimony to the fact that, for many psychologists, this search was a life's work. And they did manage to produce some 'laws' about human behaviour, usually in the form of correlational studies showing, for example, that there is a link between cigarette smoking and extraversion, there is a link between birth order and verbal intelligence, there is a link between body type and mental illness . . . , the only problem being that in order to get a significant correlation you may have to study hundreds or thousands of people. For example, over 200 000 people you may find a correlation of 0.3 between cigarette smoking and extraversion, and on a population so large a correlation of this size is statistically significant. But Kelly was worried that although this kind of endeavour might satisfy the psychologists' need for law and order in human affairs, the 'laws' thus established did not help him very much when a chubby person rolled into his office, lit up a cigarette, announced that he was an only child and would like to talk about his problems. Studies of masses of people, even if they lead to laws which hold good for masses of people, do not allow one to make predictions about people taken singly.

Kelly wanted a way of making predictions in a rigorous way about individual people.

He wanted to be able to measure the clinical problems his patients came with, to use these measurements in his therapeutic approach, and to re-measure after therapy; for what you cannot measure, you cannot control.

And of course the researcher in industry is often faced with exactly the same problem — how to get insights and make predictions, with some degree of precision, about people taken singly or in small groups. If you have ever asked yourself questions such as:

'How come Len spots sales opportunities when no-one else seems to?'

or 'I wonder if that training course did Joe any good?'

or 'I wonder if Sally and Jim will get on together if I put them on the Special Projects team?'

or 'What sort of advertising campaign does he want, for Heaven's sake? All he ever does is say No.'

then you share Kelly's problem, his need to understand and map the thought processes of individual people.

Observer bias

Diagnosticians of all kinds — if they are honest with themselves — nurse a secret worry that they might contribute to what is diagnosed. For example, if you had had a psychiatric problem in the 1930s, and money to support it, you might have shopped around between therapists to see what they said about your malady. Taking it to a Freudian therapist, you would likely have been told that it was to do with potty training, Oedipal jealousy or repressed sexual needs. Taking the same problem to a Jungian therapist, it would be interpreted in terms of religious conflicts and identity crises. An Adlerian therapist would probably interpret it in terms of birth order in the family and frustrated will to power. And if you decided to choose one of the newly emerging schools of behaviour therapy they would not concern themselves with the source of the problem at all, but would probably give you electric shocks until you stopped showing the symptoms.

Psychologists have been able to name this problem for a long time. They call it 'observer bias'. It creeps in every time we perceive something. Consciously or unconsciously our backgrounds, history and experience give us a set of expectations about the world so that we recognize familiar things and bend less familiar ones until they resemble what we already know. Pose a business problem to a committee of experts, and the marketing expert will see it as a marketing problem, the production expert as a production problem, the planning man as a planning problem, the advertising man as an advertising problem. Observer bias is a serious obstacle to understanding someone else's point of view, and it is not something that can be overcome with self-discipline and a tightening of resolve. Observer bias can have serious consequences, too; the most notable example may be that of the school-teacher whose class was randomly split into two groups. The teacher was told that all the children had been tested and that Group A children were brighter than the

Group B children (though no such difference existed in fact). She taught the class for a term; and then the children were tested at the end of term the Group A children were indeed brighter than the Group B.

Anybody who makes a living trying to intepret problems has to guard against observer bias. But though psychologists and others were fairly quick to recognize and name the phenomenon, they were less quickly able to offer a solution. Kelly's technique — Repertory Grid — enables one to interview someone in detail, extracting a good deal of information about him from the superficial to the clinically diagnostic, and to do this in such a way that the input from the observer is reduced to zero.

Many problems in industry are as susceptible to observer bias. If you ever find yourself wearing any of the following 'hats', then a knowledge of Repertory Grid will help you become a better and more objective diagnostician:

Counsellor
Accident Investigator
Company Doctor (in either sense of the term)
Trainer
Quality Controller
Head Hunter
Peacemaker
Market Researcher

The role of the expert

Another of Kelly's worries was the extent to which laymen and patients in the clinical setting depended upon the word of an expert to tell them what their problems were. The popular image of the distant, beard-stroking professor, sitting out of view of his patient and muttering authoritatively in a Viennese accent from time to time, is not so far from the truth; most of today's clinical psychologists can remember at least one member of the older generation who acted thus without self-parody. Kelly took the view that this 'expertise' was somewhat over-rated. *If you want to know what is wrong with someone, ask him . . . he probably knows.* The therapist serves a useful purpose in forcing the patient to confont problems he would rather avoid, and in guiding the examination from the superficial to the deep; but, said Kelly, most people are sufficiently adult and intelligent to know what their problems are and to take responsibility, to a great extent, for their solution.

Repertory Grid technique allows the interviewer to get a mental map of how the interviewee views the world, and to write this map with the minimum of observer bias. Kelly's practice is then *not* to have this map 'interpreted' by an expert, who judges where the problems and the stresses are; rather Kelly's approach is to discuss the map with the interviewee, to talk about things that perhaps the interviewee had not faced about himself before, to discuss with the interviewee the survival value of that particular map as a means of navigating around his life-space — but all the while assuming that the interviewee can sort out most of the solutions for himself once he has a clear grip on the problem.

The relevance of this for people working in industry? Many managers are fed up with experts offering them ready-made solutions; while at the same time wise commentators from Father Brown to Professor Revans have said that for most people: 'It isn't that they can't see the solution, it's that they can't see the problem.' Help a manager to see his problems more clearly, and the chances are that he will not need an expert to help him arrive at a solution. Repertory Grid will help to draw out and make explicit the expertise that every manager has, and help lay out his problems in such a way that solutions may become more obvious. If your interest in using the Grid lies in applications such as counselling, team building or training-needs analysis, you should bear in mind that the Grid approach is to give people responsibility for who and how they are, while allowing you to hold up to them a mirror that can reflect their problems gently or relentlessly.

So, we have three important problems — the need to look with precision at individual people, the need to avoid observer bias and the need to acknowledge that people can take responsibility for their own development and do not need experts to put them back on the rails again. All these problems confronted Kelly in his role as a clinical psychologist, and they confront with equal force anyone who wishes to do research in industry or other organizations. We promise that Kelly's Repertory Grid technique will be helpful in solving these problems; but before commencing the series of self-administered lessons that will help you become proficient in Grid technique, we would first like to outline the theoretical underpinnings that Kelly was relying on when he invented Grid. You can skip this bit if you like, and return to it later; there is a strong argument for saying that a practical book like this should contain the minimum of theory. However, Grid technique is developing so rapidly that you may well find yourself innovating, and it is as well to have a little knowledge of the theory of flight before you start to design aircraft.

1.2 Personal Construct Theory — or why people get that way

Personality differences have fascinated scientists and poets, playwrights and politicians for years. Psychologists have set themselves the task of explaining personality differences, instead of just tolerating them like other people have to do. The psychological literature is full of attempts to classify personality (extravert — introvert, conservative — radical, cerebral — emotional, group-dependent — solitary, etc.) and to explain how differences arose (heredity? environment? date of birth? balance of body humours?). Kelly's attempt to explain how people get to be the people they are relies on the basic assumption that *Man is a Scientist*.

Think of two-month-old Baby Jane. When Jane screamed and cried, her mother dipped a dummy in rose-hip syrup, popped it into Jane's mouth, and cuddled her. One thing that any parent knows about small infants is that they learn very quickly; so very soon Baby Jane will learn to expect rose-hip syrup and a cuddle when she cries, and not long after that she realizes that if she fancies a cuddle and some rose-hip syrup the way to make it happen is to bawl a lot. Little Baby Jane is a scientist. She is learning a series of propositions, of laws about the world: *if A, then B*. Baby

Susan in the next house may get quite different treatment; she could get her legs smacked when she cries, in which case she learns that crying is followed by pain, and pain by crying, and crying by smacking; and the spiral of fear, apathy and helplessness remembered by so many people with unhappy childhoods is established in her view of the world.

Human infants (maybe those of some other species as well) are born hungry for symbolic learning. The speed at which they lap up and assimilate new information makes many an older person feel envious. Kelly stresses the active nature of this experience — hypotheses are developed, tested, modified or discarded, and the child gradually builds up a network of hypotheses (*if A, then B*) based on his own unique experience of the world.

If Kelly's theory had stopped there you might be forgiven for saying 'So what? All he's done is to provide some fancy names for the fact that people learn from experience, and made it sound a little more active than some other commentators.' Kelly goes a lot further, however. He said that not only does one's network of hypotheses reflect one's experience of the world; the hypotheses also come to influence and condition it. To take a simple example; Fred goes on a course about the contribution proper marketing can make to the success of a company. Fred is now more likely to interpret issues in terms of their marketing content. He may see some issues as marketing issues where other people would not. He might be slower in seeing other kinds of problems. The expectations he has about the world conditions what he sees in it.

Think of the team member who believes he is unpopular and therefore never seems to notice friendly gestures but is quick to spot when he is being rejected.

Think of the manager who believes that women workers experience a higher sickness rate, and so notices every time his secretary is away ill but never notices when the boy from the post room is off.

Think of how expectations influence perceptions in films such as *One Flew Over the Cuckoo's Nest*.

The system of hypotheses which we begin evolving at birth and which continue to grow until death is not like a filing cabinet. Kelly says it is more like a pair of spectacles, through which you get information, but which also condition what you see and how you see it. Kelly had a good name for describing the system — he called it a 'construct system', because the word 'construct' carries with it both the sense of having been constructed or developed from experience, and also the sense of being that through which we construe — or see and interpret — the world. Thus if you can understand someone's construct system you can not only understand his history, but you can also make some predictions about how he is likely to behave in a given situation because you know something about what that situation is likely to mean to him.

Kelly invented Repertory Grid technique as a way of getting people to exhibit to him their construct systems.

Kelly's theory of personality, which he evolved from the basic notion of man-as-scientist, is quite complicated and we shall not describe all of it here. The researcher in industry may find the following points useful:

1. The degree of agreement between the construct systems of two people is a measure of the extent to which they are like each other, and the extent to which they are likely to understand each other without effort.
2. The degree to which one person can understand or mimic the construct system of another is a measure of the extent to which he understands that other person — in other words a measure of the degree to which they can negotiate sensibly, be friends, predict what the other would do, etc.
3. Construct systems change over time to assimilate new information. Of course, the construct system is predisposed to interpret new information as familiar information, but there will always be a time when the amount or significance of the new information requires a change in the construct system. People vary a great deal in the extent to which their construct systems are open to new information; someone with an over-flexible construct system would probably be described as over-reactive, because he changes his views too quickly for the importance of the information; whereas someone with an over-rigid construct system would probably be described by his associates as a stereotyped thinker or one who would not see danger when it stares him in the face.
4. Construct systems have survival value for their owners. It is sometimes difficult, when one looks at the map of someone's construct system provided by the Repertory Grid technique, to understand how anybody can bear to have that network of perceptions about the world, and perhaps if he has come for therapy or counselling he feels that way too. But it is important to remember that the construct system has got him where he is today in one piece, without too many bruises, that the apparent contradictions or gaps have actually served a purpose in their time, and you should not be too quick to strip them away because you yourself do not find them terribly pretty.

You could learn Repertory Grid technique without bothering too much with Personal Construct Theory. But most serious practitioners of Grid find that PCT (as it is often abbreviated) is helpful in planning and understanding one's task and in working out what to do in a tight corner. The key points of PCT to remember are:

1. Perceptions influence expectations, and expectations influence perceptions.
2. The medium through which this happens is known as the construct system.
3. Construct systems are unique to the individual and develop throughout life.

We began this account by telling of George Kelly in his office in the 1930s in America, trying to get a theoretical basis and a practical technique for understanding people in a more rigorous fashion. What happened to bridge the gap between that position and the many places in industry where Grid technique is making a contribution?

Kelly was a modest man, and busy. He did not write up his work for a long time, and it was 1955 before his two-volume *Theory of Personal Constructs* was published. For some reason this seems to have attracted more attention in the UK and Europe than in the US, and groups of clinicians specializing in the use and development of Kelly's technique built up – names like Don Bannister, Fay Fransella, Anthony Ryle, Pat Slater, have become well known, and you will see some of their work listed in the Bibliography. Grid technique seems to have been destined to remain in the clinical field; a valuable tool, not particularly difficult to use, often life-enhancing for the therapist and intellectually compelling for the patient, and because of its fascination making its adherents seem exclusive and group-ish. The heavy clinical usage means that most of the books on Grid discuss clinical applications almost exclusively, and there is very little else in book form about its use in industry.

You cannot keep a good idea down, however; the use of Grid in industry seems to have started at several places at roughly the same time, as behavioural scientists began to make a contribution to industrial performance. First to use Grid in industry, we believe, were the market-research experts. Here the attraction was Grid's lack of observer bias; the technique of construct elicitation, which is central to the Grid process, can be used to tell you how the consumer views your products, and your competitors' products, without the distortion caused by intimate and specialized knowledge of the product. You may have worked for months developing Wizzo washing powder, and now you want to know how it compares with Blotto, the competition's offering. Chances are that you are so wrapped up in Wizzo that you find it difficult to view objectively. Grid will help you see Wizzo as the consumer sees it, without your prejudicing the outcome.

Two applications of Grid in the personnel area come next in the chronology as we have been able to uncover it. The increased interest in diagnosing training needs and evaluating training – an interest owing something to the Training Boards and something to cost-consciousness – led several people to conclude that Grid could help here. The special appeal of Grid in this case is the opportunity it gives to map someone's construct system in detail (training-needs analysis) and to measure the later changes (evaluation). Another use of Grid in personnel work began with our own efforts in the field of identifying management potential. We used part of the Grid technique to interview managers about their perceptions of effective and ineffective behaviour at work, so as to draw up a picture of the total company view of effectiveness. This then served as a basis for strategic planning, with the question: 'Is this the picture of effectiveness that will have maximum survival value for the next n years?'

Then came a group of applications of Grid based on its ability to force people to put verbal labels onto pre-verbal concepts arose. In quality control and inspection, for example, Grid helps to discover whether Nellie sees the same faults as Sarah, and sees them in the same way; will help discover what exactly Fred, the old gaffer who can always tell when the mix is going wrong even before the instruments show it, is perceiving in the atmosphere, so that we can get his replacement trained. Grid has also been used to help people specify more closely what they mean by concepts which they express in the abstract, but want interpreted in the concrete (e.g., helping a designer get a specification from his client, helping to arrive at a man-specification).

Applications have also centred around Grid's ability to elicit people's perceptions in a value-free and incremental fashion. Applications in the field of team building, for instance, get people to share constructs about common problems.

Applications are still growing. This book will be out of date in parts by the time it gets to the printer. The reader may well find he is using Grid in a new way or on a different kind of problem. Networks of Grid users have grown up as more and more people in industry see what a useful technique it is to learn.

It is not an easy technique to learn, however, although if you saw a Grid interview or received one you might not believe this. The reason is that Grid technique can be used in various different modes, and each mode requires slightly different treatment. If you heard one piece played on the organ you might not realize what a complex performance it is, because you would now know about all the possible choices of stops, combinations, manuals, etc., which the organist was choosing between. Hear two or three and you realize the many ways this instrument can be used. It is exactly the same with Grid; and any one example probably looks simple, but you need to see the full range of examples to appreciate the complexity of choice. So this book is set out to teach you not how to play just one tune, but to play the whole repertoire (and perhaps compose some of your own). Some chapters contain a series of exercises that are stepping-stones on the way to full proficiency. The exercises are useful in themselves and will give you some simple applications of Grid to use from the start. Follow the whole book through, and try to see an experienced Grid interviewer in action, and you will find that whatever your research project, it will benefit from your knowledge of Kelly's Repertory Grid.

2. Construct elicitation

The next few chapters are practical. If you follow the instructions you will learn Repertory Grid technique and be in a position to do the kind of investigations mentioned in the first chapter and covered in detail in the last section of this book. If you just read the chapters without trying the exercises we cannot guarantee anything like such proficiency.

For the following exercises you will need a dozen or so 3 x 5 inch cards, or pieces of stout paper, and some ordinary writing paper on which to make records. You may also need the services of a friend or colleague.

Begin by taking three cards. Write on one the word CAR. Write on the next the word TRAIN. Write on the third the word DONKEY. Now put the cards on the table or desk and regard them closely. Can you think of one way in which two of the objects represented by these cards are like each other and different from the third? Can you think of something that two of them have in common where the third has something different? Write down your answer in the form of two phrases separated by a hyphen, for example:

have wheels — have legs
hard — furry

Work on these three notions for a while, producing as many of these bipolar distinctions as you can. You may find that you can put different pairs together as different distinctions come to mind. This is quite legitimate. You may also find it helpful to move the cards about in front of you to see if different positions trigger new thoughts.

When we asked Joe to produce distinctions like these about CAR, TRAIN and DONKEY he came up with the following:

have wheels — have legs
hard — furry
carry few passengers — carry many passengers
go on rails — go where they please
useful end product — polluting end product
organic fuel — inorganic fuel
born — made
fast — slow
owned personally — owned by an organization
covered — open to the elements
appeal to children — no appeal to children

What you have just experienced is the fundamental process underlying Repertory Grid work — the process known as construct elicitation. You started off with a relatively simple task, just to get used to the mechanics of the process — the business of taking three cards and asking in what way two of them are similar and different from the third. Now try something that may be a little more meaningful. Take another three cards and write on them the names of your mother, yourself and your boss. Now spend some time taking these three cards in various combinations, asking yourself: 'In what way are two of these people alike and different from the third?' or 'Is there something that two of these people have in common that they do not share with the third?' Again write down your distinctions in the bipolar form, as before.

When we asked Betty to produce distinctions like these about her MOTHER, BETTY and her BOSS, she came up with the following:

warm — cold
happy — unhappy
still hoping — given up
male — female
likes music — tone-deaf
votes Conservative — votes Labour
a graduate — not a graduate

We guess that your list about CAR, TRAIN and DONKEY was probably quite like Joe's list, but your list about MOTHER, SELF and BOSS would probably be quite different from Betty's list.

Next time, try something a little different. Think about the present job you are doing, and write down on the first card a brief description of the activity you regard as being amongst the most important in your job. The more specific you can make it, the better. On the second card, write down a brief description of an activity which you find very demanding on your skills. And on the third card, write down a brief description of an activity which you regard as a fairly routine kind of task. Now go through the triadic comparisons performance again, asking yourself the question: 'In what way can I say that two of these activities are like each other and different from the third?' You may find it helpful to think of the activities in terms of the demands they make on your skills.

We asked John, a computer salesman, to do this task for us. He named as a very important activity WRITING PROPOSALS. The activity which made many demands on his skills was COLD CANVASSING. And the routine activity was WEEKLY MEETINGS. The bipolar distinctions he produced were:

I enjoy — I do not enjoy
predictable outcome — unpredictable outcome
affects my commission — no effect on my commission
selling myself — selling the products
alone — with my colleagues
I control — other people control

Time for some definitions. The words that were written on the cards are called *elements*. They define the kind of interview you have, by selecting the subject matter. Chapters on the selection of elements follow later in the book. The bipolar distinctions are called *constructs*. They represent the dimensions the interviewee uses when he is thinking about the elements. The process of getting constructs from elements by asking the interviewee to put two of them together and separate them from the third is called *construct elicitation*.

The claims for Grid's being a technique free from observer bias can be most clearly seen if you think about the interview with John, the computer salesman. All the material in that interview came out of John's head — he wrote down the activities as he saw them, and he *construed* them to produce the bipolar constructs. The interviewer, had he gone on longer and with more elements, would have learned a great deal about John's job and his attitude towards it, without once suggesting the content of any of John's answers or leading him in any direction other than the broad one defined by the purpose of the interview.

The claims for Grid's attention to the individual are hinted at if you compare different people's constructs about the same elements. When Dora construed CAR, TRAIN and DONKEY she produced these constructs:

washable — not washable
cuddly — harsh
for boys — for both sexes
browns and greys — bright colours

but then Dora is a children's nurse and thought of them immediately as varieties of toys, whereas most people think of them as methods of transport. We guess that your constructs about MOTHER, SELF and BOSS are different from Betty's in a way that throws some light on why you are you and not Betty. John's colleague, another computer salesman, gave as his elements 1, 2 and 3 the activities: CLOSING THE SALE, FORMAL LOSS PROCEDURE and WRITING PROPOSALS, and his constructs about those three were:

making money — losing money
bad for my image — good for my image
competition involved — competition knocked out by then
on the alert — I have to force myself
fighting — recording the fight

but then he is a bit 'sharper' than John, a bit faster on his feet, perhaps, but less thoughtful, less deep.

Because the interviewer plays no part in suggesting the actual nature of the constructs, the constructs are a very personal reflection of how the interviewee sees the world, and individual differences in style and personality come quickly to the front. You can illustrate this for yourself by trying the MOTHER, SELF and BOSS combination with some good friends — but they must be good friends and you should respect their wishes if they say they do not want to proceed. The corollary to there being little or no interviewer suggestion, combined with the fact that the construct-elicitation procedure is quite searching and precise, gives the result that a Grid interview is very difficult to fake – there is nowhere to hide. People who are uncomfortable or uncooperative in Grid interviews have very little opportunity to bluster. We will return to this subject later, but bear it in mind for the moment.

Construct elicitation is the first stage in a Grid interview. Some interviews do not need to go much further than construct elicitation, others go a lot further. You will learn the decision rules later. For the sake of simplicity we started you off with only three elements; in practice the interview uses more than three – 8, 9, 12 or even 24 – taking them three at a time in combinations. Obviously this gives many more constructs the opportunity of appearing, and gives variety to both parties.

Let us eavesdrop on the interview between Pat, an internal consultant in a large organization, and the interviewer who is getting Pat's constructs about the various in-house clients Pat has in order to check Pat's progress in her new job. The interviewer has nine names on the cards – all the first names of Pat's clients.

INTERVIEWER   Now, Pat, I want to ask you some questions about these clients of yours – to get you to tell me how you feel about them. Let's take the cards TED, TONY and JOHN. Can you look at those three people and tell me which two of them are most like each other, and why?

PAT   Ted and Tony are most alike, I'd say.

INTERVIEWER   On what basis are they alike?

PAT   They're both career specialists, they're doing the job they were trained for.

INTERVIEWER   And does that apply to John as well?

PAT   No. John started out doing something else and got into his line by accident.

INTERVIEWER   So we can say that Ted and Tony are both career specialists, whereas John got into his career by accident. I'll write that down. Can you tell me anything else that two of them have got in common that they don't share with the third?

PAT   Ted and Tony tend to be a bit self-protective, John's more of a buccaneer.

INTERVIEWER   Good. This is the form that the interview is going to take – I'm going to give you these people in various combinations of three, and I want you to tell me one or more ways in which you can put two of them together so that they are like each other and different from the third. OK?

PAT   Fine.

INTERVIEWER   Right, let's take the next three. We've got Shirley and Alan and Frances – can you put two of them together so that they are like each other in some way and different from the third?

PAT   Well, there's the obvious one, that two of them are women and the third is a man – I guess you wanted something a bit deeper than that, did you?

INTERVIEWER   If you can manage it, yes please.

PAT   Alan and Frances are both likely to be drawn by the latest fad – somebody's told them that all their problems can be solved by going over to flexitime, or installing some new piece of equipment, and they don't really think it through before getting me in. With Shirley, you know that you won't get called in unless she's done some thinking about the problem herself.

INTERVIEWER   So if we were to summarize the similarity and difference what would we say?

PAT   We'd say that Alan and Frances are both swayed by fads, but Shirley knows what she wants. Alan and Frances are impulse buyers, Shirley has a shopping list.

INTERVIEWER   Thank you. Now let's look at the last three in the same way — Douglas, Bob and Louise. Can you do the same thing — tell me something that two of them have in common that the third one doesn't? Move the cards around if it helps.

PAT   That's more difficult — I don't know them as well as I do the others. Well, Douglas and Bob are both much more experienced than Louise — she's very new, they've both got twenty years or more. They would both say of themselves that they've come up the hard way, whereas Louise is a graduate entrant and maybe has her path made smooth for her.

INTERVIEWER   Can you point to any consequences this difference has, in the way they behave with you?

PAT   Yes, I think both Douglas and Bob tend to be trimmers, they are aware of the political realities — too aware, they start to compromise too early in the game, in my opinion. Louise is still at the stage where she thinks that rational argument will solve any problem and that people will do what's right even if it costs them face.

INTERVIEWER   I see. Let's take another three now — Ted and Shirley and Douglas. Can you put two of them together so that they are like each other and different from the third?

PAT   The male — female one again, of course — sorry, I have to say it to get it out of the way —

INTERVIEWER   That's all right.

PAT   There's an interesting one here, to do with whether they're still growing — let me see if I can get it straight. Is it all right to pair them one way and then a different way?

INTERVIEWER   Yes, that's splendid.

PAT   Well, if you look at them at work, Shirley is the odd one out because at work she is still growing and developing, while the other two have given up and settled into a little niche. But if you look at them outside work, in their personal life, it's Douglas who's still growing because he's taking up all sorts of new hobbies — painting, furniture restoring — and doing them seriously, whereas the other two have settled into a domestic rut.

INTERVIEWER   Thank you. That's very interesting. Can we try with the next three please?

etc., etc.

You might find it useful to go back over the record of that interview and write down the constructs as you think the interviewer recorded them.

What he actually had looked like this:

1 2 3	career specialists	— got into line by accident
1 2 3	self-protective	— buccaneer
4 5 6	woman	— man
4 5 6	swayed by fads ↓	— knows what wants ↓
	(impulse buyers)	— (have shopping list)
7 8 9	more than 20 years' experience	— very new
7 8 9	would say of self 'come up the hard way'	— had path made smooth (graduate entrant)
7 8 9	trimmers, aware of political realities (too much, start to compromise too early)	— think rational argument will solve any problem — people do right even if costs face
1 4 7	(at work) stopped growing	— (at work) still growing & developing
1 4 7	(outside work) stopped growing	— (outside work) still growing & developing

On the far left of the record are three numbers — beginning with 1 2 3. These represent the element cards used in that triad — TED is 1, TONY is 2, JOHN is 3, and so on up to LOUISE, who was card 9. The interviewer writes down the numbers of the three cards he has used, and then underlines the numbers of the two that were paired — in the first triad Pat put Ted and Tony together, so the interviewer underlined 1 and 2. Then the interviewer wrote down the descriptor of the *pair* on the left of the hyphen, and the descriptor of the singleton element on the right. This tells him all he needs to know about how this construct was derived from these three elements, should he want to go back and do further work on it later.

The way one records Grid interview data is, in fact, another great advantage of the technique. The record is extremely full — it is possible to reconstruct all the substantive points that occurred in the interview by looking at the record. If, later in our interview, the interviewer wants to question Pat about the construct *swayed by fads — knows what wants* and Pat cannot remember where it came from, the interviewer can go back to the records, check, and then say: 'You were looking at Shirley, Alan and Frances (laying the cards down again) and you put Alan and Frances together saying that they were easily swayed by fads, whereas you said that Shirley usually knew what she wanted.' It is rare for this procedure to fail to trigger the interviewee's memory. Another advantage of this full, but structured, recording system is that several Grid interviewers can work on a problem and everyone can understand everyone else's interview records without the need for long meetings where they explain, reconstruct and undoubtedly distort what went on in their various interviews. Anyone who has done research under pressure of time and resources will guess what a boon it is to be able to have interviewers send in their record sheets as soon as they are completed, able to be worked on immediately without need for further clarification.

Two more points need to be made about constructs before you move to the exercises and examples that conclude this chapter. The first is in response to the question: 'Why is a construct bipolar? Surely one word would do, instead of at least two?'

Kelly discusses this objection in his exposition of Personal Construct Theory. He says that you can only understand what I mean by 'good' if you also understand something of what I mean by 'bad'. Light is nonsense without shade; blunt is nonsense without sharp; soft is nonsense without hard. An interesting philosophical point, you may think, but of little relevance to industry. But suppose you are doing an appraisal interview with a subordinate, and he describes his present job as 'quite comfortable'. If, for him, the opposite of *comfortable* is *uncomfortable* he is telling you one thing; but if for him the opposite of *comfortable* is *challenging* he is telling you something else. Contrast the pairs of statements *he is sharp – he is honest* and *he is sharp – he is slow-witted*. It is a great discipline to have to put words into their context, a great preventer of sloppy thinking. The triadic-comparisons procedure, by asking for both a similarity and a difference, gets out both end of each construct, and as a result the data are much tighter, crisper, easier to understand and contain less dissimulation.

The second point concerns the format of the constructs themselves. A construct is not necessarily composed of a phrase and its semantic opposite; it is a contrast, but not a simple dictionary opposite. It is important to bear this in mind when interviewing, because some interviewees will guess that only dictionary opposites are acceptable to you. But you should strive to get both ends of the construct equally clear, and this usually means avoiding attaching a simple negative to the opposite pole. If you take a word such as *critical*, applied to people, there are various ways of describing its opposite: *uncritical, not critical* or (say) *accepting*. Actually, people who study these things for a living have found that there is significantly less 'meaning' or 'weight' behind modified forms such as *uncritical* or *not critical* than there is behind the unmodified, unprefixed word like *critical* or *accepting*. For this reason the interviewer should try to get a construct that consists of pairs of descriptors in their own right rather than one descriptor and its negation. You will find there are other good reasons for adhering to this practice, when we come to examine techniques such as laddering.

2.1 Practical uses of construct elicitation

The second part of this book is entirely given over to applications of the Grid technique, so we will not go into detail here. However, construct elicitation as a technique in its own right is useful whenever you want to examine the vocabulary with which someone thinks about the particular bit of the world you are interested in. For example, when we needed to get doctor's perceptions of the appeal of different medical specialties, we designed the questionnaire after construct-elicitation interviews with some doctors, using different specialties as elements. The way they construed specialties was often totally different from the way laymen construed them, with many doctors having constructs that the laymen could not have imagined for themselves; had we designed the questionnaire in laymen's language, we would have missed the systematic questioning on areas of importance that the construct-elicitation procedure allowed.

In another example of construct elicitation at work, a large American company with an operation in the UK wanted to know whether the performance-appraisal criteria that had been established by research in the USA would be applicable in the UK. We performed construct-elicitation interviews with senior managers, using as elements colleagues, subordinates and self; then we classified the constructs to see if there were any judgements the US research required managers to make which our managers did not make naturally, and whether there were any judgements which our managers made naturally but which did not appear in the US results.

Yet another example of construct elicitation at work is when it is used to force people to put into words perceptions they have but have never verbalized – in quality-control work, for example, where the little old lady sitting at the end of the line, running her fingers over the ball bearings and rejecting the faulty ones without being able to say on what basis she makes the rejection, is retiring in six months and her replacement has to be trained. Here construct elicitation using a sample of faulty and good ball-bearings has helped the inspector reveal her construct system – though she usually needs some reassurance that no-one will laugh at any private language she may have developed. This use of construct elicitation has been practised with products as varied as clothing and chocolates, ball-bearings and ladles of steel, injection mouldings and machine faults.

Our final example – though it by no means exhausts the possibilities – is an illustration of the market-research applications of construct elicitation, and at the same time shows how the technique allows the individual differences in perceptual style to emerge. A drug manufacturer asked three people to produce constructs about a list of painkillers. The housewife and mother produced:

quick-acting – slow acting
cheap – expensive
easy to carry – difficult to take with you
look effective – plain coloured
give to the kids – would not give to the kids
tastes nice – tastes nasty
big tablet – small tablet
I use regularly – I hardly ever use

whereas the doctor produced:

react with other drugs – do not react with other drugs
over the counter – prescription
liquid – tablet
active – placebo

difficult to overdose — easy to overdose
slow release — quick release
central action — peripheral action
safe — dangerous

and the drug salesman produced:

over the counter — on prescription
new products — 'me too' products
side effects — few side effects
our product — others' products
new product — old product
long shelf life — short shelf life
well packaged — unattractive packaging
good advertising — poor advertising

You might like to reflect on how knowledge of the differences between the way these three people perceive their products would help the marketing department write the promotion literature in a more tailor-made fashion — using familiar concepts if they wanted, or adding some consumer education in a measured fashion.

Before you go on to the next chapter, here are some exercises for you to try. They are designed to give you some practice in construct elicitation, and also some ideas of places where you could use the technique yourself.

Exercises

1. Elicit constructs from a friend, using nine television or radio programmes as elements. Try to do the same with another friend of different tastes from the first, and compare results. If you are using nine elements, a good order of administration is: 123, 456, 789, 147, 258, 369, 159, 267, 348. You can remember this by drawing the numbers up like this:

123
456
789

and then go across three times, downwards three times, and diagonally three times; this does not exhaust all the possibilities but it does give you every possible pair at least once.

2. Produce as many constructs as you can to the following triads of elements:

RICHARD NIXON
MAO TSE-TUNG
MARGARET THATCHER

ELIZABETH TAYLOR
MARILYN MONROE
JANE FONDA

STEAK DIANE
MACARONI CHEESE
YORKSHIRE PUDDING

THE DAY OF THE JACKAL
REBECCA
JANE EYRE

Get some other people to do the same. See how you can help them over the blank patches without suggesting any actual constructs.

3. Provide at least six possible opposites to each of the following words: new, green, dull, smooth, adult, aggressive, good, comfortable.

3. Laddering

Once you have mastered the basic technique of construct elicitation there are one or two important refinements you should know about. You may have already sensed these issues as you were doing the exercises from the previous chapter — if you were asking yourself whether one construct was more important than another, perhaps. Or you might have wondered whether despite our assertions that Grid can be free from interviewer bias, you were not biasing the interview as you sought to help your friend to produce as many constructs as possible to the sets of three elements in Exercise 2.

3.1 Asking for purpose-related constructs

One of the most difficult aspects of Grid to master is learning to cope with the fact that it can be used for various purposes, but only one purpose at a time can prevail. The selection of this purpose is up to you — though you may want to consult the interviewee about it, if it is that kind of interview — and it is also up to you to guide the interviewee into producing constructs that relate to the purpose you have in mind. With a little practice, you can do this without biasing the actual content of the constructs themselves. Usually this is done by one or two prefacing questions attached to the construct-eliciting question.

Suppose we were interviewing a salesman to see how he perceives his customers. Almost certainly we would be using the names of customers as the elements written on the cards, but we could be conducting the actual interview for a whole variety of purposes, for example:

1. The salesman is a super salesman and we want to know more about how he sees his customer so we can train other salesman to have similar perceptions.
2. The salesman is performing poorly and we want to know whether and how his perceptions of customers differs from other salesmen in the team.
3. The salesman is being considered for promotion to sales manager and we want to know the degree to which he thinks about his customers in a 'managerial' fashion.
4. The salesman is unhappy and has come for counselling because there are some customers he feels he just cannot get on with no matter how he tries.
5. The salesman is working in a highly technological environment with very sophisticated customers and we want to know more about the technical aspects of the customers' operations.

And so on. Each purpose for the interview requires that interviewer and interviewee adopt a slightly different frame of reference. It is up to the interviewer to indicate the frame of reference he requires. Thus for purposes (1) and (2) above, the eavesdropper might hear the question: 'Now, Bloor, Geary and MacKenzie — can you tell me something that two of them have got in common that makes them different from the third, *in terms of what they are like to sell to?*' Eavesdropping on an interview for purpose 4, one might hear: 'Now, Bloor, Geary and MacKenzie — can you tell me something that two of these have got in common, that makes them different from the third, *in terms of the way you feel about them?*' Eavesdropping on an interview for purpose 5, one might hear the same question, but qualified *'in terms of the way they run their operations?*' And for purpose 3 the interviewer might use a mix of questions.

Some of the constructs will be the same, of course, no matter what the qualifying question. Some constructs may appear to you to be irrelevant to the stated purpose, but the interviewee cannot concentrate on your purpose until he has cleared that particular construct out of the way. You learn to tolerate this, especially in the early stages of a Grid interview when the interviewee is settling down. But when the interviewee gets stuck on a particular kind of construct, or makes gestures that indicate that he cannot see the wood for the trees, then you can help him by asking the qualifying question that relates back to your purpose and tells him which bit of the field of constructs you are interested in.

The qualifying question nearly always takes the form 'in terms of . . . ' or 'from the point of view of . . . '. You can do this without actually suggesting the constructs themselves. It would be nice and simple if we could give a list of qualifying questions, with occasions to use them, but this would put an evolving technique into a strait jacket. We can give examples, but feel free to invent your own:

Qualifying questions about material attributes of the elements, e.g.,
. . . in terms of the way they run their operation?
. . . in terms of the way they affect people?
. . . in terms of their physical properties?
. . . from the point of view of safety?
. . . in terms of the demands they make on maintenance?

Qualifying questions about the interviewee's actions regarding the elements, e.g.,
. . . in terms of the demands they make on your skills?
. . . in terms of your responsibilities towards them?
. . . in terms of the approach you have to take towards them?
. . . from the point of view of your response to the demands they make?

Qualifying questions about the interviewee's feelings regarding the elements, e.g.,
. . . in terms of how you feel about them?
. . . in terms of the impression they make on you?
. . . in terms what they feel like to you personally?
. . . in terms of your own gut reactions to them?

and so on. Elements can be construed through spectacles of different 'focal lengths', from striving-to-be-objective through to totally subjective. You have to decide which one — or which combination — is best suited for your purpose, and then use a skilfully selected qualifying question or two to get the interviewee and yourself working on the same focal length.

To check your understanding of this point, let us suppose that you are doing a construct-elicitation exercise with a safety officer, using as elements a series of accidents that have happened within the factory recently. What qualifying question or questions would you use for each of the following purposes?

1. Checking to see whether a training course would do him some good.
2. Checking to see whether the accidents were genuine accidents or could have been prevented.
3. Checking to see whether he had a 'blind spot' about certain kinds of accident and did not see them coming as well.

For purpose 1 you probably want a question such as: 'Construe these accidents in terms of the demands they make on your skills'. For purpose 2 you probably want a question such as: 'Construe these accidents from the point of view of prevention'. For purpose 3 you could well need two kinds of qualifier; the one about prevention, as in 2, and one such as: 'Construe these accidents from the point of view of how you personally feel about dealing with them.'

Exercises

1. You are interviewing a doctor about his patients, using the names of patients as elements. What qualifying question would you ask (a) to discover what was wrong with the patients, and (b) what was wrong with the doctor's attitude towards his patients?
2. You are interviewing an architect about buildings, using particular buildings as elements. What qualifying question would you ask (a) to discover what skills the architect thought were used in designing such buildings, (b) what his aesthetic feelings were towards such buildings and (c) what the architect thought such buildings would be like to live in?

3.2 Laddering

Here we come to the question of the relative importance or salience of different kinds of construct, and to a technique that is vital, and easy to misuse.

The construct system is not just a jumble of assorted perceptions; it is a hierarchy, with some constructs closer to the centre, to the essence of the person, and others more peripheral. One way of picturing the construct system is as a series of interlocking ladders, getting smaller in number and stronger in influence/strength as one reaches the top. A good Grid interviewer needs to know what to do in the interview to expose as much of this construct system as is necessary for the purpose of the interview.

Try this experiment with yourself. Take three cards and write down the names of two close business associates and yourself. Produce a construct about those three in the normal way. Then ask yourself whether in general you prefer to work with people who are at one end of the construct, or at the other. Make a note of your answer. Then ask yourself why you have that preference. Make a note of your answer, and ask yourself why it should be so. Make a note of your answer, and ask yourself why it should be so. Now make a note of *that* answer, and ask yourself why it should be so — or are you already at the arm-waving, head-scratching stage of saying 'I'm sorry, that's just the way I prefer it' or 'Can't take it any further, that's the way it is for me'.

When we went through this procedure with Jill, for instance, her interview went as follows.

INTERVIEWER   John and Joe and Jill — can you tell me something that two of these have in common that makes them different from the third, in terms of the way they are at work?

JILL   Joe and I are both fairly thorough, but John tends to be a bit slapdash.

INTERVIEWER   Now, forgetting these three for a moment, can you tell me whether in general you prefer working with people who are thorough or people who are slapdash?

JILL   I'd have to say the slapdash ones.

INTERVIEWER   Why is that, can you tell me?

JILL   I think the slapdash ones tend to get more inspiration.

INTERVIEWER   And do you prefer working with people who get inspiration?

JILL   Yes.

INTERVIEWER   Why is that?

JILL   They're more exciting to be around.

INTERVIEWER   Why is that important to you?

JILL   Well, because exciting people are — well, exciting.

INTERVIEWER   Why is excitement important to you?

JILL   It's the opposite of routine, and routine's awful.

INTERVIEWER   Why do you dislike routine?

JILL   I'd just rather have change and excitement, that's all. It's just the way I am, I suppose.

Jill is getting to the stage where she cannot explain herself any further. Taking her through the sequence of 'why' questions gradually elicited more constructs, each of greater importance and personal relevance to Jill, until we came to a construct *exciting – routine* which she could not take further. The process of going 'up' the ladder to the centre has happened, as it often does, in very few stages with skilful use of the 'why' question.

Coming down the ladder, you use the 'how' question. Given a construct $x - y$, you come down the ladder by asking questions like: 'Can you tell me some more about how x and y are different?' or 'Can you give me some more examples of how x is not the same as y?' You use this kind of question when you have a construct that is so big, so global, as not to be useful unless you can break it up into its component constructs. Try it on yourself. If you were interviewed using as elements activities that you do in your job it is a fair bet that the construct *high job satisfaction – low job satisfaction* would emerge. Write down some examples of how activities with high job satisfaction differ from activities with low job satisfaction. Be careful to write down both ends of each construct. Be careful, too, not to give examples of activities with high and low job satisfaction — what we want is features of those activities with high job satisfaction which differentiate them from activities with low job satisfaction.

When we went through this process with Colin, for example, the interview went as follows.

INTERVIEWER   Colin, you said that some activities were high on job satisfaction and others were low on job satisfaction. I wonder if you can tell me something of the ways in which high job-satisfaction activities are different from low job-satisfaction ones?

COLIN   I think the high job-satisfaction ones are ones that result in other people taking action, and the less satisfying ones produce recommendations or results that people ignore.

INTERVIEWER   Thanks very much. Any more differences that occur to you?

COLIN   The low job-satisfaction ones are often the ones that I have to do just because I'm in this job with this title.

INTERVIEWER   And how does that make them different from the high job-satisfaction ones?

COLIN   Well, a high job-satisfaction one would be something like the Martinstown project, or the job for NKM —

INTERVIEWER   Sorry to interrupt, but I'm not looking right now for examples of actual activities, I'm looking for features of activities — for instance you said that low job-satisfaction jobs were the ones you had to do just because you were in this job with this title, and I'm wondering how this makes them different from the high satisfaction ones. How would you describe them in contrast?

COLIN   Oh, they tend to be the jobs I do because of my own skill and expertise in my field.

Were the interview to carry on like this Colin would provide more and more constructs, laying the construct *high job satisfaction — low job satisfaction* open into its component parts. The process of going 'down' the ladder to the periphery is beginning to take place.

'How' questions come down the ladder, 'why' questions go up it. 'How' questions usually take the form 'Tell me more about how *x* differs from *y*'. 'Why' questions can take at least two forms: asking for a preference between *x* and *y* on some parameter, and then asking for the reason for the preference; or when the construct *x — y* has been generated, to ask 'Why is that an important distinction to make about (naming the class of elements)?'

You have to know how to use laddering questions to get some depth and perspective into the interview, to get from the general to the specific and back again, and to accomplish changes in focal length similar to those used when asking qualifying questions. However, there is a danger in using the 'why' question when you get close to what in PCT terms are called *core constructs*.

Construct theory says that everyone has some fundamental constructs which he uses to interpret the world, and that these constructs are difficult and traumatic to change. *Good — bad*, for example, is likely to be a core construct with most people.

Many religious bigots have a core construct *Catholic – Protestant*, or *Jewish – Muslim*. A paranoid would probably have a core construct *for me – against me*. The character who cannot exist on a quiet beach without chewing gum, cigarette, radio, newspaper, can of beer and a good scratch probably has a core construct *being stimulated – nothing going on*. These core constructs – usually four to six in number for most people – are so closely personal that one clinical expert on Grid states that a person's core constructs represent, in a real sense, his God.

You can tell when you are approaching core constructs in the actual interview because they become self-defining; the interviewee can give no more reasons, only reiterate the construct in some way; and often the gestures used are an instant give-away. But the amateur user of Grid should be very careful of revealing core constructs, for several reasons.

1. Self-deception. People often have an image of themselves that is different from the reality. They may be very disturbed when the Grid interview reveals to both of you that their core constructs are different from their treasured self-image. Counselling work with senior managers in Northern Ireland who have discovered to their chagrin that the construct *Catholic – Protestant* influences their behaviour more profoundly than they had believed is an interesting test of skill, as we can testify, but it is one that both parties should go into with their eyes open and not find themselves in by accident.
2. Internal contradictions. It is possible to have mutually contradictory core constructs, which are kept apart by the exercise of considerable (and often unconscious) psychological energy. There is, for example, a fundamentalist evangelical Christian who is also a biologist; with one half of his head he believes in the Bible account of creation, and with the other half he believes in Darwinian theory, and he manages to keep the two apart by not admitting the contradiction. If in a Grid interview he were presented with this contradiction in his core constructs the resulting trauma might be quite difficult to resolve.
3. Need to know. Most of the industrial and organizational uses of Grid that the reader of this book is probably concerned with do not require core constructs to be investigated. When you reach the sections on counselling, team building, etc., you will find reference to core constructs, but we strongly advise you to try some of the less inner-directed uses first; and for applications such as questionnaire design, quality control, market research or training-needs analysis, which we believe you should try first, there is absolutely no need to extract core constructs.

A good rule of thumb is not to go more than one level of 'why' questions upwards on any one construct until you are confident that you have all the administrative skills of the Grid technique well in command, and experience of Grid interviews in various 'safe' purposes with interviewees who trust you. Unless you already have experience in counselling, you should probably give yourself about a year's experience with Grid before attempting closer work with core constructs – and then you had better have a good reason.

If you ladder upwards using the technique of asking your interviewee to express a preference for one end of the construct over the other — as Jill was asked whether she preferred working with people who are thorough or people who are slapdash — there are two points to be aware of. The first is that you can ask various preference questions, depending on the purpose for which you are doing the interview. Jill was asked which she preferred to work with — people who were thorough or people who were slapdash. She could also have been asked questions such as: 'Which puts more test on your skills, people who are thorough or people who are slapdash?' or: 'Which sort of people is it more important to be good at dealing with in your job, people who are . . . ' or: 'Which sort of people does your boss ask you to be better at dealing with, people who are . . . '. The variations are enormous, but most preference questions take the form either of asking for *liking* or of asking for *importance*. Interviews for counselling or team-building purposes usually cover the *liking* aspect more, whereas investigative interviews (to draw up a man-specification, for instance) most often stress the *importance* aspect.

The second point to be aware of when laddering upwards through the preference technique is that you must be sure to ask for a preference for one end of the construct over the other, *in general*. Do not be drawn into asking for a preference amongst the elements that gave rise to that construct, and do not be drawn into trying to establish a rank order between the constructs. In most Grid interviews the elements are used to generate constructs that, one hopes, will be relevant not only to those particular elements, but also to the family to which these elements belong; so you ladder about the constructs themselves, as separate entities divorced for the moment from the elements that generated them.

If you have come to the Grid technique completely new, this is probably a good point to reflect on what you have learned already. This chapter concludes with a series of exercises that will give you more practice in construct elicitation, and in the techniques of laddering and asking for purpose-related constructs that we have been discussing in this chapter. But this pause is not just a stepping-stone to higher things; it is also there to allow you to reflect on the technique of construct elicitation, which is useful in its own right. You can use construct elicitation whenever you want to know the vocabulary with which someone understands and labels the part of the world you happen to be discussing. This is useful if you want to address someone in his own vocabulary — e.g., attitude surveys, advertising, questionnaires — or if you want to alter or enhance someone's vocabulary — e.g., career counselling, negotiation, the transfer of inspection skills. Later in this book you will learn how to use the full Grid technique when what you want to know is not the vocabulary structure alone, but also its function; but for the moment construct-elicitation technique is worth practising in its own right.

Most people who learn construct-elicitation technique say that they feel it has made them a better interviewer and conversationalist even when they are not consciously practising it. The discipline involved in asking for both ends of the label, the compare-and-contrast techniques, and the practice in keeping quiet, together with the enhanced awareness Grid gives of the difference between receiving information from the interviewee and interpreting it — all these combine to make the Grid practitioner a more skilful interviewer, a better extractor of information from others. So – keep trying! If you felt any hesitancy at the beginning because of the cards and paper you had to manipulate, you will probably find by now that you have developed sleight of hand to overcome this; most interviewers keep the element cards in their hand like a hand of cards, with the numbers written in the top right hand corner so that they are displayed when the cards are fanned; then they can select the next three cards to hold ready between the second and third fingers while the interviewee is poring over his present triad.

Another point to notice as you practise construct elicitation on your friends or captive interviewees is the management of silence. In a conventional interview, though they may not admit it, both parties are talking together for a good part of the time; there are many unfinished sentences, interpretation, suggestion; there is often the feeling that you are not so much listening to what the other chap's saying as preparing your next remark. It is not like that in Grid; here the burden of the conversation passes completely from interviewer to interviewee and back again – like the conch shell used to control conversations in *Lord of the Flies*. You, the interviewer, ask the construct-eliciting question laying down a new triad of elements. Then he works out a construct or two and tells it to you. You write it down. Perhaps you ladder it, or ask for more constructs. Then you produce your next triad . . . either the interviewee is talking and you are writing, or you are asking him a question and he is listening. There is very little waffle. The important thing to remember is this: do not be afraid of silence in a Grid interview. Do not feel you have to fill it. Silence means that the interviewee is working – particularly just after you have given him a new triad to work on. Soon you will learn to use that silence to complete your notes on the previous triad, and to pick the cards ready for the next one, and your control over the speed of the interview will increase dramatically.

In the exercises that follow, we suggest that you do some real construct-elicitation interviews on real people. Most people find that when they are practising Grid like this it does not pay to go into long explanations about how this is a new technique, you are only just practising, and will they bear with you if it makes them feel uncomfortable – that is guaranteed to bring Murphy's law into operation. Try to look quietly confident, and you should soon settle down.

Exercises

1. Try a spot of career counselling (teenage children make good subjects for this). Get someone to write down the names of nine careers – some he would like to follow, some he would dislike, and his present career if he is in one. Get as many constructs as you can about careers; if you have to specifically tie the constructs to a particular purpose (often not necessary in this sort of interview because it happens automatically) ask for the careers to be compared 'from the point of view of what it would be like to work in them'. Do make sure to ladder on the constructs, particularly upwards; if you use a preference question it should be along the lines of 'which in general do you prefer, careers which are x or careers which are y'.

It is likely that you and the interviewee will discover how few constructs people actually have about careers — particularly people on the verge of choosing a career — and that this interview could reveal areas of ignorance, i.e., potentially useful constructs about careers that the interviewee does not have — and you can also use the results of the preference question to build up a specification for the most preferred career.

2. Practise asking for purpose-related constructs. Get your interviewee to name some shops of stores that he or she regularly shops at. Using these as elements, elicit some constructs:
   (a) about what these places are like from the shopper's point of view;
   (b) about what these places must be like to work in;
   (c) about the 'image' these places try to present to the public through advertising.

3. Practise laddering. Write down the names of three colleagues at work, and construe them (produce some constructs about them) in terms of their effectiveness at work. Now ladder yourself upwards ('why?' questions) and downwards ('how?' questions). For example, you might have a construct:

high work standards — low work standards

Laddering *up*, you would ask: 'Why is that an important distinction to make about people at work?' or 'In general, do I prefer working with people who have high work standards or people who have low ones? Why?'

Laddering *down*, you would ask: 'In general, how do people who have high work standards differ from people who have low work standards? How does the behaviour of one class of people differ from the other?'

Note that you can ask the second *why* question in several ways, e.g., 'Do I prefer to work with . . . ', 'Do I regard as more effective . . . ' or 'Do I regard as promotable in this organization . . . '.

4. More laddering practice. With a friend, ladder *up* and *down* with the following sets of elements:
   (a) Houses I have lived in.
   (b) Jobs I have had.
   (c) Mistakes I have made at work.
   (d) Things I would wish for if I could have three wishes.
   (e) Boy friends/girl friends.
   (f) Places I have been to on holiday.

4. Choosing elements

If by now you have more than a little competence in eliciting constructs from triads of elements, you will doubtless be wondering where the elements come from. Until now we have suggested or provided the elements, but you have to learn to choose them for yourself.

The elements help to define the kind of conversation you have. You decide that you want to interview for a particular purpose — say quality control, where you want to know more about what the inspector sees when he is looking at faults. Already you have narrowed down the range of things you want to talk to the inspector about; you do not want to know how he gets on with his mother, or whether he is good at picking Derby winners; you want to know how he sees faults, and in particular how he discriminates between them. So it makes sense to use faults of various kinds as elements in the interview.

There are some guidelines for selecting elements. They may appear to be complicated, but in fact they are fairly simple to remember, and when you have mastered them you have freedom to plan almost any kind of Grid interview with confidence.

The best analogy when thinking about choice of elements is to consider what a surveyor does when he is mapping out a new piece of ground. He starts by selecting a series of key points on that piece of ground — salient features, such as church spires, hilltops or ponds. Then when he has his salient features identified he takes a series of measurements between the features which give him more and more data about the territory until he is ready to draw the complete map. It is rather as if when eliciting constructs one is looking at the relationships between features on the map, and the elements themselves can be thought of as the features themselves — the points from which the surveyor starts when mapping the territory.

All analogies break down, of course, and this one only holds so far; but there are three points you might like to remember when choosing elements, or bring to mind when you have difficulties.

1. The more specific and precise, the better. Elements really should be as precise as you can get them. An imprecise element, struck against another imprecise element or two to produce a construct, will not produce much clarity of contrast and therefore will not produce good clear constructs. If you find yourself in trouble with imprecise elements, remember that to the surveyor a church spire is better than a church building is better than a church yard when it comes to using it as a triangulation point.

2. A rough scatter over the element area is acceptable. You do not have to strive for elements that are somehow 'evenly' distributed over the available territory. As long as there is a rough coverage of the area the surveyor will be satisfied, and so can you be.

3. If you are interested in the border between one kind of element and another, then you have to include some elements from the other side of the border. If the surveyor wants to plot the course of a river, he has to take triangulation points

from both banks. If you want to know whether your salesman thinks about products you manufacture differently from products you buy in, you must include both kinds of product in your element set. If you want to know what your managing director's stereotype of an effective country general manager is, obviously you will ask him to construe elements that include effective country general managers as he sees them, but to know how he differentiates between effective and less effective ones you must include some less effective ones in your element list.

4.1 Rules for selecting elements

Elements must be discrete

Elements most often used are people, objects, events and activities — in other words, nouns and verbs. Nouns should hurt when you drop them on your foot — specific people, specific objects. Abstract nouns such as 'my ideal subordinate' or 'leadership' should be avoided. Verb elements — events and activities — should be pinned down as closely as possible in space and time; the kind of event that one could have taken a short film clip of, or an activity that one could have observed if one was a fly on the wall. Loose descriptions that cannot be pinned down so clearly — such as 'negotiating' or 'thinking' — should be avoided.

People learning Grid often feel uncomfortable with this rule. They feel that the elements thus produced are too trivial. It is possible to select too-trivial elements; but it is a less reprehensible and more recoverable fault than selecting as elements notions that are so broad as to be imprecise. The sophistication of the conversation increases as you move to eliciting constructs, and still further as you ladder the constructs and/or progress to full Grid; you want to select elements that are a level or so below the level of sophistication that you want to have your final conversation about.

A common manifestation of this fault is when people first try their hands at market-research type interviews. If, for example, you wanted to interview someone to discover his preferences about cars so as to recommend him to a particular car, what elements would you choose?

If you chose varieties of car as elements, you have learned the lesson about elements being discrete. If — like many people the first time around — you chose features of cars (4-DOOR, SUN ROOF, ECONOMY, etc.) then you will find yourself very lost in the actual interview because you have chosen as elements things which should really appear as constructs.

Avoid adjectival and adverbial phrases as elements. It can be done, but with difficulty, and you are safer sticking to nouns and verbs. Do not use features of elements as elements; use the elements themselves. See if you can make yourself produce an 'opposite' to your element (not to the question you may have used to elicit it) and if you can (2-DOOR or HATCHBACK, SOLID ROOF, GAS-GUZZLING, etc., in the car example) then you are probably jumping the gun by using as elements things that should really emerge in the construct-elicitation process.

Elements must be homogeneous

Do not mix classes of elements; do not mix people with things, or things with activities. A little private practice with one or two non-homogeneous sets will show you how difficult the procedure becomes and how few constructs you can get this way.

Elements should not be sub-sets of other elements

The surveyor will get into trouble if one of his landmarks is a churchyard and another landmark is a tombstone within the churchyard. With objects or events/ activities as elements it is sometimes possible to make a similar mistake; if one element described your whole range of coffee products, for example, and another element names just one line of coffee; or one element is MAKING PRESENTATIONS and another element MAKING PRESENTATIONS TO THE MANAGING DIREC-TOR. The reason should be obvious; the smaller element will contain so many features similar to the larger element that they will be difficult to compare and contrast during the construct-elicitation process.

Elements should not be evaluative

It is easy, particularly with events and activities, to allow the element description to contain an evaluative flavour — to become cliches of the kind that the Americans call 'motherhoods'. LEADING THE TEAM, PARTICIPATION and MOTIVATING MY STAFF are all examples of elements that seem to contain a high degree of implicit evaluation which would make them difficult to handle in the actual interview. Of course, the rule about making elements as specific as possible will help here, but it is a caution worth uttering in its own right.

To test your understanding of these rules, try spotting what is wrong with each of the following lists of elements (either in themselves or because you do not think they will achieve the stated purpose).

1. To discuss the qualities required in a successful manager:

NEGOTIATING	COMMUNICATING	MEETINGS	CONTROLLING
LEADERSHIP	REPORT-WRITING	PLANNING	OPERATING

Just about everything! They are evaluative (LEADERSHIP), they are not homogeneous (some nouns and some verbs), they are highly abstract in most cases and concrete by contrast in two (REPORT-WRITING and MEETINGS), and they have the flavour of the well worn cliché that might not have much personal relevance to the interviewee (PLANNING, CONTROLLING and OPERATING come straight from some management textbooks).

2. To discuss the qualities thought to be necessary to be a successful woman in public life:

MARGARET THATCHER	BETTY FRIEDAN
ANGELA RIPPON	REBECCA WEST
MARJORIE HURST	DOROTHY HODGKINSON
DIANA RIGG	SHIRLEY WILLIAMS

Assuming that the interviewee knows all eight women (an assumption worth checking), the error lies in the fact that these are all successful women. To get the contrast between successful and unsuccessful women, you need to include some unsuccessful women in the list; and to get the contrast between successful women and successful men, you would need some successful men in the list as well. Remember that 'you can only understand what I mean by *good* when you understand what I mean by *bad* as well'.

3. Career counselling:

WORKING WITH PEOPLE	EQUAL OPPORTUNITIES
HIGH SALARY	GOOD BOSS
PROMOTION	PAYMENT BY RESULTS
STAFF DISCOUNT	TRAINING
PENSION SCHEME	TEAM-WORK

This one has fallen into the trap of providing as elements things which should really emerge — if at all — as constructs. Features of careers have been used as elements, when it should really have been the careers themselves. Apart from providing a set of elements that are difficult to work with (try it, especially laddering, and see if you feel you want to shout for help), this list has also pre-empted some of the possible constructs by suggesting them to the interviewee and thereby has introduced an element of bias.

4. To discuss Jim's relations with the rest of the management team:

BARRY	PAT	KEITH	SUSAN
JOE	ALAN	MAUREEN	BOB

You can assume that all the above names represent people in the management team. One mistake is not to include Jim himself — you need to see how Jim sees himself in relation to the rest of the team, and you will not see that if you leave Jim out. Another possible mistake, which you do not have any data on but might have asked about, is that if the above list leaves out any members of the management team besides Jim himself, then the picture could well be lopsided.

Working within these basic rules you also need a touch of flair — which will come with experience — before you can be completely confident about choosing the right kind of element for a particular purpose. It is often possible to achieve the same purpose starting with different elements; and with goodwill and experience on both sides you can even break some of the basic rules. If you practise the exercises and study the examples, especially in the second half of this book, you should be well on the way to developing your flair.

4.2 Strategies for selecting elements

One more series of rules — this time rules of thumb — about choosing elements. You will probably have noticed that in the previous examples the elements sometimes appear to have been chosen by the interviewer, and at other times the actual elements have been chosen by the interviewee in response to the interviewer's promptings. You have, in fact, three choices of ways of eliciting elements: you (the interviewer) can provide them; or you can ask the interviewee to generate a list of elements spontaneously once you have told him broadly what class of elements you want; or you can come equipped with a list of questions, the answers to which will be the elements. To study the advantages and disadvantages of each strategy, let us suppose that you are the manufacturer of indigestion remedies and you want to know how family decision-makers think about indigestion remedies. As part of the procedure you decide to do construct-elicitation exercises with several family decision-makers, one of whom is Mrs Smith.

Strategy 1 has you preparing a list of indigestion remedies to use as elements in the interview: GRIPENOT, ENO'S, RENNIES, MILK OF MAGNESIA, ACTAL, ALKA-SELTZER, ACHE-O and SUPERTUM (your product). You would do this if you had a particular reason for wanting to see how your product SUPERTUM compared in the public eye with its main competitors (say ACTAL and RENNIES). You might feel that you did not want to take the chance of people not mentioning ACTAL and RENNIES if you used a variety of free-response element elicitation, so you put them into the interview from the beginning to be sure of getting the information about your product compared with them. The price you pay for this is that some of the products may not be as familiar to the interviewee as if she had generated them herself (try a few constructs including ACHE-O and GRIPENOT, which we can guarantee you will not know, since we invented them). As it is just not possible to do a Grid interview about a topic about which you are ignorant, the interview will be much less useful on that account. The other price you pay is that supposing Mrs Smith, having heard that you are interested in her views on indigestion remedies, prepares herself to extol the merits of her granny's patent jollop, discovers that none of the element cards are to contain her own contribution, she may feel less commitment towards the interview than she would if GRANNY'S JOLLOP had been one of the elements.

The remedy for the possible unfamiliarity of some of the elements is to have one or two in reserve, though even then they might not all share the same degree of salience. And if you think that lack of 'ownership' may get in the way then you can either allow a couple of extra elements *ad lib*, or try hard in your general bearing to overcome the problem. You pay this price whenever you want to have constructs elicited about this particular group of elements for internal comparison between the elements themselves, *or* when you want to interview more than one person as part of the same project because you want to investigate or reconcile different construing styles. It is like doing a Grid with a supervisor about his staff, and then using those same members of staff in a Grid interview with the supervisor's manager as part of an investigation into why staff say there are inconsistencies in management style.

Strategy 2 has you prepare a series of blank element cards, and at the interview you ask Mrs Smith if she will write on the cards the names of (say) nine indigestion remedies she uses or knows about. Where this could be very illuminating for you is that it gives you a notion of what she regards as an indigestion remedy; so that if she and others like her write ANADIN or HOT WATER — not to mention GRANNY'S JOLLOP — on the cards you will know you had competition from an unexpected quarter. The price you pay for this is a slight but definite bias in Mrs Smith's responses towards remedies she is familar with and likes. It is less likely that she will rack her brains for the name of one she saw last advertised six months ago, even though she may remember it and the advertisement if you were to suggest the name as in the first strategy. And it is less likely that she will produce the names of remedies that she has tried but does not like, or that have a bad reputation.

There are many circumstances other than the market research one where you could be interested to see what the interviewee does with the broad classification of elements you give him. If you ask a manager to reel off the names of the people working for him, does he include contract staff? If you ask a doctor to reel off the possible career choices open to him, does he confine himself to medical specialties or does he mention selling drugs or going into forestry? If you ask the safety manager to reel off a list of recent accidents, does he take your question to mean only incidents where chance has played a large part, or does he also include incidents that could have been foreseen and prevented? You will certainly get elements of personal relevance to the interviewee this way, and if you are happy to pay the price of the slight bias towards favour and familiarity then this is your strategy.

Strategy 3 has you preparing a set of blank cards before the interview and also a list of eliciting questions which will get you elements written on cards. Interviewing Mrs Smith, for example, you might have prepared the following questions:

1. – When I say 'indigestion remedy', what is the first product you think of?
2. – Can you tell me the name of an indigestion remedy you have tried recently?
3. – Is there an indigestion remedy that you have tried but did not like?
4. – Can you tell me the names of a couple of remedies that your friends have recommended or talked about favourably?
5. – Can you tell me the names of a couple of remedies that your friends have found unsatisfactory?
6. – What is the cheapest indigestion remedy you know?
7. – And the most expensive?

To these questions, Mrs Smith would produce the names of indigestion remedies until you had nine names on the cards. By asking for the names of products she did not like or had heard ill of, the technique above has avoided the favour and familiarity bias inherent in the free-response method, while at the same time ensuring that there is a good degree of ownership of the elements on Mrs Smith's part. Obviously the interviewer must have additional questions ready if the same product is generated in response to two different questions.

The price you pay for using this strategy is chiefly time. Getting out a list of elements this way is often longer than the two previous ways. However, you do get more detailed information as a result, by compiling a list of the answers to each element question; in your role as market researcher for the SUPERTUM company you would know if you employed this strategy what remedies people had recently tried, what remedies were being bad-mouthed wherever people meet to talk about such things, what remedies had a reputation for being expensive and which were thought of as cheap. The trends and patterns in this kind of information can be tremendously valuable. For example we did some Grid interviews with new graduates who had just joined a large organization that was interested in the image it presented to new graduates, so we asked the graduates for the names of six other organizations they would have worked for and two that under no circumstances would they work for, to use, with the sponsoring organization, as elements in a Grid interview. By listing the organizations graduates said they would have worked for we could provide the sponsoring organization with a very clear picture of the firms it was in competition with for its graduate entry. In another case, we asked managers to name recent events that they had enjoyed and not enjoyed at work, and to name the nicest and the worst possible things that could happen, to use as elements in a study of managerial motivation; a content analysis of the things managers enjoyed and did not enjoy was very useful indeed.

Think of the surveyor's map when you are deciding on eliciting questions; you want to scatter the map with your questions, so your element-eliciting questions will often come in pairs, for example:

one you like
one you do not like

a frequently used or occurring one
an infrequently used or occurring one

a successful one
an unsuccessful one

a happy one
a sad one

one you can plan for
an unexpected one

a new one
an old one

a demanding one
an easy one

and so on. Make out a list before each interview — do not rely on inspiration at the time unless you really have no choice — and try them on yourself.

Three strategies, then: you can supply elements, you can get them by free-response; or you can use eliciting questions. Either of the last two strategies puts you within reach of the interviewer-bias-free interviewing procedure that was one of our original goals. There is nothing stopping you mixing strategies, either, though you should be clear about why you do it; if you do mix strategies then it is probably best to begin with any eliciting questions you want to use, then go on to free response, and finish with supplied elements, making sure you check that the interviewee knows them.

Noun elements are easier to work with than verb elements, because it is easier to be precise with a noun phrase than with a verb phrase. Using people as elements, however, is potentially dangerous once you stray into the area known as 'significant others' — the people who are close to your interviewee or who have played a part in moulding his personality. Remember that Grid started life as a clinical technique. In Kelly's original formula you would be asked to name your parents, spouse, best friends, most admired person, most pitied person and so on. The constructs produced about these have obvious deep personal relevance. You can get into deep waters very quickly if you try using significant others as elements; and even in the industrial setting you might find more under the surface than meets the eye. Care, therefore, when using people as elements.

Exercises

What elements would you use for each of the following purposes? If you decide to supply a list, write it out. If you decide to use eliciting questions, write them out. See if you can try some of the interviews on a friend. (Do not forget the lessons of the two previous chapters.)

1. How does British Rail compare with its main competitors in the eyes of the public?
2. What exactly does Bill Jones do in his job and what are the demands it makes on him?
3. How much do people's perceptions of a particular employer change after they have been working there a while?
4. How security conscious are our employees?
5. 'I'm used to negotiating with my opposite numbers in other plants in the group, but the thought of having to negotiate with some outside loss adjuster terrifies me. Can you help?'
6. 'The buyer accepts cloth with faults in it that she doesn't even seem to see, and then it passes our inspector in the assembly room only to get bounced back by Sales.'

5. Full Grid

If you have followed the exercises and examples so far, you should be getting fairly proficient at eliciting constructs from a set of elements of your own choosing. Do not worry if you do not feel totally confident; most people's learning curve for Grid rises fairly sharply to begin with, has plateaux followed by great Aha! experiences when some of the rules we have tried to articulate are seen as roads to freedom and not as restrictions, but the curve itself continues to go upwards for several years.

Construct-elicitation technique allows you to invite the interviewee to tell you the constructs he uses about a particular part of his world. It is useful whenever you want to investigate, share or modify someone's vocabulary. But it does not tell you everything that you (and he) may be interested in; it does not tell you how the construct system actually works. Two people can produce the construct *powerful — passive* when discussing the decision-makers they try to sell to, but if they use those constructs in a different way then they have not got the same construct. Full Grid procedure allows you to exhibit not only the constructs themselves, but in detail how they are used.

It is basically quite simple. Instead of regarding each construct as a pair of words, you regard it as a scale — most often a five-point scale. Then you get the interviewee to rate each element on each construct, so that you build up a matrix of elements x constructs. By doing this you get closer to the functional meaning of the elements and constructs — you understand how they are actually used by the interviewee.

In Chapter 2 we eavesdropped on part of an interview with Pat, an internal consultant in a large organization. The elements Pat was using were TED, TONY, JOHN, SHIRLEY, ALAN, FRANCES, DOUGLAS, BOB and LOUISE. In the course of construct elicitation the interviewer extracted the following constructs before he stopped to enter them into the Grid:

1 2 3	career specialists	— got into line by accident
1 2 3	self-protective	— buccaneer
4 5 6	woman	— man
4 5 6	swayed by fads ↓	— knows what wants ↓
	(impulse buyers)	— (have shopping list)
7 8 9	more than 20 years' experience	— very new
7 8 9	would say of self 'come up the hard way'	— had path made smooth (graduate entrant)
7 8 9	trimmers, aware of political realities (too much, start to compromise too early)	— think rational argument will solve any problem — people do right even if costs face

37

| <u>1 4 7</u> | (at work) stopped growing | — (at work) still growing & developing |
| <u>1 4</u>7 | (outside work) stopped growing | — (outside work) still growing & developing |

Now he begins asking Pat the questions that will lead to the full Grid:

INTERVIEWER   Pat, let's stop the triadic comparisons procedure for a moment, though we'll probably return to it later. What I'd like to do now is get you to place all the people on all the dimensions we've talked about so far. I'm going to turn each of these bipolar dimensions into a five-point scale and ask you where each of the people falls on it. Now you said that Ted and Tony were career specialists, so let's make them 1 on the scale, whereas John had got into his line by accident so let's make him 5. If you think now about Shirley, would you say she's a career specialist or did she get into her line by accident?

PAT   She got into her line by accident.

INTERVIEWER   As much as John?

PAT   Yes, just as much.

INTERVIEWER   So we could give Shirley a 5 on that scale. OK? Right, now think about Alan. Is he a career specialist or did he get into his line by accident?

PAT   He's more of a career specialist.

INTERVIEWER   As much as Ted and Tony?

PAT   No, not as much as them, he's more of a 2.

INTERVIEWER   Right, we'll give him a 2. Next is Frances — which end of the scale is she?

PAT   She's a 2 as well.

INTERVIEWER   How about Douglas?

PAT   Douglas is more of a 4.

INTERVIEWER   You mean he got into the line by accident, but not so much as John?

PAT   That's right. John really goes with the tide, but Douglas does try to manage his accidents a bit.

INTERVIEWER   How about Bob?

PAT   I'd give Bob a 4 as well.

INTERVIEWER   And Louise? Where does she fit?

PAT   She's a 3, I would say.

INTERVIEWER   You mean exactly half-way between the two ends of the scale?

PAT   Yes, that may be because I don't know her as well as the others — she is a career specialist of sorts, because she's a trained economist, but at the moment she's not actually using her skills as an economist but allowing herself to be used as a trained person who can think. She may drift off into personnel work or she may give herself a good shake and go into corporate planning where she can use what she's been trained for.

INTERVIEWER   Thanks. I just want to be sure that when you give someone a 3 it's because he or she really does fall in the middle as you see it and not because you don't know or think the question doesn't apply.

PAT   OK, I understand.

INTERVIEWER   You see I've got one line of the picture completely filled in now. Can I do the same with the next scale – you described Ted and Tony as being self-protective, so let's give them a 1 on that scale, whereas John you said was a buccaneer, so we'll make him 5. So if self-protective is 1 and buccaneer is 5, where do you place Shirley?

PAT   I'd give her a 2, though she wouldn't be pleased to hear it.

INTERVIEWER   Well, I'm interested in how you see her, not in how you think she sees herself, so feel free! She gets a 2, right?

PAT   Yes.

INTERVIEWER   How about Alan?

PAT   A 1, definitely.

INTERVIEWER   Frances?

PAT   A 1 again.

INTERVIEWER   Douglas?

PAT   Douglas gets a 5. He'll take on anything.

INTERVIEWER   Bob?

PAT   Give him a 2 – he's not as bad as the others, but he's very unadventurous for someone in his position.

INTERVIEWER   Finally Louise – what shall I write for her?

PAT   A 4, I would say – she is quite adventurous.

INTERVIEWER   Good. Now the next construct you gave me was *woman – man* – am I right in thinking that this is going to be difficult to turn into a five-point scale?

PAT   Right. Shirley, Frances and Louise are females, the rest are males, and I don't think there are any doubtful cases!

INTERVIEWER   Let's have a look at the next one. You said that Alan and Frances were both easily swayed by fads – so let's make that 1 on the scale – but that Shirley usually knows what she wants, so let's make that 5. Would you say that Ted is easily swayed by fads, or does he usually know what he wants?

PAT   He's easily swayed. Give him a 1. Tony's the same, too.

INTERVIEWER   Tony gets a 1?

PAT   That's right.

INTERVIEWER   How about John? Easily swayed by fads, or knows what he wants?

PAT   He knows what he wants.

INTERVIEWER   So we give him . . . ?

PAT   Give him a 5.

INTERVIEWER   How about Douglas?

PAT   Douglas gets a 2 – he can get out of his depth very easily.

INTERVIEWER   And Bob?

PAT   I think I want to give Bob a 3.

INTERVIEWER   Sure?

PAT   Think so.

INTERVIEWER   How does he compare with Shirley?

PAT   He's a bit less pliable than Douglas.

INTERVIEWER   How does he compare with Shirley?

PAT   Oh, nothing like — yes, 3's the right score for him.

INTERVIEWER   And Louise?

PAT   I'd say she was a 4 — better than Bob, but not as sharp as Shirley.

INTERVIEWER   Do you want to just check those ratings that I've written down here and make sure they're OK?

PAT   Yes, that's fine.

INTERVIEWER   Right, now the next scale you gave me is about experience. 1 is more than 20 years experience — Douglas and Bob both get a 1 — and 5 is very new — Louise gets a 5. Can you fit everyone else in there? Starting with Ted?

As the interview proceeds, the interviewer builds up the matrix of elements x constructs as we overheard. When he has finished getting the first group of constructs rated he goes on to some more triadic comparisons, and then maybe some laddering; then he builds the new constructs into the grid through the rating procedure as before. The finished product looks like Fig 5.1.

1	TED	TONY	JOHN	SHIRLEY	ALAN	FRANCES	DOUGLAS	BOB	LOUISE	5
career specialist	1	1	5	5	2	2	4	4	3	got into his line by accident
self protective	1	1	5	2	1	1	5	2	4	buccaneer
easily swayed by fads	1	1	5	5	1	1	2	3	4	knows what he wants
20 years' exp.	1	3	2	2	4	5	1	1	5	very new
would say had come up the hard way	1	3	2	3	3	4	1	1	5	hard path made smooth
trimmers, aware of political reality	1	2	1	5	3	3	1	4	5	think rational argument will solve any problem
stopped growing (at work)	1	2	3	5	2	1	1	3	5	still growing & developing (at work)
stopped growing (at home)	1	3	1	1	2	1	5	4	5	still growing & developing (at home)
thin-skinned	2	1	4	3	5	5	5	1	3	does not notice insults
high opinion of himself	4	5	1	2	1	2	3	1	3	believes he is going to fail
is influenced by personal feelings	3	2	5	3	1	1	4	3	1	does not let personal feelings influence him
allows people to sell him pups	3	2	4	5	1	1	1	1	2	sceptic
ignores others' professional standards	4	5	3	4	4	2	1	1	2	recognizes that other professions can contribute something useful

Figure 5.1

This displays not merely Pat's constructs about her clients but something of the way she uses the constructs. It is a very detailed picture. Later on we shall describe in more detail how to analyse the Grid (or get it analysed for you). But for the moment you might like to examine the Grid and ask yourself the following questions:

1. Which two people does Pat see as most like each other, and which two does she see as the most different?
2. Does Pat think that people who are aware of the political realities are likely to ignore other people's professional standards?
3. If Pat had to write a one-paragraph briefing on Shirley for the benefit of someone going to negotiate a piece of work for Shirley, what do you think she would say?
4. Do you think that in Pat's organization there might be a conflict between older managers and graduate entrants?

All the answers are there, in Pat's Grid. As you look for them, you are coming to grips with two of the main kinds of information a Grid interview gives you: it allows you to see how each element is rated on each construct, so that you can compare elements if necessary; and it allows you to see how each construct is used and to compare constructs if necessary. Do not be frightened of pitching in to what may seem a great slab of undifferentiated information; the answers to each of the questions can be worked out in your head or on a small piece of paper, and you will find that the inspection skills come quickly with practice.

Time now to find a cooperative friend again and practise a couple of Grid interviews to the specifications below. Then we will try to anticipate the administration questions that will doubtless come to mind as you experiment.

1. Begin by doing a Grid on your cooperative friend about potential employers. Use as elements his present employer, five employers he would like to work for and three that he would under no circumstances work for. From the Grid work out the characteristics of his present employer as he sees them, and the characteristics of his most and least preferred choices (or *next-most — next-least* if his present employer qualifies for either of those descriptions).
2. Now try one using holiday resorts he has visited or knows a lot about. From this try to work out what he means when he says he likes a resort.
3. Now try one using customers or clients or work colleagues, to find out more about his likes and dislikes.

You will probably find that the experience of doing these Grid interviews has been as interesting for the recipient as it has for you. The process of clarifying his thoughts may be quite enjoyable. You may find that in this process he has given you some more constructs, or re-defined the old ones. The first two exercises were designed really to give you some skill in inspecting the Grid as you go along, but in the third one you might even have found some surprises for you both as you discover patterns in the Grid that you and he did not know were there. We will discuss analysis later; this chapter ends with a question-and-answer session, trying to cover the points people raise when they have had their first experience of conducting a Grid.

5.1 Your questions answered

Do I have to use a 1 to 5 scale?

No. Practitioners of Grid use anything from a two-point to a nine-point scale. There is evidence to suggest that a seven-point scale is getting close to most people's limits of discrimination, and much above five points is very difficult to examine visually, so five points suits us. If you need a very fast visual inspection of the grid then use a two-point scale — tick and cross, or red and blue. This sacrifices detail for speed and simplicity.

What if the element will not rate on that construct?

Not every element in the world can be rated on every construct in the world; few people could place the element FALSE TEETH on the construct *religious — atheist*, or the element MY FIRST BIRTHDAY on the construct *present — future*. You should not try to force such a rating. There is a very useful concept here — the *range of convenience* of the construct. A construct's range of convenience is described by the number and kind of elements that can be rated on it. Some constructs, such as *good — bad*, have a very wide range of convenience for most people — most people can classify most of their experiences into good and bad. A construct such as *two-legged — four-legged* will not have such a big range of convenience. Mary might have a construct *likes me — does not like me* with a very wide range of convenience which reflects her need for affection and possible insecurity, whereas tougher-skinned Linda might have the same construct, but apply it to fewer people. In a full Grid interview you are testing the range of convenience of each construct — you will find that worth bearing in mind when we look at analysis later. If you find you have one or two constructs on which one or two elements cannot be rated — after discussion — put a N/A or 0 symbol in the box. Do not force your interviewee into making silly judgements for their own sake. But if you find that you have an element or a construct that has many N/A judgements applied to it, you must ask yourself or the interviewee whether it is in fact consonant with the other elements or constructs and if it is not, drop if from the Grid.

What do I do with a construct where the two ends are completely unconnected?

This happens from time to time — you give someone OMO, DAZ and STERGENE to construe and they say 'Two of them are powders but the other comes in a pretty package' — and despite our earlier warning that a construct is not necessarily composed of semantic opposites you feel like despairing. Usually the problem sorts itself out if you say to the interviewee: 'I'm going to have trouble turning those two statements into a nice smooth scale. Have we got one scale here, or two, do you think?' and if you leave this question until the middle of the Grid, when he has got used to the procedure of turning constructs into scales, he will usually be able to help.

Is it OK to re-define the constructs?

Yes and no. In our study of doctors' career choices, one doctor gave us the construct *working with women only — working with men only*. When we came to apply that construct to elements other than the three specialties that had generated it, of course there were two constructs there: *working with women only — working with both sexes* and *working with men only — working with both sexes*. Constructs such as *past — future* or *works too hard — does not pull his weight* might well need re-defining into *past — present* and *present — future*, and *works too hard — works adequately* and *works adequately — does not pull his weight*. Listen for any difficulty the interviewee might be having, and ask whether it would be better to split that construct into two parts. Where it is less OK to re-define the constructs is if the interviewee wants to make his constructs prettier or more socially acceptable. This usually needs resisting.

Do you get all the constructs out and then fill in the Grid, or rate each element on each new construct?

Either is permissible, and the stages in between. The two methods do seem to have slightly different outcomes for the conduct of the Grid interview, though. If you take each construct as it emerges and get all the elements rated on that construct before proceeding to the next construct (call that the Across-method) then you are asking the interviewee to switch attention from one element to the next. If you wait until all the constructs have been elicited (call this the Down-method) then you are asking the interviewee to switch attention from one construct to the next. The Across-method probably leads to neater constructs — there is more opportunity and incentive to re-define the construct in use. In favour of the Down-method we would say that it allows you to present the interviewee with a single element card and say: 'Concentrate on that one element and I'm going to ask you some questions about it.' When the elements are activities or events this seems to make life easier for the interviewee, who can concentrate on one element at a time. We also find that the Across-method imposes a discipline very quickly on the interviewee, so it is useful when you have a very talkative interviewee who will easily distract himself away from the purpose of the interview; whereas the Down-method, by encouraging the production of constructs, is better at drawing out a less talkative person.

For most Grid purposes whether you use the Across- or the Down-method seems to be a matter of personal choice and experiment. Some work suggests that there may be the possibility of slight differences in the actual Grid depending on which method you use, but for most industrial purposes you need not worry about that. Most often the way we do a Grid is to do about five triads, laddering *downwards* as constructs emerge but laddering upwards at the end of the five; writing the constructs resulting from the laddering into the Grid, and then using the Down-method (with verb elements) or the Across-method (with noun elements) get the elements rated on the constructs before proceeding to the next five triads. This seems to control the pace of the Grid to something comfortable while allowing the interviewee to see what is going on and why he is being asked all these questions.

It is sometimes difficult to get ratings — the interviewee keeps changing his mind

What helps here is to write down the two ends of the construct on two pieces of card and lay them some distance apart on the table. Then you can ask the interviewee to sort the element cards according to how he thinks they fall between the two construct cards. You can ask him to sort into two piles, or to create his own scale, or if you want to use a five-point scale you can create five 'depots' between the two ends of the construct and ask him to put the element cards on the appropriate depots. Obviously this is a bit more cumbersome, but with people who are not used to attitude scales you might find it helpful. There is a similarly helpful device for helping people who have difficulty with construct elicitation — spread all the elements out on the table and ask the interviewee to pick up the two that are most alike, to say why, and then to pick out the one that is most different in those terms. Then you re-shuffle and ask for another similiarity judgement on a different dimension. Usually you do not have to do this more than two or three times before the notion of triadic comparisons establishes itself and you can get back to the regular procedure.

Can I suggest constructs?

Yes, if you know why you are doing it. You might well want to offer elements or constructs if they had not been produced naturally and you were interested to know how the interviewee would use them. If Pat had not rated her clients on the scale *good manager — bad manager* and we wanted to know more about the kind of attributes she thought a good manager had, we could well ask her to use this new construct. Or we could suggest that now it would be fascinating to see how Pat rated herself on the scales she had produced, so we could slip in a tenth element — PAT. As soon as we do this we create some expectations in Pat's mind of the kind of answers we are expecting of her, so care is needed in offering constructs or elements — usually it comes fairly late in the interview procedure, so as not to set an unduly restrictive example in the early stages.

When do I stop?

When you have got all the information you need. That is an unhelpful answer, but if you read the rest of the book — on analysis, feedback, and practical examples — you will see examples of Grids stopped at different points simply because they had met their purpose. You could go on for a long time; the key thing is to remember your purpose, what you want to achieve with the Grid interview, and keep it in mind when controlling the flow of the interview. Bear with the examples for a while, and it should soon become clear.

No exercises for this chapter, but try some items from the reading list:

FRANSELLA, F., and D. BANNISTER, *A Manual for Repertory Grid Technique*, Academic Press, London, 1977.

BANNISTER D., and F. FRANSELLA, *Inquiring Man: The Theory of Personal Constructs*, Penguin, London, 1971.

6. Analysis of Grid Data

If you have been reading elsewhere about Grid technique you may have a touch of trepidation as you approach this chapter. Are you heading for a confrontation between mathematics and computers on the one hand, and your dimly grasped inability to imitate an abacus on the other? Fear not. You do not need a computer to start analysing a Grid, though a computer will do things for you that you could not do yourself; and as there already exist a fair number of programs for analysing Grids we shall outline what they do, give you examples of their outputs, and give you some consumer advice with which to select the program to meet your requirements.

There are five principal methods of analysis to cover: frequency counts, content analysis, visual focusing, cluster analysis, and principal-components analysis. The first two methods are concerned with analysing the content of the Grid, and the remaining three analyse not only the content but also the interrelationships. Therefore the first two methods involve nothing more complicated than counting, whereas the rest ask for correlations.

A preliminary word of warning. Before you start on a Grid study you should have a clear view of the purpose of the exercise, and in taking this clear view you should think about how you are going to analyse the Grid. There is nothing worse than the experience of discovering, after much hard work collecting data, that your data do not fit the computer program you were hoping to use, or that they will not allow you to do the statistics you would like. It is also fairly disheartening to be caught with more data than you actually need. So, if you are a computer buff, be warned that you do not always need a computer, and Grids collected for computer analysis may contain much material redundant for your purposes. If it is a big Grid study then a pilot interview and analysis will be invaluable.

Now to qualify our word of warning. There is one concession to the computer which we believe you should *not* make in the actual interview process. It concerns the occasion when an element cannot be rated on a particular construct despite the interviewee's best efforts. It is psychologically important to be able to record and discuss the Not Applicable rating. For example, during interview, the manager of a Design Studio produced the construct *old – young* about his subordinates, but then had great difficulty applying it, and retreated into 'I don't know' whenever he had to rate a subordinate older than 40. This gave us a very fast insight into his problem – that he thought 40 was over the hill, and he himself was pushing 39. Most computer programs in common use for Grid analysis turn a Not Applicable judgement into a mid-point of scale judgement, and do some damage to the structure of the Grid in the process. You probably have to go along with the computer people for a while, but in the actual interview you should be sensitive to the Not Applicable rating.

Enough of cautions. Before doing a Grid, ask yourself the following questions:

1. – What do I want to achieve with this interview?

2. — Who do the data belong to?
3. — What resources have I got for analysis?
4. — What form of analysis do I want to use?
5. — Is speed of analysis important?
6. — Will the Grid be interpreted as a cooperative effort, or by me alone?

Then you should be able to select the right mode for your Grid, and plan your analysis accordingly, using one or more of the following techniques.

6.1 Frequency counts

In a frequency-count analysis you simply count up the number of times particular elements or particular constructs are mentioned. Although this method can be applied to individual Grids, it is most often used when a sample of people have been interviewed and you want to look for common trends.

One example of the use of frequency counts is a study we conducted on sales-people in the travel industry, to analyse their training needs and give the marketing department some information on products to promote. We asked the salespeople to name (a) examples of products they found easy to sell, (b) examples of products they found difficult to sell and (c) examples of products they believe the public do not understand or know about. Obviously the construct-elicitation stage of the exercise was the most valuable part, but we got much useful data — and got it quickly — just by assembling lists of the most frequently mentioned products under each heading.

If you use eliciting or free-response questions, a frequency count of the resulting elements is often very helpful. The number of times a particular product or person or job activity is cited in response to your eliciting question is a useful insight in itself and may help when you want to compare different groups of people. Frequency counts of constructs are usually a little more difficult, because it is not often that the same constructs are produced by several people. You can, however, select a fairly common construct or group of constructs and make a pattern to see how they are used. For example, in a Grid study with managers' activities as elements, several managers produced the construct *with staff — with customers*, but when asked the laddering question (in this case 'For you to be effective in your job, which is it more important to be good at dealing with, the staff or the customers?') the managers in one department unanimously said *staff*, and the managers in the next department unanimously said *customers*. Much complaint, from customers and staff alike, about inequitable treatment between departments was thus exemplified, and work began to try to effect an improvement.

Another example of frequency counts of constructs comes from a rule-of-thumb measure of organizational health which we use but have not tested exhaustively. Grid interviews with managers using job activities as elements usually produce a series of constructs such as: *with staff — with customers, with my boss — with my peers, with my peers — with my subordinates, with my boss — with my subordinates*, and so on. If these are laddered using the preference question quoted in the previous paragraph ('For you to be effective ... ') it is possible to construct a pyramid showing the relative preferences given to boss, peers and subordinates. Our rule of thumb is that in a healthy organization the proportions look like this:

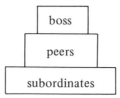

with about 50 per cent of the preferences going to the subordinates (in other words, about 50 per cent of the time the managers say that it is more important that they be good at managing their subordinates — we are definitely not talking about likes and dislikes), about 30 per cent of the preferences going to the peers, and about 20 per cent going to the boss. If the proportions were reversed the pyramid would look like this:

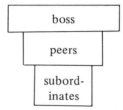

and in practice the consequences of this is that people devote more time and effort to managing their boss well than to managing their subordinates: which leads to politicking, angling for the boss's approval and licking of boots. In a pyramid where the boss : peer : subordinate proportions were more like 10 : 15 : 75 — a pyramid with a very narrow top and wide base — our guess is that the top—down guidance could be getting too strong and that channels of communicating information from the shop-floor upwards might be too weak for comfort.

This rule of thumb works fairly well for us, but we cannot elevate it to the status of a research finding; we have not tried it too often in matrix organizations, for example, where things might well be different. The principle underlying it is that of the frequency count; in this case the relative frequencies with which different poles of a family of constructs were thought to be important.

Frequency counts work best when the elements or constructs you are counting are discrete and well defined, and have a consistent public meaning. As soon as you have less well-defined and discrete elements or constructs you need an analysis technique with a little more latitude, and this is what content analysis is for.

6.2 Content analysis

To perform a content analysis you select a series of categories into which the elements or constructs fall, and then assign the elements or constructs to categories. In doing this you have more latitude than in a simple frequency count, because the category widths can be as broad as you like.

You can categorize either the elements or the constructs or both. An example of content analysis of elements is the study we conducted in five countries on the motivation of managers of service engineers. Elements were elicited by asking for the following:

Two job events where the interviewee had felt highly motivated.
Two job events where he had felt demotivated.
One event outside the job where he had felt highly motivated.
One event outside the job where he had felt highly demotivated.
The best possible thing that could happen in his job.
The worst possible thing that could happen in his job.
The most significant event which had occurred yesterday.

The elements cited to each eliciting question were then grouped together by content area. For example, the main content areas for the two job events where one manager had felt demotivated were: lack of management support, lack of spare parts and poor-quality machines, lack of information, engineers not being able to do the work, low level of pay and benefits, relations with unions, poor treatment compared with the salesmen, poor customer relations induced by lack of spare parts, lack of own training and being set impossible targets. We were able to produce a table showing the relative proportions of each kind of problem in each country studied, as well as an analysis of the overall figures, by means of a frequency count of the number of items in each category.

An example of the content analysis of constructs is shown from a study undertaken for a firm who wanted to know whether the categories used in its performance appraisal forms were 'right'. Here we did construct-elicitation studies on many managers, using as elements colleagues or subordinates (whom they were allowed to identify with initials or nicknames, this being quite a sensitive area). The constructs were then content-analysed to see whether they corresponded at all with the labels used on the performance appraisal form. A simplified version of the final picture is shown in Table 6.1.

Table 6.1

Present appraisal form	Construct groupings
motivation of staff	
training of staff	
industrial relations	
cost control	
technical competence	technical competence
crisis action	crisis action
accuracy	accuracy
customer relations	customer relations
	socially acceptable
	easy to manage
	works long hours
	long-serving (20 + years)

We are faced with two problems: the present appraisal form asks people to make judgements on four dimensions that do not occur naturally in their construing of these others; and conversely in making judgements of these others the managers use four dimensions that are not represented on the appraisal form at present. Several actions resulted. First, we asked the question: 'How important is it that people be judged on the dimensions of motivation of staff, training of staff, industrial relations, and cost control? Because, if it *is* important, then we know that in your appraisal-training and associated instructions you will have to undertake special remedial training to give people practice in using these dimensions.' Next, we asked the question: 'Would it be a good idea to incorporate into the appraisal system any of the dimensions used by managers naturally but not presently represented, i.e., social acceptability, easiness to manage, working long hours and being a long-serving employee?' There were two answers to this question. The dimension 'easy to manage' was re-christened 'relations with boss', though keeping much of the same content, and incorporated into the new scheme. The other three dimensions came as a warning; social acceptability should not be used as an appraisal dimension (it has very little to do with performance, and lends itself easily to unfair discrimination). The same could be said in lesser degree about the other two dimensions. The lesson for the re-design of the appraisal system was that much more attention should be given to weaning people away from these dimensions − a difficult task, as we knew they were dimensions they regularly used − and towards less dangerous dimensions.

Two examples, then, of content analysis at work. How do you actually set about doing it?

The first task is to develop the category system. Occasionally there will be a system ready-developed, as in the second example above where we had to try to fit constructs to the categories provided by the appraisal system. More likely, though, you will find yourself with a pile of constructs or elements, and you will wonder what to do next.

If you know in advance that you will use content analysis at some point, then it is worth adapting the original Grid procedure so that you get your constructs written on cards to begin with. One construct per 3 x 5 inch card − which can also carry comments made when laddering the construct − will simplify the content analysis considerably. If you go on to do a full Grid the labour of writing out the constructs twice in the actual interview − once on cards, once in the Grid − does not seem anything like as bad as the labour of rewriting constructs onto cards from a pile of Grid forms.

Then the best way is to clear a big table and just sort your cards into piles until you have sensible-looking, relatively homogeneous piles. Most people have absolutely no trouble doing this once they have taken the plunge and started to let the cards run through their fingers. Just occasionally we meet someone who cannot develop a category system unless someone tells him the system to develop, and we do not know a way of unblocking that jam.

Now label the categories − if you have a lot of cards, we mean physically writing a label for each depot and attaching it − and if you can, get a colleague to look at the cards you have assigned to each label and see what label he would give to those cards. If there is a big difference between his labels and yours, either start to negotiate or re-sort the cards.

Now that you have a category system, take all the cards and assign them to categories. If it is a good category system there should not be too many left over in the Miscellaneous heap, and there should not be too many that you want to assign to more than one category. If you find a problem with overlapping categories, think about re-defining the categories. Almost inevitably one or two category boundaries get shifted at this stage.

Now take a sample of cards, and code them so that you know the categories to which you assigned them. Give them to your colleague and ask him to assign them to categories. If you disagree, start to negotiate or re-sort the cards.

The services of a friendly colleague are important whenever you are construing someone else's construing — which, if you think about it, is a fancy name for what you have just been doing by categorizing other people's constructs. There is always the possibility of unconscious bias creeping in at such times. You want a reliability check with a colleague to test that what you see in the elements or constructs is the same as what anyone else who shared your purpose would see; and you must be sure to take the reliability check in two stages, one for the category names, and one for the category assignments.

The piles of cards are now ready for counting and interpretation.

One construct categorization often used is a tripartite division of constructs into *propositional*, *sensory* and *evaluative*. A *propositional* construct is one that describes easily observable properties of the elements, e.g., *black — white*, *in the office — out of the office*. *Sensory* constructs describe how the person feels or perceives the elements, e.g., *wet — dry*, *hard — soft*, *quiet — loud*. *Evaluative* constructs describe how the person evaluates the elements, e.g., *comfortable — challenging*, *liked — disliked*, *high priority — low priority*. This categorization is helpful to bear in mind when eliciting a Grid, as the purpose of the Grid usually determines the kind of constructs it would be most useful to elicit, and the balance between them. In a counselling Grid, for example, it would be necessary to elicit a high proportion of evaluative and sensory constructs; in a Grid for investigating the perceptions of quality controllers the propositional and sensory constructs would need emphasizing; in a market-research Grid it would be necessary to see how the evaluative constructs map onto the propositional ones, so the interviewer must be careful to elicit both kinds.

Frequency counts and content analysis are both simple methods that involve no complicated statistics — the most complicated you will get is a chi-squared if you want to compare the relative distributions of categories across two or more groups of people — and they are both concerned with counting how many times different semantic groupings occur in the elements or constructs. They are used most often on groups of people rather than data from people taken singly.

The next three methods all examine how constructs or elements relate within a particular Grid; they involve more mathematics and are more difficult (but not necessarily impossible) to apply to groups of people.

6.3 Visual focusing

This is a raw Grid, with the elements and constructs omitted, using a tick/cross system rather than a five-point scale:

	E1	E2	E3	E4	E5	E6	E7	E8
C1	✓	×	×	×	✓	×	✓	×
C2	×	✓	×	✓	×	✓	×	✓
C3	✓	×	✓	×	✓	×	✓	×
C4	×	×	✓	×	×	✓	×	✓
C5	✓	✓	×	✓	✓	×	✓	✓
C6	✓	×	×	✓	✓	✓	✓	×
C7	✓	✓	×	✓	✓	×	✓	✓
C8	×	×	✓	×	×	✓	×	×

To analyse this Grid using the method of visual focusing you get a narrow strip of paper and copy on to it, in position, the pattern of ticks and crosses given to Element 1. Then you compare this strip in turn with each of the other elements, writing down the number of times there is agreement (a tick with a tick, or a cross with a cross):

thus:

E1	E2	
✓	×	= 0
×	✓	= 0
✓	×	= 0
×	×	= 1
✓	✓	= 1
✓	×	= 0
✓	✓	= 1
×	×	= 1
		total = 4

and:

E1	E3	
✓	×	= 0
×	×	= 1
✓	✓	= 1
×	✓	= 0
✓	×	= 0
✓	×	= 0
✓	×	= 0
×	✓	= 0
		total = 2

and:

E1	E4	
$\sqrt{}$	x	= 0
x	$\sqrt{}$	= 0
$\sqrt{}$	x	= 0
x	x	= 1
$\sqrt{}$	$\sqrt{}$	= 1
$\sqrt{}$	$\sqrt{}$	= 1
$\sqrt{}$	$\sqrt{}$	= 1
x	x	= 1

total = 5

The maximum agreement score is 8 (the total number of constructs in the Grid) and the minimum zero. The next step is to draw up a matrix showing the agreement scores between every possible pair of elements, thus:

	E1	E2	E3	E4	E5	E6	E7	E8
E1	x	4	2	5	8	1	8	3
E2		x	2	7	4	3	4	7
E3			x	1	2	5	2	3
E4				x	5	4	5	6
E5					x	1	8	3
E6						x	1	4
E7							x	3
E8								x

Inspect this matrix, looking initially for the high numbers. E1 and E5 are totally in agreement (score 8) and E7 is in total agreement with both of these. E2 and E4 are in agreement almost as much (score 7 out of 8) and E8 is in agreement with E2 to the same extent.

To understand what these numbers mean and why you should bother with them, let us suppose that you are the promoter of indigestion remedies we visited earlier, and this is the Grid from the buyer of the major chain of chemists whom you are hoping to interest. The code for the elements in the buyer's Grid is:

E1 : GRIPENOT
E2 : ENO'S
E3 : RENNIES
E4 : MILK OF MAGNESIA

E5 : ACTAL
E6 : ALKA-SELTZER
E7 : ACHE-O
E8 : SUPERTUM

SUPERTUM is, you remember, the product behind which you have sunk your fortune. You will see that in the eye of the buyer your product is very little different from ENO's — because seven times out of eight, SUPERTUM and ENO's are given the same rating by the buyer. You will also see that there is an agreement score of 6 out of 8 between SUPERTUM and MILK OF MAGNESIA (E4).

Before you let this depress you, though, you might reflect on the fact that the manufacturer of ACHE-O is in even worse straits than you are. In the mind of this influential buyer of indigestion remedies, there is no apparent difference between his perception of ACHE-O and his perception of GRIPENOT and ACTAL (because they have an agreement score of 8 one with another).

In other words, where there is a high agreement score between two elements you may assume that those elements share a good deal of meaning. You might want to test this:

'Tell me, Mr Buyer, you seem to see my product SUPERTUM as very similar to ENO's. Is that really how it looks to you, or can you perhaps tell me some features on which the two products are different?'

In doing this, of course, you are asking for additional constructs, on which E2 and E7 score differently. These constructs can be written into the Grid and all the other elements scored on them — a good way to build up a reasonably full Grid from small beginnings.

The next stage is difficult to do correctly by eye, but it might interest you to try to re-sort the Grid so that similar elements are placed close together. Here we would start with elements E1, E5, and E7, so we could put these together to begin with:

	E3	E6	E8	E2	E4	E1	E5	E7
C1	x	x	x	x	x	√	√	√
C2	x	√	√	√	√	x	x	x
C3	√	x	x	x	x	√	√	√
C4	√	√	√	x	x	x	x	x
C5	x	x	√	√	√	√	√	√
C6	x	√	x	x	√	√	√	√
C7	x	x	√	√	√	√	√	√
C8	√	√	x	x	x	x	x	x

This re-sorting of the Grid places E1, E5 and E7 together because they are totally in agreement. Next E4, E2 and E8 are placed together because they are in close agreement, with E4 closest to E1 because of those two groups of three E4 and E1 have the highest agreement; then E6 and E3 are fitted into place.

This re-sorting involves a good deal of visual inspection, and if the reader can think of a better way to re-sort the Grid visually he is probably as right as we are; you can be exact about the correct location for the major columns of similar elements, but after that the picture gets a bit hazy. However, it could be the case that all you are really concerned about in the Grid is the degree of similarity between certain selected elements, as in our example of indigestion remedies; or if E3 = MYSELF, E5 = MYSELF AS I WOULD LIKE TO BE, E1 = MY FATHER and E7 = MY BOSS, in the above Grid.

You can apply exactly the same principle to the constructs, only this time it is a bit more complicated; if you examine C2 and C3 you get:

| C2 | x | ✓ | ✓ | ✓ | ✓ | x | x | x |
| C3 | ✓ | x | x | x | x | ✓ | ✓ | ✓ |

which appears to be total disagreement, until you reflect that if by chance the construct C3 had emerged the other way around — as it could well have done — there would be total agreement.

If you draw up the agreement matrix between constructs (using the Grid re-sorted for elements), ignoring the point about reversing constructs, you get the following matrix:

	C1	C2	C3	C4	C5	C6	C7	C8
C1	x	1	7	2	5	6	5	3
C2		x	0	5	4	3	4	4
C3			x	3	4	5	4	4
C4				x	1	2	1	7
C5					x	5	8	0
C6						x	5	3
C7							x	0
C8								x

Now with 8 elements, an agreement score of less than 4 makes the case for reversing that construct. Constructs C2, C4, and C8 have collected rather some low scores, so let us reverse these three constructs and see what we get:

	E3	E6	E8	E2	E4	E1	E5	E7
C1	x	x	x	x	x	✓	✓	✓
C2R	✓	x	x	x	x	✓	✓	✓
C3	✓	x	x	x	x	✓	✓	✓
C4R	x	x	x	✓	✓	✓	✓	✓
C5	x	x	✓	✓	✓	✓	✓	✓
C6	x	✓	x	x	✓	✓	✓	✓
C7	x	x	✓	✓	✓	✓	✓	✓
C8R	x	x	✓	✓	✓	✓	✓	✓

Note that an R is tacked onto those constructs that have been reversed. Our matrix now looks like this:

	C1	C2R	C3	C4R	C5	C6	C7	C8R
C1	x	7	7	6	5	6	5	5
C2R		x	8	5	4	5	4	4
C3			x	5	4	5	4	4
C4R				x	7	6	7	7
C5					x	5	8	8
C6						x	5	5
C7							x	8
C8R								x

which, satisfactorily, gives us no agreement score lower than 4 — in other words, no construct whose relationship to any other construct would better be represented if one of them were reversed. (It is not always as neat as this, so that sometimes an element of trial and error is required.) However, we can re-sort our Grid now for constructs as well, bearing in mind that the range of possible scores is 4 to 8, not 0 to 8 as with the element re-sort. Now we get the re-sorted matrix:

	E3	E6	E8	E2	E4	E1	E5	E7
C2R	√	×	×	×	×	√	√	√
C3	√	×	×	×	×	√	√	√
C1	×	×	×	×	×	√	√	√
C6	×	√	×	×	√	√	√	√
C4R	×	×	×	√	√	√	√	√
C7	×	×	√	√	√	√	√	√
C8R	×	×	√	√	√	√	√	√
C5	×	×	√	√	√	√	√	√

in which those constructs which are used in a like manner are placed close together in the Grid.

A schoolteacher was asked to do a Grid interview using as elements some of the children she taught. By some strange chance the pattern of her Grid corresponded with the one we have been using as a working example. Her construct C5 was *tidy — untidy*, and her construct C8 was *creative — uncreative*. The Grid analysis, which reversed C8 revealed that every child in the Grid who was judged *tidy* was also judged *uncreative*; and that every child in the Grid who was judged *untidy* was also judged *creative*:

'Tell me, Miss Jenkins, do you really think that tidiness and creativeness go together? Or can you think of a child you teach who is both tidy and creative? Or maybe one who is untidy and uncreative?'

This technique of re-sorting the constructs in the Grid is a splendid device for revealing stereotypes. It is rather complicated to do by hand — whereas the element sort is quite simple with practice if you stick to the tick/cross system — and this is where the computer will help. If you are only interested in the relationship between a selected number of elements and/or constructs it becomes more feasible, of course, as you can afford to lose some detail when it comes to the finer points of the re-sort.

6.4 Cluster analysis — The FOCUS program

The idea of revealing the meanings in a Grid by re-sorting it so as to place like elements together and like constructs together is carried further by various computer programs which use a variation of the cluster-analysis technique. There are several cluster-analysis based programs, using slightly different procedures; perhaps the best of those currently in use are the program developed for the Open University, and the FOCUS program and its related programs developed by Mildred Shaw and Laurie Thomas at Brunel University. We shall describe the FOCUS program from a user's point of view; detailed questions about the statistics underlying it should be addressed to Dr Thomas or Dr Shaw.

The FOCUS program operates in a way similar to the manual analysis you have just studied, except that where we used simple differences, the FOCUS program makes correlations. This enables it to be much more sensitive and to cope with five-, seven- or even nine-point scales.

Figure 6.1 is an example of the output from the FOCUS program. This was a Grid performed on a quality assurance engineer in a medium-sized manufacturing

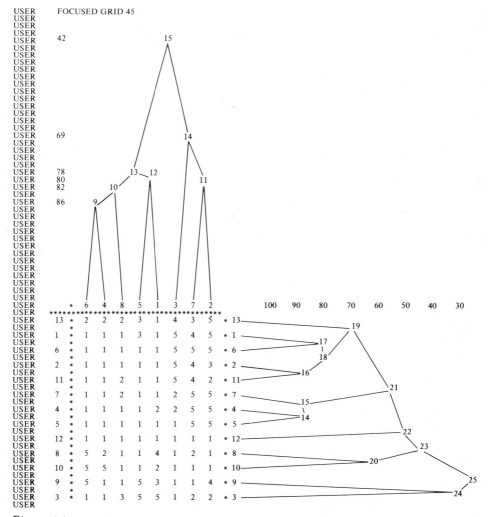

Figure 6.1

plant, as a method of getting a job description/man specification; he was someone who had virtually created the job (it was a fairly esoteric job) and conventional methods of writing a job description would have been time-consuming and may well have missed some detail.

The FOCUS program examines the raw Grid, first of all looking at the correlations between elements. It searches for the two elements that are most highly correlated; in this case elements E6 and E4 are the most highly correlated, at a level of 86 per cent. The program then melds these two elements together to create a new element which it christens E9 (there were 8 elements in the original Grid). It prints the element E9 at point 86 on the vertical scale running on the left-hand side above the Grid, to correspond with the correlation of 86 per cent, and it prints E9 between E6 and E4, its component elements.

The program now searches between the remaining elements for the next two most intercorrelated ones. It is searching through the list E1, E2, E3, E5, E7, E8 and E9, because elements E4 and E6 have now been dropped from the search. The next most highly intercorrelated elements are E8 and E9, at the 82 per cent level. So an additional new element, E10, is created from the marriage of elements E8 and E9, and printed in the appropriate place. The search continues: E7 and E2 form elements E11; E5 and E1 form E12; E10 and E12 form E13; E3 and E11 form E14; and finally E13 and E14 form E15. The program then re-sorts the Grid and prints the complete element 'tree' with the intercorrelations on the scale at the left.

The same thing happens with the constructs, with the program primed to reverse any construct necessary; this it prints so that the interpreter can annotate the Grid accordingly. Looking at the constructs we see that C4 and C5 are most closely correlated (they form C14) with C7 almost as closely correlated (with C14 it forms C15); then C2 and C11 form C16, and so on, until all the constructs have been joined into the 'tree'. The Grid is then re-sorted so that similar constructs are placed together and the final output is what we have here: a re-sorted Grid with a vertical tree of elements and a sideways-on tree of constructs, ready for interpretation.

Before discussing how to interpret computer output from a Grid analysis, it is worth discussing the philosophy behind interpretation. (Also, you will see much more about the interpretation of Grid in specific circumstances in the examples in the second half of this book.) Be cautious about construing other people's construing. The business of putting a Grid through a computer tempts one to do this. Unless you have a computer on the spot primed to analyse your data, the computer analysis separates the Grid interview from the Grid analysis. You might Grid 20 managers in their offices over the country; bring the data back to your office to get them analysed; are you really going to get on the company bicycle and visit all 20 again to talk about interpretation?

However, if you do not involve the interviewee in the interpretation process, you miss out on the following:

1. The freedom to claim that your study has been completely free from observer bias. You put your interpretation on what the interviewer means by the words

he uses to describe elements and constructs and on what he means by the way the elements and construct function.

2. The opportunity to question the interviewee further about any interesting-looking correlations.

3. The opportunity to generate feelings about a need for action, etc., on the part of the interviewee which you could have achieved by involving him more deeply in discussing his Grid.

You may be happy to pay that price; for it is a price and not a prohibition. It depends why you are doing the Grid. When you are doing it to extract information from the interviewee (market research, job descriptions, questionnaire design) you lose less than when you are doing it as a service to the interviewee (counselling, therapy, team building, training-needs analysis). With some of this latter group you may be faced with a choice of doing a less sophisticated Grid and analysing it on the spot, or doing a more sophisticated Grid which involve breaking contact while the computer does its work.

Happily, the advance of technology is reducing this problem. Desk-top computers now do things that were inconceivable ten years ago, so the difficulties of having to break off to analyse the data (or having to conduct your interview in the room next to the computer terminal) will soon be a thing of the past. Nonetheless the warnings about construing other people's construing will always apply, and you should read the section on interpreting the output of this and other computer programs with caution.

Back to our quality assurance man. To interpret his Grid we need to know what the elements and constructs are. In this interview we used job activities as elements; reading from left to right in the re-sorted Grid they are:

E6 : Advising production on simple faults that can be eliminated during production

E4 : Getting people to react to a technical fault

E8 : Checking the finished product to ensure it meets the required technical standards

E5 : Ensuring that staff are doing what they should be doing

E1 : Supervising solvent analysis

E3 : Collecting information on an unknown technical problem

E7 : Reading technical reports

E2 : Writing technical reports

Let us just concentrate on the elements tree for a moment. E3, E7 and E2 form a group that does not meld with the rest of the Grid until a fairly low level of inter-correlation — there appear to be two 'families' of elements, E6, E4, E8, E5 and E1, on the one hand, and E3, E7 and E2 on the other. Is there anything in the content of those two families of elements that tells you anything about why they should be separate?

Yes there is. The bigger family — E6 to E1 in the Grid — you might describe as 'doing', or 'up-front', work, and the smaller family is 'back-room' work. Because these two families are fairly well separated we can conclude that our man sees them as quite different from each other. *How* different you can see by looking at the constructs used to describe each family of activities — and by asking him for more information.

Within the left-hand family, E6 and E4 together with E8 form a little group. Is there any reason why these activities should be judged so alike? They are all concerned with faults; they are all concerned with something he does directly. E5 and E1 have more of an element of supervision in them. They are judged to be quite like each other, too. It might be interesting to ask our man whether he thinks that E5 and E1 require similar skills from him, or require him to take similar actions.

Basically the principles underlying this analysis are concerned with inspection for close similarities between elements, and for separated families of elements. Then, bearing in mind the purpose for which you are doing the Grid, you ask yourself or the interviewee questions such as:

1. — Does this make sense to you? Are there good reasons why things should be so?
2. — Has this pattern of looking at your world got survival value for you/your organization?
3. — Does this Grid reveal stereotypes or areas of ignorance that you were not aware of?

You may like to complete the interpretation process by looking at the patterns in the constructs. The constructs in order of appearance (with reversals already performed) are:

C13 : short-term — long-term

C1 : will cost a lot of money if I do — not likely to result in a loss of
       not   money

C6 : day-to-day activity — 'after' function

C2 : I get others to do something — other people get me to do something

C11 : grey-area — know what you are looking for

C7 : highlighting problem areas during — highlighting problem areas afterwards
        the event

C4 : looking at product this very — looking to improve next time
        minute

C5 : current situation — after the event

C12 : important — not so important

C8 : out of the ordinary — straightforward

C10 : queries take longer to answer — can answer queries after a few minutes

C9 : grey areas — can be determined before we start

C3 : fault has been found — looking for faults

HINTS

1. Remember why we did the Grid. This is a good performer and we want to draw up a description of the man in the job.
2. Look for the way elements are rated on constructs to tell you something more about the construct functions.

TEST YOURSELF

1. If you now had the chance of interviewing this man to find out more about how he sees his job and the demands that it makes on him, what would you want to ask?
2. If you could stand in his shoes for a moment and write on his behalf some homely advice to his successor, what would you say?

There are other programs available that use the principles underlying FOCUS. Two of the most useful, from the same authors, are PEGASUS and SOCIOGRID. In PEGASUS the Grid is built up interactively with the computer, the interviewer being taken out of the procedure altogether. The computer begins by asking for the purpose of the Grid, and asks for six elements; then it asks for constructs, and gets each element rated on each construct. It builds up the size of the Grid by looking for high degrees of intercorrelation between elements or constructs and asking for new constructs or elements that reduce the intercorrelation. SOCIOGRID allows the Grids of two or more people to be mapped onto the same space, provided that either the elements or the constructs (but not both) are held in common between the various Grids. This is particularly useful for applications such as team building, negotiations or investigating differences in points of view.

6.5 Principal-component programs

Imagine that you have nine elements and have calculated the correlations between all possible pairs. Let us assume that the resulting matrix of correlations looks like this:

	E1	E2	E3	E4	E5	E6	E7	E8	E9
E1	x	.9	.8	.9	.2	.1	.0	.0	.2
E2		x	.7	.8	.2	.0	.1	.1	.3
E3			x	.8	.2	.1	.1	.3	.2
E4				x	.2	.2	.0	.0	.3
E5					x	.9	.7	.2	.1
E6						x	1.0	.1	.1
E7							x	.0	.1
E8								x	.9
E9									x

How many independent variables are we looking at here? E1, E2, E3 and E4 all seem very highly correlated with each other, and hardly at all with the rest of the elements; E5, E6 and E7 similarly form a tightly knit group; and E8 and E9 are very highly correlated. So if we wanted to represent the number of and relationships between the independent variables underlying this correlation matrix, maybe we could do so with a three-dimensional diagram with three axes at right angles; one axis formed from E1–E4, one formed from E5–E7, and one from E8 and E9.

This is the basic principle underlying principal-components analysis. This analysis asks the question: 'How many independent dimensions do we need to describe all the relationships within this matrix?' When mathematicians speak of independent variables they have in mind a graphical representation that puts these variables at right angles; obviously this limits what one can actually draw to two dimensions, or three with some use of perspective; but it is possible to think in the abstract of any number of independent dimensions.

Several principal-components programs are available to analyse Grid data. Perhaps the best known are those developed by Pat Slater, Jane Chetwynd and others, known collectively as the INGRID suite. The development of the INGRID suite used to be funded by a grant from the Medical Research Council, but since the cessation of the grant, development work is going on in various places. The Post Office Psychological Services Division offers a commercial INGRID service to industrial users.

An example of the output from a typical principal-components program is given in Fig. 6.2. The program has extracted the two main independent dimensions, I (the horizontal axis), and II (the vertical axis). It prints also the percentage of the total variance accounted for by each axis; I accounts for 60 per cent of the total variance in this case, and II accounts for 25 per cent, leaving an extra 15 per cent which should be shown on other independent axes, but which has been omitted. The computer will also print out the labels of the elements and constructs which are most closely associated with each axis, thus allowing the interpreter to label the axes if he wishes. In this case we have a Grid where the elements were people at work, and from a judgement of the constructs that were used to describe those elements the interpreter christened the two major axes *weak – strong* and *I do not get on well with – I get on well with*. The computer also prints out the relative positions of each element on the two major axes; so BOSS'S BOSS scores somewhat on the *strong* side, and very high on the scale *I get on well with*, whereas SELF is seen as a little *weak* and he seems to like himself a bit, but not a lot.

The interpretation of this output involves looking at the relative positions of the various elements (or constructs, for a similar analysis can be performed for the constructs, or both elements and constructs can be mapped onto the same plot). Thus our man here, who has come for counselling, appears to be in rather a bad way. The three subordinates he gets on well with – 1, 3 and 4 – are all seen as rather weak, whereas the one he sees as strong he does not get on with at all. He sees his boss as strong, but he does not get on well with him – he gets on better with his boss's boss. It does not take much imagination to translate this into a difficult management situation for all parties. Our man has two clients, both seen as weak, both seen as not people he can get on with. What sort of service is he going to give them if this is how he thinks about them?

The cautions about construing other people's construing apply just as much here

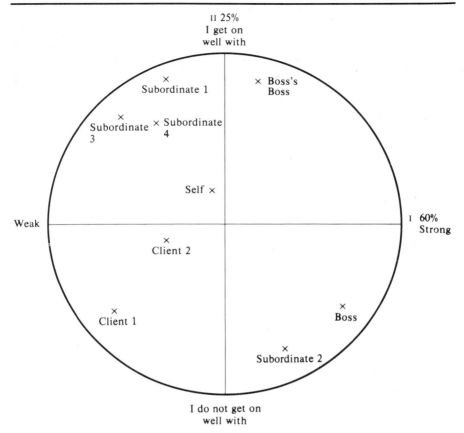

Figure 6.2

as they did to the FOCUS program; so do the underlying questions one asks in interpretation, such as the survival value of a particular perceptual structure. Instead of having to follow through the relationships element by element to build up the picture, the picture is ready built up here by the computer.

Another apparent advantage of this approach is the ease with which change can be shown in the Grid. Suppose we give our man counselling, coaching, therapy, job re-design or whatever we think necessary as a result of examining his first Grid; then we could run a second Grid (Fig. 6.3) in which the new positions of the various people were shown. Indeed we could lie the pre-therapy Grid over the post-therapy Grid to show clearly the relative changes. (In Fig. 6.3 the old positions are in lower case and the new positions in capital letters.)

We can thus assess whether the therapy has made much difference. Do you think it has? In the right direction?

The great appeal of the principal-components approach lies in this simple striking visual presentation of the data. There are however two cautions that many Grid practitioners feel reduce its usefulness.

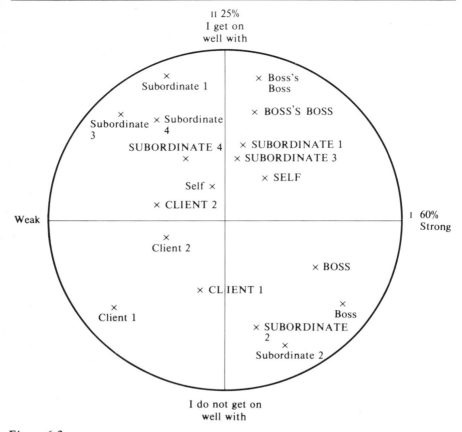

Figure 6.3

1. Not all the variance is represented by the two axes on the paper. It is usual to find only two axes used; sometimes three are given. You could well find that there are important relationships between elements or constructs that are not presented for analysis because they do not figure totally on the two (or three) main axes. To have 15 per cent of the variance left out is by no means unusual; we have seen papers where nearly 50 per cent is left out, without comment, by the authors. This sacrifices detail of unknown importance for the sake of easy visual inspection.

2. In before-and-after Grid studies — as with our example of change after therapy — there is no guarantee that the main axes produced for the second Grid will be the same as the ones in the first Grid, if you analyse the two Grids separately. You should really combine the two Grids — which means using the same elements and constructs for the second Grid, no more and no less. Thus if your change after therapy includes the availability of more elements or constructs, there is no way to introduce them into the second Grid and have it comparable with the

first. Many people do not bother to take note of this point; they analyse the second Grid separately from the first, lie the one over the other, and hope nobody notices that the axes do not match.

As both the cluster analysis and principal-components approaches have their adherents, we thought it might be useful to draw up Table 6.2 comparing the two kinds of program from the user's point of view. We have omitted many statistical comparisons which, while relevant to clinical users of Grid, might not have so much salience in industry.

These considerations tend to swing the argument in favour of cluster analysis for an increasing number of Grid practitioners. The fact that the relationships do not jump out of the page at you, but have to be traced, is not an enormous disadvantage — it helps you to get into the Grid and learn about its nuances. And when you remember that the person best motivated to make sense of the computer output is the person who generated it, many of the problems of interpretation recede still further. The process of analysing his own Grid is likely to increase the interviewee's feeling of ownership and commitment, whereas to be presented with a ready-mapped pair of axes with most of the work done from him may actually induce a barrier.

Table 6.2

Cluster Analysis	*Principal-components analysis*
1. Throws away no detail of the relationships between elements/constructs in its visual presentation of the data	Throws away some details of the relationships between elements/constructs in its visual presentation of the data
2. Requires some inspection before relationships between elements/constructs can be grasped completely	Relationships between elements and constructs retained for presentation are easily grasped
3. When two Grids are being compared, only elements *or* constructs need be held constant between the two	When two Grids are being compared, both elements *and* constructs must be held constant between the two
4. Uses non-parametric statistics on the data, i.e., treats 4 as more than 2 and less than 5, but makes no assumptions about the absolute size of the differences	Uses parametric statistics on the data, i.e., assumes that the distance between 4 and 2 is the same as between 5 and 3; and that a score of 4 on a construct indicates twice a score of 2
5. Can be easily administered interactively, building up a Grid and analysing it as you go along	Difficult to administer in interactive mode
6. Relatively easy to demonstrate what the computer has done to get from the Grid to the map	Rather more difficult to demonstrate what the computer has done to get from the Grid to the map
7. Cheaper to process (usually)	Dearer to process (usually)

Take your choice of analysis methods, bearing in mind the purpose for doing the Grid, how deep you want to go, what need for speed you have, and how and by whom the Grid is to be interpreted. If you work in a big firm with its own computer services people, do not expect them to be able to handle your data; they will be used to stock control or payroll or process applications, and a social sciences application may be totally unfamiliar. Most Grid analysis programs can be accessed either by sending your data away to be processed, or by your leasing the program directly, or through a time-sharing link.

If this chapter was heavy going, we apologise; statistics never make light reading. Try reading it again after dipping into the section of the book on applications, and try yet again before embarking on your first study — actually having the problem in front of you concentrates the mind wonderfully.

7. Before you begin . . .

By now you should be competent to undertake most forms of Grid interview successfully, though if you get the chance to see an accomplished Grid practitioner at work the experience will be beneficial. Before you begin in earnest, though, you should make yourself familiar with the remaining section of this book, which deals with some applications of the Grid technique to industry. The following list of hints and tips will be helpful.

7.1 Decide your purpose

You should know before you start why you are doing the Grid interview. For whose benefit is the Grid being done? Who will own the final data? What, if anything, will happen to the data after the interview ends? Where on the construct *extractive — reflective* does your proposed interview fall?

And what are you going to use as elements? What kind of constructs are you going to ask for? If you are going to ask for a preference for one end of the construct over another, on what parameter (importance, liking, difficulty, etc.) is that preference to be expressed?

7.2 Pilot

You may need two separate kinds of pilot; the first, never to be discarded, is when you run through one or two triads of elements to see whether they seem to be producing the kinds of constructs that suit your purpose. When you become practised this is the kind of thing you can do in your head without involving the interviewee, but it should always be done. The second kind of pilot is for the times when you have several extractive-type Grid interviews to do; then it is a good idea to do one or two full interviews, including analysis of data, before embarking on the complete study.

This second form of pilot study should allow you to make an estimate of the total time and resources required to complete the work. If you plan to use a computer in the analysis of the data, do not forget that you will have to go to a specialist source for your analysis; programs such as the FOCUS and INGRID suites are not yet widely available, and even simple social science statistics may not be available on a computer used for industrial purposes. Do not forget to allow for feedback time in the estimate.

7.3 Beware of interpreting

You can use Grid to extract information from someone, or to reflect back to him his thought processes, or you can take up one of many positions in between these two poles. In any case, you should think long and hard before construing someone else's construing. You have worked hard to control your observer bias, using a technique that gives you a lot of control over it; be careful before stepping back into the role of interpreter. You, as the experienced interviewer, may legitimately apply various kinds of statistics to highlight the pattern of meaning in the Grid, but you should then try to feed back that pattern to the person who produced it, get his comments and reactions, give him the chance to offer additional elements or constructs if these could reconcile patterns that he (or perhaps you) find strange. For most Grid studies, good politics and good research go hand-in-hand; it is only in the most extractive of studies, where both parties accept that this is so, that you should work without feedback — knowing the price you pay for doing this.

7.4 Listen to the conversation

The actual process of eliciting a Grid generates a conversation of great value. For some purposes the Grid conversation is more useful than the Grid itself — although without the Grid technique to help, the conversation may well not have happened.

Listen when you elicit the elements. Constructs may be generated then — not always in neat bipolar form, but enough to give you a lead you can use later on.

Listen to the ease or difficulty the interviewee experiences when generating elements to your eliciting questions. You may be asking a manager to think of events he has learned from, or activities he finds demanding on his skills — perhaps these are things he has never verbalised before. Listen to the things he says as he tries to name them.

Listen when you elicit the constructs. Do they come easily or with difficulty? Do you have to encourage the use of private language? What does he say while he tries to think of words for distinctions he has been using pre-verbally and probably unconsciously?

Listen when you ask him to rate an element on a construct when he may never before have made that judgement. Does he surprise himself? Does he show reluctance? Does the process itself generate new elements or constructs you can write into the Grid?

And look. Look at the body language — it is a very clear indicator of attitude. You will find that people use a lot of circular, impatient, encompassing gestures when you approach closer to core constructs in your questioning — or they go tight and enclosed in an effort to hide their feelings. The process of the Grid interview is usually so absorbing for the interviewee that he finds it difficult to control his body language, so you can use it as a valuable guide to feelings.

7.5 Rules are freedoms

The exercises in this book have taken you through a series of rules — rules for eliciting elements, rules for getting constructs, rules for feedback, etc. The rules are not in any sense restrictions. They are guidelines you can choose to follow to achieve your purpose with the kind of Grid interview you have in mind. You can do practically anything you want with a Grid interview, once you have learned the rules to follow and choose between. You can concentrate on the elements, on the constructs or on the full Grid; you can supply elements, supply constructs, share and swap elements and constructs between people; you can be mechanistic or free, extractive or reflective, as it suits your purpose. All the examples of Grid that follow in the second half of this book are examples of different applications of Grid for different problems, with the researchers adapting the Grid approach to suit their needs. Finally, you may find the summary shown in Table 7.1 a helpful *aide-mémoire* as you start to practise.

Table 7.1

To administer a Repertory Grid

1. (a) Decide *purpose* — why, for whom, with what expected action?
   (b) Decide *mode* — interviewer-guided, interactive, interviewee-guided, shared amongst a group?
   (c) Decide *analysis* — computer or manual, content or structure, etc.?

2. Choose *elements* by:

   (a) interviewer nomination if he wants the interviewee's views of those elements specifically; care to check that the interviewee is familiar with them.
   (b) interviewer elicitation of elements by questioning the interviewee to get a spread of elements over the available range.
   (c) interviewee nominating elements *ad lib.* after the interviewee has specified the family. This method produces elements that are familiar to the interviewee and with a possible bias towards preferred elements.

   Care

   Elements should be specific — people, events, objects, activities. Avoid features, relationships, etc. If you can hear an implied opposite to your element set (not to the questions used to elicit it) you are probably nominating as elements things that should arise as constructs.

   An element set should be homogeneous and discrete. Do not choose elements that are sub-sets of other elements.

3. Elicit *constructs* by presenting the elements three at a time with the questions such as:

   'In what way are two of these similar to each other and different from the third?

   or

   'Tell me something that two of these have in common which makes them different from the third?' etc.

If appropriate, refine the constructs by qualifying the question, e.g.

'Tell me something about two of these people that makes them different from the third in the way they go about their job?'

or

'Tell me about the demands these activities make on your skills — are any two of them similar in demands and different from the third?' etc.

4.   Obtain *higher-order* constructs by *laddering*. Present each construct to the interviewee and ask for a preference for one pole of the construct over the other on a parameter which is decided by reference back to the purpose of the Grid, e.g.,

'Which do you prefer to work with, people who are x or people who are y?'

or

'Which do you think it is more important to be good at doing, activities which are x or activities which are y?'

Take care before laddering the higher-order constructs; core constructs can be reached very quickly and this should not be done unless the interviewee has covenanted for it in his understanding of the purposes.

5.   If going on to administer a full Grid, turn each construct into a five-point scale or a two-point (tick/cross) scale. The former is used when fine judgements are required and the Grid will be analysed later; the latter is used when quick visual inspection of the Grid and manual analysis will be used.

Each element is then rated on each construct. Elements appear as columns, constructs as rows. The Grid can be filled in by columns or by rows, whichever is easier. New constructs may appear during this process; existing constructs may be re-defined; and new elements may be offered.

The purpose of this process is to test the range of convenience of each construct. Not every element may be rated on every construct, but constructs with a narrow range of convenience within the Grid may be discarded or re-defined.

6.   It is not necessary to exhaust all the possible constructs by triadic comparison before going on to full Grid. Many people find that the best way is to elicit a few constructs and put them into the Grid after laddering, and then produce some more; this makes the procedure more obvious to the interviewee.

7.   The Grid is now ready for discussion, sharing or analysis.

Part Two

Uses of Repertory Grid in Industry

8. Using Repertory Grid in market research

8.1 Background

As far as we can tell, the area of market research was one of the first business applications of the Grid. We add the qualification because many market-research people are reluctant to share their experience of it, preferring to keep their techniques secret. This is a pity, because many of the market-research people we have talked to about Grid have only a hazy idea of what they are doing with it.

The usefulness of Grid in market research lies firstly in its potential to give the researcher descriptions of his products in the consumer's own terms, and secondly in its ability to provide hard data showing how the researcher's product differs from its competitors in the consumer's own terms. Some market-research studies stop at construct gathering, if all they want is new insights about the product's appeal; others go on to full Grids, but usually without complex computer analysis because the main requirement is for one or two comparisons between elements.

We discuss here three examples of Grid in market research, showing (a) construct elicitation only, (b) individual Grids and (c) group Grids. Obviously we have had to change the names of the products and organizations under discussion, and if you think you recognize the name of a product, it is there merely to add verisimilitude, not necessarily because these were the products used when we did the research.

8.2 Example 1: Product design

A publisher decides that he wants to commission a book that will be a best-seller. To do this, he decides to conduct construct-elicitation interviews with a sample of typical book buyers (at several levels: buyers for shops, buyers *in* shops and buyers for libraries). He uses as elements the names of existing best-sellers mixed with names of books supplied by the interviewees, who are asked to name some recent books they have enjoyed reading. As he is in the fiction market, he confines his questions to fiction books.

One interviewee named the following four books as ones she had read recently and enjoyed:

The Last Enchantment (Mary Stewart's book on Merlin)
Lord of the Rings (Tolkien)
Little Big Man (Thomas Berger's novel of the West)
William's Happy Days (Richmal Crompton's schoolboy)

Then she was shown a selection of 20 cards bearing names of recent best-sellers. She was asked to pick five that she had read and liked or disliked. From this process came the remaining five elements:

The Day of the Jackal (Forsyth)
Five for Sorrow, Ten for Joy (Rumer Godden's convent novel)
A Coat of Varnish (C. P. Snow's detective novel)

73

The Thorn Birds (Colleen McCullough's Australian epic)
All Things Bright and Beautiful (James Herriot)

Construct elicitation produced the following constructs:

$^+$English — foreign

myth $\overset{=}{-}$ reality

all-round appeal — 'man$^+$'s book'

research based $\overset{=}{-}$ pure fantasy

I will re-read$^+$ — I will not re-read

serious $\overset{=}{-}$ funny

adult$^+$ — children's book

old author $\overset{=}{-}$ new author

vivid writing$^+$ — pedestrian

dialogue realistic$^+$ — wooden dialogue

easy to parody — less so$^+$

characteristic words and phrases — not so$^+$

a manufactured bestseller — took a long time to get published$^+$

dirty bits put in to shock — dirty bits part of the plot$^+$

well connected story$^+$ — series of episodes

crafted$^+$ — thrown together in a rush

told in first person $\overset{=}{-}$ told in third person

spiritual values $\overset{=}{-}$ 'worldly'

short $\overset{=}{-}$ long

historical/social interest permeates$^+$ — historical/social interest put in
the whole book   only by one or two markers — rest
of action could be anywhere,
anytime

historical reconstruction $\overset{=}{-}$ based on experience

The interviewee was then asked to express a preference for one end of each construct over the other, giving the pattern of crosses on the list above; and was then asked to rate each construct in terms of how important she felt it was to her enjoyment of the book — high, medium or low importance. This gave the following re-arrangement:

HIGH PRIORITY CONSTRUCTS

+		−
vivid writing	—	pedestrian
dialogue realistic	—	wooden dialogue
not easy to parody	—	easy to parody
few characteristic phrases	—	characteristic phrases
not manufactured bestseller	—	a manufactured bestseller
dirty bits part of the plot	—	dirty bits put in to shock
well connected story	—	series of episodes
crafted	—	thrown together
historical/social interest permeates the whole book	—	historical/social interest put in only by one or two markers — rest of action could be anywhere, anytime

MEDIUM PRIORITY CONSTRUCTS

+		−
English	—	foreign
I will re-read	—	I will not re-read
adults	—	children's book

=		=
pure fantasy	—	research-based
funny	—	serious
historical reconstruction	—	based on experience

LOW PRIORITY CONSTRUCTS

+		−
man's book	—	all-round appeal

=		=
myth	—	reality
old author	—	new author
told in first person	—	told in third person
short	—	long

Looking at the left-hand side of the high-priority constructs the publisher is able to assess what kind of book appeals to this interviewee. Obviously the next stage is to do some laddering – it would be interesting to know more about her notion of realistic dialogue, for example. A good bookseller would probably be able to put together an acceptable selection of books for this interviewee based on these data; the publisher needs to interview more people, to discover other people's thoughts on the same topic. Assuming that most of the other interviewees produced constructs like the person quote here, the publisher then briefs his authors and literary agents:

'I'm looking for a new book. It's important that it have vivid writing, with realistic dialogue, and if it's a period piece then the historical flavour should be all through the book, not just the odd mention of dinners costing 3/6d and people riding on trams. I want a well interconnected story, with different story lines weaving in and out of each other, not the 'this happened here and then that happened there'. Careful about the sex appeal – I don't mind dirty bits but they've got to look like a legitimate part of the action. Doesn't matter whether it's funny or serious, doesn't matter whether you're re-telling a myth or trying to base it in reality. Length is immaterial, and a new author stands as good a chance with this one as an existing author.'

Of course, we have simplified this example a little: the publisher would take other things into consideration besides readers' preferences when putting together his list, and this might well have led him to prefer novels of a certain length, or established authors. The use of Grid allows him to make a judgement about how important these factors are, and allows him to specify what the market wants in the market's own terms, rather than him relying on guesswork and his existing product range.

Other similar uses of Grid in product design:

1. – Architects wanting to elicit a specification from a client for whom they are designing a building.
2. – Manufacturers of toys and sweets for children, wanting a product that will meet current tastes.
3. – Car manufacturers wanting to know about their products as the public sees them, not as the designers or engineers see them.

If you use this application of Grid be sure to think about your element-selection strategy. You will want some preferred products and some disliked products; do you want to supply all the elements (risking the feeling of lack of ownership that sometimes goes with this) or to have free-response or elicitation (in which case you may encounter unexpected elements). In the example above, we used a mixed strategy – some free-response and some supplied by being chosen out of a large range.

8.3 Example 2: Impact of a new product

A manufacturer of cosmetics and perfumes has a panel of home testers whom he regularly consults for their views on his product range. In the early stages of setting up his panel he had Grid interviews conducted with each person, using as elements his own products and some of the competition's products. This allowed him to set up a form based on commonly used construct names; at regular intervals the home testing panel are asked to fill in the form, which is shown in Fig. 8.1.

FRAGRANCE EVALUATION FORM

			PRINCIPESSA							
woody									sharp
sweet									musky
young									middle-aged
well packaged									badly packaged
sexy									ladylike
unusual									much as the rest
daytime									nightime
feels expensive									feels inexpensive

Figure 8.1

The manufacturer produces a perfume called Principessa, and uses the form to collect comparisons between Principessa and its main competitors. When the Fragrance Evaluation Form is sent out, three or four times a year, together with samples of the fragrances to be used as elements, the home testers have to fill in their views on each of the elements, using some constructs already provided and adding some of their own if they feel like it. A complete Fragrance Evaluation Form from one tester is shown in Fig. 8.2.

The tester has tested the eight samples provided, and has added in the free space her comments on two perfumes that she has tried for herself, by adding two more elements and two more constructs. This process enables the manufacturer to see how his product compares with its major competitors, and also allows him to check the unanimity with which certain descriptions are used; he can test whether terms

FRAGRANCE EVALUATION FORM

1	JE REVIENS	MISS BALMAIN	VENT VERT	PRINCIPESSA	TAPESTRY	BLASE	GRASS OIL	STEPHANOTIS	In Love	Wistaria (Quant)	5
woody	2	1	1	4	2	4	1	2	3	3	sharp
sweet	3	5	1	4	3	2	5	1	1	3	musky
young	4	5	1	2	2	1	2	1	1	3	middle-aged
well packaged	3	5	5	3	2	5	2	2	2	2	badly packaged
sexy	4	4	4	2	3	1	3	5	4	1	ladylike
unusual	4	2	1	1	1	4	2	1	2	1	much as the rest
daytime	3	3	2	5	4	4	2	1	1	3	nightime
feels expensive	2	2	2	1	1	5	2	2	3	1	feels inexpensive
feels like me	5	3	2	4	2	5	2	2	5	1	feels like I've put it on
my husband likes it	3	2	1	2	1	5	2	1	5	3	my husband doesn't notice

Figure 8.2

like 'young' and 'sexy' are used in the same way by all his testers, and thus make a judgement about how if at all to use these words in his advertising.

With the existing panel, too, he can check the impact of new products on the market. When a new perfume, called Charlie, was introduced, Principessa took quite a knock, as you can see in Fig. 8.3.

Our manufacturer is in some trouble. First he sees that the introduction of the new element, CHARLIE, into the comparison table has stimulated the production of many new constructs (many of the testers filled in all four free-response constructs and added some more, whereas two free-response constructs were the normal pattern). So another manufacturer has managed to create a product which seems different and which stimulates new ideas about perfume in the minds of the users. That is bad news enough — in an evanescent field like cosmetics *different* often means *better* just by itself. Then the manufacturer looks at the constructs and sees that the new product CHARLIE is seen as an outdoor fragrance, with notions of laughter, independence, and the wearer wearing it to please herself, whereas his PRINCIPESSA is seen as a perfume to be worn indoors when occupied with the serious pursuit of catching a man. Before CHARLIE came along, PRINCIPESSA scored 1 on *unusual* and 1 on *feels expensive*; now CHARLIE has knocked those down to 3 and 2, respectively. Before CHARLIE appeared, PRINCIPESSA scored 2 on *young*; now CHARLIE has knocked it to half-way between *young* and *middle-aged*. Clearly our manufacturer will have to do something to restore the image of

FRAGRANCE EVALUATION FORM

1	JE REVIENS	MISS BALMAIN	VENT VERT	PRINCIPESSA	CHARLIE	TAPESTRY	GEMINESSE	SORTILEGE			5
woody	2	1	1	4	4	2	4	2			sharp
sweet	3	5	1	4	3	3	4	2			musky
young	4	5	1	3	1	3	5	3			middle-aged
well packaged	3	4	4	2	1	2	5	4			badly packaged
sexy	4	5	4	2	1	4	2	3			ladylike
unusual	4	2	1	3	1	1	3	5			much as the rest
daytime	4	3	2	5	1	3	4	2			nightime
feels expensive	3	2	2	2	1	1	2	3			feels inexpensive
outdoors - free	4	5	1	5	1	4	5	4			indoors - confined
laughing	5	5	2	5	1	5	5	4			all very serious
I'd wear it alone	5	4	2	5	1	2	4	4			I'd put it on for company
woman independent	5	5	2	5	1	3	5	4			woman trying to catch a man

Figure 8.3

his PRINCIPESSA in the eyes of the fickle female public, or he will have to bring out a new perfume designed to capture part of the CHARLIE market.

The regular panel of testers, experienced in Grid procedure, can be used either to test the impact of your product on the competition, or the competition's impact on yours. The example quoted here used Grid to produce the Evaluation Form, and asked the testers to add new constructs if they had any come to mind; a more subtle, but more time-consuming method, is to conduct Grid interviews from scratch each time, but if you are going to use a panel of testers anyway — as many manufacturers of consumer goods do — then the Grid information is more precise and comes in the consumer's own language.

Example 3: Graduate recruitment

You may be forgiven for asking why this topic figures in a chapter on market research, but the answer is quite simple; the organization concerned was worried that it somehow was presenting the wrong image to its graduate recruits, because so many of them left employment after a very short time. The principles behind the research can be applied to a much wider range of problems.

The organization is a nationwide retailing firm, with a reputation for being among the best employers in the retail area. Nonetheless, its turnover of new graduates was unacceptably high, and far too many left within a very short time —

days or weeks — of joining. Exit interviews revealed many comments like 'I didn't realize it was like this,' and 'It all seemed different from outside.' There was a case, therefore, for thinking that we should look at the image the firm presented to the new graduate, to try to identify more precisely the area of mismatch.

We obtained discussion groups of three different kinds of graduate: Group A, graduates who had been offered a job and had accepted but had not yet taken up employment; Group B, graduates who had joined the firm the previous year and were still there, having had almost a year's experience; and Group C, this year's graduates who had been offered a job by the firm but had turned the firm down. For each of these three groups we ran small discussion groups of 6 to 10 people at a time, using Repertory Grid.

After a short introduction, each person was given a group of cards and a Grid record form with room for 9 elements and 20 constructs. They were first asked to fill in the element cards thus:

CARD 1 — the present employer (in the case of Group C, the employer sponsoring the research)

CARDS 2 to 6 — other employers you would consider working for

CARDS 7 to 9 — other employers you would not consider working for.

The principle of construct elicitation was then illustrated by a couple of examples, using CAR, TRAIN and DONKEY as one group of elements, and WILSON, CALLAGHAN and BENN as another group. When everyone had grasped the idea they were asked to do the same with their own element cards, putting the constructs straight into the record form. After 20 constructs or failure of inspiration, whichever came first, they were then told to rate each element on each construct, using a simple tick-cross scale; finally they were asked to tick the side of each construct that represented their preferences. An example of the output from one person (rendered fictional to preserve anonymity) is given in Fig. 8.4.

There then followed a group discussion; in Group A it centred on their expectations about this employer, and what they thought about the recruitment process; in Group B it centred on the difference between early expectations and the reality of employment there; and in Group C it centred on the reasons why the graduates had been put off joining the firm even when they had received a job offer.

Analysis of the results is fairly selective; a good deal of data is collected, but not all used. The first step is to compile a list of all those other employers who were thought of as potential alternative employers by the three groups of people. Obviously, the most frequently occurring names represent the employers who are competing with this firm (Tomkin's Stores) for graduate recruits. Here was the first shock: the most frequently mentioned competitors were firms like BP, ICI, IBM or Unilever — not firms in the retail sector at all. Then we compiled a list of frequently mentioned retail firms — mentioned as potential alternative employers, that is, not as employers they would resist. Then using the Grid record forms we listed all the adjectives that were applied to Tomkin's Stores, all the adjectives that were applied to the most frequently mentioned competitors, and all the adjectives that were applied to the most frequently mentioned retail competitors. This gave three lists, and a much-simplified version of those lists is given in Table 8.1.

✓	TOMKIN'S STORES LTD	BRITISH PETROLEUM	IBM	UNILEVER	ICI	BBC	WOOLWORTHS	HM PRISON SERVICE	BRITISH LEYLAND	X
profit-making ✓	✓	✓	✓	✓	✓	X	✓	X	X	spending taxes
bureaucratic	X	X	X	X	X	✓	X	✓	✓	no red tape ✓
go-ahead ✓	✓	✓	✓	✓	✓	X	X	X	X	stick-in-the-mud
look after staff ✓	✓	✓	✓	✓	✓	✓	X	X	X	poor staff policy
competitive ✓	✓	✓	✓	✓	X	X	✓	X	✓	monopoly
place to develop ✓	✓	✓	✓	✓	✓	✓	X	X	X	place to stagnate
fixers ✓	✓	✓	✓	✓	✓	✓	✓	X	X	panickers
good reputation ✓	✓	✓	✓	✓	✓	✓	X	X	X	low reputation
getting better ✓	✓	✓	✓	✓	✓	X	✓	X	X	getting worse
equal opportunity ✓	✓	X	✓	X	X	X	X	X	X	women looked down on
9 - 5 job	✓	X	✓	✓	X	X	✓	X	X	work all hours ✓
high technology ✓	X	✓	✓	X	✓	X	X	X	X	low technology
high standards ✓	✓	✓	✓	✓	✓	✓	X	X	X	low standards
quick promotion ✓	✓	✓	✓	✓	✓	X	✓	X	✓	wait for promotion
good staff ✓	✓	✓	✓	✓	✓	✓	✓	X	X	poor staff
solving problems ✓	✓	✓	✓	✓	✓	✓	X	X	✓	just caretaking
good locations ✓	✓	X	✓	X	X	✓	✓	X	X	poor locations
not innovative	X	X	X	X	X	X	X	✓	✓	open to ideas ✓
selling =	✓	X	✓	X	X	X	✓	O	X	production =
ephemera	✓	X	X	✓	X	✓	✓	O	X	permanent products ✓

Figure 8.4

Table 8.1

TOMKIN'S STORES	UNILEVER	SAINSBURY'S
look after staff		
good public image		
high quality		
equal opportunity		
place to develop	place to develop	
good staff	good staff	
vertical integration	vertical integration	
profit-making	profit-making	profit-making
competitive	competitive	competitive
innovative	innovative	innovative

Even this over-simplified list retains the essence of the research: that Tomkin's Stores was seen as more like the big industrial firms (e.g., Unilever, ICI, IBM) than like other retail firms; that Tomkin's therefore attracted people who would not otherwise go into retailing; and that other retail firms were often cited as examples of places where the graduates would not want to work.

This news came as part shock to Tomkin's, part confirmation of what they had already guessed. The difficulty lay in their good reputation as being head and shoulders above most other retailers; they therefore attracted graduates who would not normally consider going into retailing, but would join a firm as prestigious as Tomkin's. However one branch of retailing is pretty much like another in essence; whether you are working for a high- or low- status retailer you still need to be able to stand till your feet bleed, to have a butterfly mind that does not care if there are always 20 different claims on its attention, to put up with rudeness from the public, to accept the Head Office way of displaying merchandise when you could think of a better way to do it yourself . . . and the graduates did not realize this before joining. Part of the 'image' problem was therefore that they were projecting too up-market an image, and appealing to the wrong sort of graduate. The research results also forced them to think hard about the level of graduate they actually wanted; with the usual lack of analysis they had gone for the Upper Second from the Good University, and we were able to question them about whether it would not be better to go for the ordinary degrees and the polytechnic students.

In this method, the advantage of the full Grid procedure was that it enabled comparisons to be made between elements — a selected few elements chosen after counting the most frequently named elements in each category. Doing the Grid in groups reduced the time taken to complete the exercise, and also provoked some very lively discussion afterwards, probably livelier than one would have got with individual interviews. The end results were simple to present, and had the advantage of coming obviously from the graduates themselves without intervening interpretation — a useful point to remember when faced with a potentially tricky internal political situation, as nobody likes to be told that his recruiting policy has been wrong even when people are voting with their feet in large numbers.

These three examples of Grid in market research are all 'extractive' rather than 'reflective' uses of the technique. Other uses veer towards the 'reflective' end: the architect using Grid to help specify a client's dream home, or the travel agents who use disguised Grid techniques to help people plan their holidays by clearly eliciting their needs. Data from individuals are used much less often than aggregated data from groups of individuals, with consequent loss of subtlety. The gain is to hear the product described as the user sees it, to know that you have not been blinded by previous work on product development or seduced into a one-sided view, so that you can produce a product that the customer finds acceptable and describe it in terms that represent the customer's needs.

9. Using Repertory Grid in quality control

9.1 Background

The principles of Repertory Grid are used by several firms wanting to improve various aspects of quality control. Here the main attraction of Grid is its role in the development of a vocabulary, and the structure it provides for turning a pre-verbal vocabulary into a verbal one. Many production industries have someone in the quality-control department who is expert at detecting faults, without being able to put words to the faults; in a ball-bearing factory, for example, all the quality-control work is done by one elderly lady who runs here hands over the ball-bearings as they come off the line and consistently picks out the bad ones. The problem is that she is retiring in a few months' time and her successor has to be trained to the same degree of dexterity — trained to recognize things for which she has at present no adequate labels. There are also problems wherever two or three quality controllers are gathered together: how to make sure that they all have the same standards and a common language. Training a new quality controller to work alongside the old ones, or bringing together a team of quality controllers — all areas where construct elicitation or full Grid will help. We give here three examples, sometimes translating the idiosyncratic language of the particular product concerned into a more accessible area.

9.2 Example 1: Learning from experienced operators

The problem here is to learn from an experienced quality controller who is good at picking out faults exactly what it is he sees or feels in the products. It is therefore appropriate to use construct elicitation, using as elements a selection of faulty objects and some perfect ones. The actual objects themselves should be used wherever possible — ball-bearings, moulded plastic figures, cups of tea, or whatever. Only when the elements become physically impossible to manipulate should they be written on cards — ladles of steel, for example — and if it is possible to include a photograph or similar representation on the card then this should be done.

Quality controllers vary a great deal in their verbal sophistication, depending on the industry they are in, but mostly they need a little help settling down to the construct-elicitation process. The process of analysis itself may be unfamiliar, and they are certain to have private language to describe some of the faults which they may be shy of revealing. So it is important to set them at ease first, and to explain that you are expecting to have the faults described in their own language rather than in any authorized language they may expect to have to use. It is also useful to use the 'full context' administration of construct elicitation, rather than the more usual triadic comparison. So an excerpt from a 'full context' interview, using as elements a range of children's stuffed toys that the controller was responsible for passing, runs as follows:

INTERVIEWER   Now we have here ten toys, some with faults and some without. Could you please look at the ten and pick out for me two which are most alike?

INTERVIEWEE   These two.

INTERVIEWER   And could you pick out from the rest the one which is the most different?

INTERVIEWEE   This one.

INTERVIEWER   So if we put these two together because they are like each other, and say that this one is the most different, can you describe to me what these two have in common that makes them different from the third?

INTERVIEWEE   With these two the legs don't match, but this one's got legs the same length.

INTERVIEWER   And having legs that don't match is a fault, while legs that do match in length is what you're looking for, right?

INTERVIEWEE   Yes, that's right.

INTERVIEWER   Fine, now let's put these three back into the pack and I'm going to ask you to pick out two more that are like each other in some way — a different way this time.

INTERVIEWEE   These two.

INTERVIEWER   And could you pick the one that's most different to these two?

INTERVIEWEE   This one.

INTERVIEWER   Now could you tell me what they've got in common that's different from the third?

INTERVIEWEE   This one's got its buttons on wrong, but the other two are O.K.

INTERVIEWER   When you say wrong, what exactly do you mean?

INTERVIEWEE   Well, actually there's two things wrong, the buttons are on out of line —

INTERVIEWER   Out of line?

INTERVIEWEE   Slanting off-centre, like this, you see.

INTERVIEWER   Thanks.

INTERVIEWEE   And the distance between them isn't the same, and it should be — four buttons equally spaced down the front.

INTERVIEWER   So a good one would have its buttons down the centre and equally spaced?

INTERVIEWEE   Yes, that's right.

INTERVIEWER   Can we do the same thing again? You draw out two that are like each other, and then the one that's most different . . . .

INTERVIEWEE   Well, there's these two . . . and this one opposite . . . .

INTERVIEWER   And what are you seeing in the two that are like each other?

INTERVIEWEE   Those two will sit upright by themselves, but this one falls over.

INTERVIEWER   And they are supposed to sit up by themselves, are they?

INTERVIEWEE   Yes, we had a right to-do in the advertising about it, they have 'em on telly sitting up and a little boy wrote in and complained that his didn't.

INTERVIEWER   I see. Can we do another three?

INTERVIEWEE   Well, there's this one, and these two . . .

INTERVIEWER   And what's the difference here?

INTERVIEWEE   I don't rightly know how to put words to it . . . it's just something I see about it, this one, I know it won't sell, it'll be the last one left on the shelf . . . .

INTERVIEWER   What do you call it to yourself, in your head, when you're checking them off?

INTERVIEWEE   I call them mardy buggers. It's what my mother used to call me, you see.

INTERVIEWER   I like that. And you're saying that this one here is a mardy bugger, and these two are not.

INTERVIEWEE   You can say mardybugs if you like, since you're writing this down.

INTERVIEWER   Thanks. What is it about this one that makes you call it a mardy-bug? How is it different from these two?

INTERVIEWEE   It's something about the face, you see. A mardy kid is someone who's always miserable and grizzling, and this one looks like that to me.

INTERVIEWER   Can you say what it is about the face that makes it look mardy?

INTERVIEWEE   Can't really.

INTERVIEWER   Is it the shape, or is it the features themselves, do you think?

INTERVIEWEE   It's not the shape, the shape doesn't change much . . . it's something about the eyes . . .

INTERVIEWER   Let's put the mardy one against a good one and let me ask you what things about the mardy one you would have to change to make it not so mardy. Put them side by side, like this . . . . What would you need to change?

INTERVIEWEE   The nostrils need to come down a fraction, there's too much between them and the mouth. And the black eye-bits are too close together — the whites of the eyes are in place, you can hold them together and they match, but the black part of the eyes is stitched too close together . . . .

INTERVIEWER   So how do you reckon they should be done?

INTERVIEWEE   Well, I suppose if you look at this good one there's the same distance between the eyes and nose as between the mouth and nose, so that's probably the rule there . . . . And when you're putting the black eye bit on the white bit you want the same amount of white on both sides. Something like that, anyway.

etc., etc.

In this example we can see how the use of full context enabled both parties to start off with easy triads. Full context was also helpful in making sure that each construct was defined by its extreme ends (within the context of the elements present) so that good clear comparisons were possible. You can also see a nice example of 'private language' and the interviewer's reaction to it, and observe how laddering takes place, assisted by the presence of the actual objects as elements.

The end-product of this exercise is a list of constructs with a good and bad end, defined in observable terms, but with the private language terms appended in case they should come in useful later. When our quality controller retires and leaves the inspection of calico dolls to someone else, the newcomer will not have to work it out all for herself but can borrow the crystallized experience of her predecessor.

Stuffed dolls is perhaps not a very earth-shattering example, but it was one we thought most readers would be able to understand without having worked in a stuffed-toy factory. Wherever the quality-control judgements are partly aesthetic, or use senses other than sight and hearing, you can use this procedure, and it has been applied successfully in industries ranging from engineering to food preparation.

9.3 Example 2: Training new operators

If you are successful in applying for a job as a chocolate taster in one of Britain's major chocolate manufacturers, you will early on be faced with three chocolates. Your task is simple – to decide which two of those three are the same. If you get it right, you are taught the firm's accepted label for that differentiation – it may be as simple as *milk – plain*. Your reward for doing so well is another three pre-selected goodies, which you have to differentiate in the same way; when you are confident of this differentiation you are taught the accepted label for it (*bitter – sweet*, for example) and so on.

The constructs themselves (*milk – plain*, *bitter – sweet*, etc.) were derived from interviews similar to the one illustrated above, except that a further stage was added of getting all the quality controllers to agree common names, and to give advice on which were the easiest differentiations to learn. Thus the training programme for newcomers begins with triads pre-selected to illustrate a given progression of 'official' constructs, getting progressively more difficult as the training goes on. The advantage of learning the 'official' label is that it prevents private language proliferating and means that quality controllers achieve a high degree of inter-rater reliability.

At a later stage in the training, when basic constructs have been absorbed, the experience becomes more complex. Instead of being given chocolates three at a time, they are given the full context – 10 or 20 chocolates of different quality, and they must do as our inspector of stuffed toys did, only this time there are right answers for the construct labels. And when they are proficient at this, and have broadened their skills to include not only taste but degree of cover and quality of decoration, the next stage involves learning to grade along the constructs. From the full context the trainee selects the two most alike and the one most different on a given construct – say *glossy coat – matt coat*. These chocolates are then laid out in front of the trainee and he has to assign all the rest to places between the two extremes, thus learning to use the constructs as scales. His assignments of elements on constructs are checked with those of an expert and any differences discussed.

This method allows the trainee to be trained in a controlled fashion, with the minimum possibility of error, at his own pace, and with a maximum of 'discovery learning' – the best kind of learning. Formal instruction is very difficult in quality-control areas, and until the use of Grid the alternatives were most of the 'pick-it-up-as-you-go-along' variety. Using the Grid-based method above, newcomers to quality control can be trained quickly and effectively.

9.4   Example 3: Resolving differences between existing operators

Maureen Pope, at the Institute for Educational Technology at Surrey University, has helped several firms where quality-control procedures were in difficulty because of 'lack of communication' between different departments. Dr Pope used Repertory Grid, and one of its more unusual computer programs, to help solve the problems.

One company concerned manufactured children's clothing. There were four quality-control operators, and several management staff involved in the quality-control process at some point – the production manager, the sales manager, etc. Dr Pope began by getting them all together – in itself an unusual occurrence – in a room containing many faulty garments. The object of this session was to obtain some garments, later to be used as elements, that everyone agreed were faulty in some way. She thus had a set of common elements, and was interested to know how different people construe these common elements.

She conducted Grid interviews with all the staff involved, using the faulty garments. The first analysis was a simple content analysis of the constructs; this proved highly revealing. The quality controllers themselves had constructs about the actual appearance of the garments (*seams crooked – not, tabs OK – not, elastic too tight – not*, etc.). Their supervisors tended towards constructs expressing blame for the fault, or its ease of repair, e.g., *fabric fault – construction fault, cutting fault – our fault, can be redone – must be thrown out*. And the managers involved in selling the garments had constructs such as *affects saleability – does not, will make a second – cannot sell at all*, and so on. So Dr Pope was able to identify clearly one of the causes of 'lack of communication' – that they could all be looking at the same fault, but the quality controller could be thinking: 'My stitching slipped there,' while the supervisor thought: 'It's on an inside seam, so no-one'll notice,' and the sales manager thought 'I can probably get this past as a sample, but it had better not get any worse,' and they had never sat down together and shared the different implications they saw in the same fault. One of Dr Pope's first steps, therefore, was to bring the group together again and show them the different kinds of constructs she had got from the different people, say how they related to the job each one had to do, but also start a discussion about how one person's constructs related to another.

She also put the individual Grids through the SOCIOGRID program, developed by Dr Mildred Shaw to analyse a number of Grids where the elements are held in common but the constructs are individual. One output of the SOCIOGRID is a 'socionet' – a multidimensional map showing how closely each person's perceptions of the similarities and differences between the elements resembles each other person's. Socionets can often be reduced to a two-dimensional drawing without great loss of detail; when Dr Pope drew the socionet for the various people involved in this exericise she saw that three of the quality controllers were very close together on the map (indicating a good deal of similarity between their perceptions of the elements), but the fourth quality controller was very much different. Interestingly, this fourth controller had worked for the firm for 20 years, but had her own private language for faults, different from that of her colleagues; she referred to 'spiders' (a particular cloth fault) when the other three called them 'pulls'. SOCIOGRID will not tell you that three are right and the other is wrong, but it did highlight the differences; and it so happened that as part of another exercise in the factory the eye-movements of the four were being filmed, and the fourth quality controller had a completely different pattern of scanning the garments from the other three.

The end-product of the exercise was therefore a clear identification of the areas of agreement and disagreement between the quality controllers and their managers, and an equally clear insight into the different languges they used. Remedy was fairly simple — getting them to talk to each other, sharing constructs and percep-tions and labels, so that there developed both a common language and an under-standing of one another's points of view.

10. Using Repertory Grid in questionnaire design

When you measure people's attitudes you need to be sure that you are asking them the right questions. You might want to investigate why people choose particular careers; it is difficult to make sure that you present them with all the possible reasons to choose between. You might want to know what the different attitudes to the job are between stayers and leavers so that you can cut recruitment costs; it is difficult to be sure that when you ask questions about their attitudes to the job you test all the possible attitudes they may have formed. If you want to know whether people like working for your company, you need to ask them questions on all possible areas of liking and disliking, and it is difficult as an outsider to be sure that you have covered all your options. Repertory Grid procedure is an invaluable help with the design of questionnaires. Used in the pre-pilot stage, when interviewing to discover the areas the questionnaire should cover and the best ways of expressing them on paper, Grid — most often just construct elicitation — usually shows up important areas that other techniques might miss.

10.1 Example 1: Doctors' career choices

We took part in a study designed to discover doctors' attitudes to particular medical specialties. The background was one of constant shortage in some specialties despite what were thought to be attractive inducements, and constant over-supply in others despite the fact that every medical student knew these specialties were difficult to get into. Specifically, specialties such as psychiatry, geriatrics, dermatology, mental handicap and community medicine find it difficult to attract doctors, whereas specialties such as cardiology, obstetrics and neurosurgery are usually oversupplied.

Our research design used a questionnaire on which doctors were asked to rate the characteristics of (a) their present specialty, (b) their ideal specialty and (c) some known popular and unpopular specialties. From this we would have a clearer idea of how the unpopular specialties were perceived, and how important the drawbacks were, so that remedial action might then be addressed to the real problem. Obviously the first step in this design is to get a list of parameters on which the doctors rated the specialties. We took 'expert' advice from the administration staff, who mostly thought that the problem was one of pay, conditions and promotion rates — put those right and doctors would flock into the unpopular specialties. We wondered if there might be more to it than that.

A national sample of doctors was interviewed, using construct-elicitation techniques. The elements were chosen by each doctor, who was asked to name his present specialty, some others that he would have liked to go into and some that he would have disliked going into. In piloting the interviews we found that our original eight-element set did not provide enough variety and lost the doctors' interest, whereas a set of twelve elements gave better results. Constructs were elicited from the elements, the doctor being asked to construe them in terms of the way he felt about them.

For example, in one interview the doctor had as his set of elements:

E1: ANAESTHETICS	E7: OBSTETRICS
E2: CARDIOLOGY	E8: PATHOLOGY
E3: PSYCHIATRY	E9: BLOOD TRANSFUSION
E4: GENERAL PRACTICE	E10: GERIATRICS
E5: PEDIATRICS	E11: INDUSTRIAL MEDICINE
E6: OPHTHALMOLOGY	E12: COMMUNITY MEDICINE

and produced constructs like the following:

mental illness — physical illness
no feedback — can tell when you are doing well
really ill patients — no real demand on my skills
maintenance — putting people right
putting people right — finding out what went wrong
etc, etc.

There were several surprises when we did our analysis of the interviews. The first step in analysis was to count the number of times a given specialty had been mentioned as a preferred or not-preferred element. Some specialties — such as general practice, pediatrics — turned up under both headings quite frequently. The next surprise was that there were some constructs about medical specialties that very few of the lay people we consulted had predicted would occur — the laymen had not even thought of them, let alone thought of them as important. Among these important constructs were the following:

patients die or get well — patients linger
sick patients — healthy patients
unconscious patients — patients can talk back to you
old patients — young patients
clear aetiology — unclear aetiology
I experienced at school — I had no experience of at medical school

For many doctors these were crucial constructs in their choice of specialty; and not all doctors evaluate the poles of each construct in the same way. Doctors who prefer their patients to either die or get better, rather than to linger, are likely to choose surgery as a career; doctors who prefer to deal with more subtle, difficult-to-diagnose ills are more likely to choose medicine. There is a similar differentiation between doctors who like to work on problems whose cause is clear, and those who like to unravel mysteries; usually each has a definite preference for his own type of work and would not be happy with a transfer. One construct that surprised us was the *sick patients — healthy patients*. We had assumed that people do not become doctors unless they want to help the sick. But there are a surprising number of doctors who dislike working with sick people; they go into specialties where the patients are basically healthy but have one or two problems, e.g., into obstetrics, blood transfusion. There are doctors who do not like it when their patients talk back when they are busy; they are likely to choose anaesthetics or perhaps pathology. And it was fascinating to hear doctors describe their preferences for the different poles of the construct *old patients — young patients*, particularly thinking of pediatrics; doctors who liked pediatrics said: 'It's nice because if you actually save a life you've saved so much life, and it's a test of your medical skill to be able to diagnose when the patient often can't talk.' Doctors who disliked the idea of going into pediatrics said: 'It's dreadful to think that if you lost a life you'd be losing so much life, the responsibility would be awful; and I can't imagine practising medicine without being able to talk to the patient and get some feedback from him.'

Besides learning a great deal about the feelings doctors had about the various specialties, we noted how often the construct *I experienced at medical school — I had little or no experience at medical school* appeared. In Britain, attempts to give young medical students a wide range of experience of the different specialties, and to provide decent disinterested career counselling, are left very much to the discretion of the individual Dean. One reason why many specialties are not chosen is because students are not exposed them as often as they are to the more glamorous and obvious choices.

With the results of the Grid interviews we were able to design a questionnaire that asked the right questions — asked questions about feelings and perceptions that we knew came from the doctors themselves, instead of retreating into the personnel-department officialese that so often seems the alternative. When the questionnaire itself was piloted we had far fewer problems with the content and nature of the question than we expected, going on experience with other surveys. And, of course, we were able to claim to anyone who made objections ('It's just another academic exercise . . . ', 'Why should doctors have to explain themselves to laymen?') that the questionnaire had not been put together by a group of lay academics, but was taken almost directly from records of doctors' own feelings and preferences as they were expressed in the interviews.

We cannot quote the final outcome, unfortunately, as the report has yet to be made officially available. We can, however, testify that Grid gave us a very early and systematic grip on the problem, gave us data of a kind and detail we were not able to anticipate, and made the actual design of the questionnaire much simpler than if we had used ordinary interview methods.

10.2 Example 2: Wastage studies

Most organizations lose too much money by poor recruitment and early training practices. The prediction of who will stay and who will leave is one important area for research, but it is often difficult to do well.

A good paradigm to follow, if time allows, is to take a sample of newcomers and find out as much about them as you can. Then in six months' time — or whatever period of time seems appropriate for a significant number of them to have left — go back over the data and see what factors differentiate stayers and leavers. Unfortunately for this simple paradigm, the differentiating factors are not usually the simple ones — age, number of previous jobs, educational background, etc. To find good differentiators you need to look at the attitudes people bring to the job, and look in some detail. Obviously Grid will help a great deal here in revealing people's attitudes to work and expectations about the job.

Kate Keenan, an industrial psychologist with a great deal of experience with wastage studies, used Grid to help with a study of the wastage of milkmen in the London area. She took a sample of around 900 milkmen and interviewed them using job activities as elements; at the end of this procedure she also asked them to describe what they thought a good milkman should be like. With the data so gathered she put together a questionnaire in which the milkmen were asked to describe themselves and their attitude to the job, and also to describe the ideal milkmen. When she returned in six months' time she was able to differentiate in two ways: between stayers and leavers, and within the group of stayers between effective and less effective performers.

Among the attitudes that distinguished stayers from leavers were: attitudes towards working in bad weather, attitudes towards working alone with no-one around to help if you got into a mess, and attitudes towards being your own boss. People who stayed were more likely to be able to tolerate bad weather — often they had had experience of it before. They could shrug and smile when they had a disaster with no-one around to help (like the one who overturned a float full of milk at the bottom of a hill on a main road on Saturday morning just after he had been let out on his own). And they liked being able to control their work even if this meant that they worked seven days a week to maintain personal control over the work. Attitudes that did not differentiate stayers from leavers included the one which most laymen would think of as being crucial, and which many depot managers used in their interviewing, i.e., attitudes to getting up early. You do not even apply for a job as a milkman unless you can face the thought of getting up at 03.30. Managers who asked new applicants: 'How do you feel about working these hours?', got the answer 'Fine,' and then felt aggrieved because the man left within the month, can now be given a little more guidance as to the right areas to probe.

Miss Keenan also found interesting differences in attitudes between successful and less successful milkmen who had remained in the job. One crucial difference had to do with selling. In their Grid interviews the milkmen had hardly mentioned selling. The closest they came was with phrases like 'You've got to know your customers,' implying that they knew their customers' needs ('Mrs Bloggs has six children and they'll all be home from school next week'), but rarely seeing the need to go beyond this into suggesting that she would like some extra milk and as she would be finding it difficult to get to the shops, and how about some eggs and bread and potatoes? When the questionnaires were analysed, however, it was found that the more effective milkmen were more likely to think of themselves as salesmen rather than as delivery men.

Grid is here being used in a purely extractive sense — take a sample of new starters, Grid them for information about their feelings about the job and their attitudes to work, perhaps use the Grid information for the design of a questionnaire, and later on when the sample has sorted itself into stayers and leavers go back to see whether there were any differences in attitude between the two groups. Grid can also be used in a semi-counselling sense, if the researcher has a remit not only to gather the data from the employees, but also to feed it back to them in a way that will help them perceive and make plans to overcome any obstacles to early job satisfaction. This has been done with graduate recruits and similar level staff, where the expense of the counselling interview is small compared with the possible cost of losing valuable staff before they settle down and start to make a contribution.

10.3 Other attitude surveys

The two previous examples show Grid used to help in the design of specific attitude surveys. Many other examples can be offered. We once asked managers to rate their most and least successful performance appraisal interviews on a series of bipolar scales, e.g.:

we wanted the same — — we wanted different
outcomes from   outcomes from the
the interview   interview

I had a clear idea — — I had no clear idea
of his career path   of his career path

I had picked him to — — I had inherited him
do the job   or been forced to accept him
etc., etc.

With a sample of managers filling in the questionnaires, each reporting on two appraisal interviews, we were able to show which of the bipolar scales differentiated between successful and less successful interviews as the managers saw them. This allowed us to write the training material, and the other literature associated with the appraisal programme, in such a way that it directly addressed managers' problems. Of course, we derived the bipolar scales from Grid interviews — two or three managers who had had a lot of experience with appraisals, using actual interviews as elements.

Exactly the same procedure has been used to gather people's attitudes to selection interviews, disciplinary interviews, sales calls, customers, advertisements, products, etc. For example, a construct-elicitation interview with a salesman using as elements customer calls he had made in the last month, produced the following list of constructs:

customer knew what — customer did not know what
he wanted   he wanted
customer took notes — customer did not take notes
customer took control — I was in control
old customer — new customer
customer wanted cheap — customer wanted value for money
quick call — call took a long time
had to wait with others — proper appointment system
competitive sell — breaking new ground
etc., etc.

These statements were amalgamated with those from other salesmen to produce a questionnaire on which all the sales force were asked to describe their most and least preferred customers. A composite picture of the most-preferred and the least-preferred customers was then used in several ways: the marketing people used it, the training people used it, the management course used it, bits of it were incorporated into the territory-management diary so that individual salesmen's problems could be detected early, and so on.

We asked several people who design questionnaires and attitude surveys, and who have used Grid technique as part of the process, to give examples of how they use Grid or how Grid helps them. Here are some of the answers:

'I wanted to study people's attitudes towards pay and equity. The person who commissioned the survey thought that fair pay consisted of 'rate for the job' and that was it. I took him with me on some Grid interviews and it became crystal-clear to him – and me! – that in fact there are at least three points of comparison: rate compared with what you could get for the same job outside, rate compared with what your mates get inside, and rate compared with the amount of effort you put in. When I'd put this point to my boss before he thought it was a piece of academic nonsense, but he couldn't resist the evidence of his own eyes.'

'Our organization does regular surveys of the morale of its employees. I conducted some group Grid interviews before we ran the latest survey and found that there were all sorts of issues which were important to people outside Head Office but which we didn't think about – like how close you live to your work – and issues that have become more important over the last few years, like the state of the labour market for women. I think I could have probably got most of these issues identified anyway, but I'm not sure I could have done it so quickly without Grid and it certainly gave me some notion of the relative priorities of the different issues.'

'We do consumer surveys to see how people like our product (confectionery). From time to time we'll pay people to sit in our laboratories and fill in forms on all the products. Using Grid approach – not just the construct elicitation, the full Grid – we were able to state clearly that there is a relationship between the size of a sweet and its perceived flavour. That's why the Yorkie chocolate bar is such a success, of course, though we weren't quick enough to spot it! Or we learn new things that people say about our products, or new things that they think are important. Then we can put what we've learned to use in the smaller questionnaires that we send to our market-research agency for use with the public.'

To summarise, then, Grid technique is useful in questionnaire design when you want to be sure that you have addressed the issues as the person filling in the questionnaire sees them, and maybe need information about the relative priorities of different items. There is an additional political advantage in being seen to use the 'customer's' language. Grid may reveal important areas of concern for inclusion in the questionnaire, or it may just give you a feeling for relationships and a knowledge that you have probed as deep as you can so you will not have left much out. As any questionnaire needs to be based on pilot interviews, the Grid procedure is no more costly, and often takes less time – and is more interesting for the recipient.

11. Using Repertory Grid to investigate motivation at work

11.1 Background

Several organizations have asked us to investigate motivation at work, usually the motivation of managers. This subject is a good candidate for the use of Grid technique, in many variations. However the problem usually needs refining first; the personnel executive says he wants to know more about motivation at work, and we then have to ask whether this is a matter of academic interest, or whether his concern is linked to more practical issues. This has mostly led to a re-definition of the problem: 'We want to know more about what motivates people at work so that we can organize things for them to be more productive.' Motivation is such an odd, changing and seemingly irrational topic that it is easy to get seduced into studying the phenomenon at the expense of making recommendations about how to manage it. So you will not find the last word on motivation in this chapter, but you will find a method of studying it in sufficient depth to make confident recommendations for short- or long-term action, and some of the results that can be revealed without also revealing the organizations where the work was done.

Why use Repertory Grid to study motivation? As with all these chapters on the applications of Grid, we have to keep clear of using Grid for its own sake; if there is another good instrument that could be cheaper and easier to use, then that should be the one. Our reason for using Grid to study motivation was based in Grid's ability to produce data without observer bias. Motivation as a topic has been worn to death; every researcher in industry is familiar with countless theories of motivation, and quite a lot of line managers are also familiar with terms such as 'job satisfaction', 'hygiene factors' and 'self-realization'. Besides the proliferation of jargon that can get in the way of doing good research, there is an additional problem that several researchers experience. In getting to know the industry or the jobs one is studying, it is very difficult not to form opinions about the motivation of the people doing the job on the basis of how one would feel oneself if one were doing it. If you hate getting up early in the morning, you will probably think that this must be a considerable demotivator in the life of the average milkman; whereas most milkmen reckon that you do not become a milkman without knowing that you will have to get up early, and anyway they view it in terms of being finished by mid-day and having the afternoon free.

So we chose to use Grid to get a fresh look at motivation, uncontaminated by pre-existing theories as far as possible, trying to interpret the data in their own terms rather than in terms of existing theoretical frameworks.

11.2 Methods

Of the organizations where this kind of study has been carried out, two methods

are selected for description in detail, illustrating two different and equally successful approaches to the problem.

Method 1

This involved individual interviews with a random sample of people doing the kind
of job under study. After the usual explanations and reassurances (e.g., making sure
that the interviewee knows he has not been chosen because his motivation is particularly low, or high) the interview commenced. Elements were elicted according
to the following set of questions:

E1 : A short description — half a dozen words or so
that will enable you to recollect later what you
were saying — of an event in the last eighteen
months or so where you felt strongly motivated to
try as hard as you could.

E2 : A short description of an event in the last eighteen
months where you have felt disillusioned, dispirited,
fed-up.

E3 : Another event like E1.

E4 : Another event like E2.

E5 : A routine event or activity that you enjoy doing.

E6 : A routine event or activity that you dislike doing.

E7 : Now imagine that a good fairy were to appear and
say that you could wish for something to happen
— an event like all the other events we have listed
so far. Money and resources are no object, but you
have to wish for something involving you personally,
rather than someone else or the whole organization.

E8 : And now imagine that a nasty fairy has appeared
in the good fairy's place: with the same sort of
constraints, what would be the worst possible
thing that could happen to you?

E9 : Finally, what was the most significant thing you
remember about yesterday? Not necessarily from
the point of view of motivation, but just the event
that stands out most in your mind as you think
about yesterday (or the previous day at work).

These elements were relatively easy to elicit, but if you try this method you
should be aware of the following points.

1. The events have to be personally relevant. So if, for example, to Element 2 the
answer had been: 'When the Board announced that Grade III managers were not
going to get company cars after all', and you are talking to a victim of the
decision rather than to the person who made it, then the actual element needs
making more personally relevant with a question such as: 'And how did that

affect you personally?' or 'Did this make you do something different from how you would have previously done it?' It needs practice, and trial-and-error, before you can judge how much to refine the elements this way; a skilled interviewer and committed interviewee can manage with less concretization than a less practised interviewer and/or less committed interviewee.

2. The 'good fairy' and 'bad fairy' elements may be difficult to get in terms of 'an event that would happen to you' but it is worth persisting, and worth recording any attempts before you get a personally relevant event. The different kinds of best and worst have often given us very illuminating insights into interfunctional differences within an organization, and into differences between different organizations in the same industry.

3. Some interviewees have objected to the word 'routine', saying that at their level (whatever it is) they do not have routine tasks. In this case we have re-defined by saying something along these lines: 'Well, you can see that in the first four questions we have been trying to look at some peaks and troughs in your job; what we want to look at now is the bread-and-butter activities, the ones that do not get you very excited either way . . . ' and this usually solves the problem.

4. People often begin to describe the events themselves, in great detail, at the elicitation stage. You need to make it clear that all you want for the moment is a brief description of the event itself, and later on in the interview you will be seeking to record their feelings about it.

5. A helpful phrase to explain what you are doing is: 'It's as if I were a film camera-man following you around, and I want to capture on film the essence of your job by filming different kinds of event that you get involved in.'

Construct elicitation then takes place, with the question: 'Can you tell me something that two of these events have got in common, that they do not share with the third, *in terms of how you feel about them?*' That is usually enough direction about the kind of construct you want — asking for constructs *in terms of your motivation* is probably prejudging the issue and less likely to be successful. One skill the interviewer needs very early on is the ability to ladder *down*. A typical exchange in the early stages of the interview goes like this:

INTERVIEWER Please look at those three events and tell me a way in which two are like each other and different from the third?

INTERVIEWEE In those two I got lots of job satisfaction, whereas in the third the job satisfaction goes very low.

The interviewer wants to know what the component parts of job satisfaction are in this context — the construct *high job satisfaction — low job satisfaction* is a much higher-order one than we require. So there has to be a laddering question or questions:

INTERVIEWER What was it about those two that gave you job satisfaction and which was different in this one?

How could I tell a high job-satisfaction event — as you understand the term — from a low job-satisfaction event?

What do you feel about the high job-satisfaction events that differentiate them from the low job-satisfaction events?
etc., etc.

Though construct elicitation itself tell you something about the conditions under which the interviewee feels highly and less highly motivated, it is worth going on to full Grid to look at the interrelationships of constructs and elements. The full Grid is best if it is then discussed with the interviewee rather than it being analyzed without reference to the person who generated it.

Figure 11.1 is the full Grid, after it had been put through the FOCUS program, for a senior manager in an industry connected with transport. His elements were:

E1 :   A new building in his area was opened by the Queen.

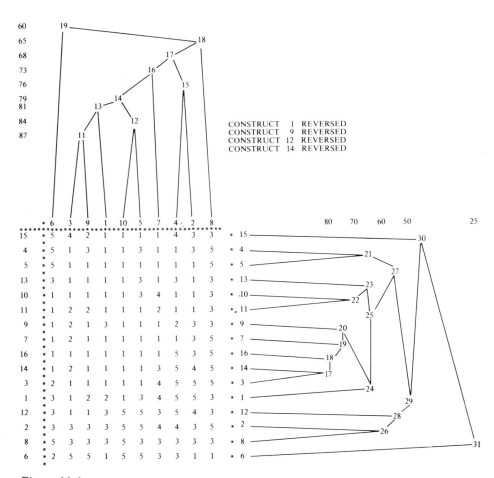

CONSTRUCT   1   REVERSED
CONSTRUCT   9   REVERSED
CONSTRUCT 12   REVERSED
CONSTRUCT 14   REVERSED

Figure 11.1

E2 : Manning problems and customer complaints for him to resolve, caused by equipment failures.

E3 : Being nominated to a local working party whose aim was to get more business to his part of the world.

E4 : Loss of freight business due to a series of one-day strikes and working to rule.

E5 : Visiting staff at various termini in his area, talking to them and assessing their stewardship.

E6 : Repetitious award ceremonies which are time-consuming and dull.

E7 : A business reorganization.*

E8 : Being moved from this part of the country.

E9 : Selling a lot of business and advertising space locally in connection with an open day being held next year.

This manager's constructs were:

C1	:	many rules and guidelines	— no rules and guidelines
C2	:	acting alone	— part of a team
C3	:	things happening at the right speed	— things happening at the wrong speed
C4	:	chance to impress senior management	— no opportunity to do so
C5	:	chance to impress the public	— no opportunity to do so
C6	:	no choice about getting involved	— I could choose whether to get involved
C7	:	easy to discover how well I am doing	— difficult to discover how well I am doing
C8	:	using technical skill	— using people skills
C9	:	preparing material for others to use	— acting on my own authority
C10	:	spending money	— saving money
C11	:	quick results likely	— results in long term
C12	:	I had had formal training to do this	— I had had no formal training to do this
C13	:	doing something new	— doing things as they had always been done

* N.B. Although the interviewee was specific about the kind of reorganization he wanted, we have suppressed the details here for obvious reasons.

C14 : atmosphere of   — atmosphere of cooperation
       conflict
C15 : all the necessary   — none of the necessary
       resources available   resources available
C16 : feel that if I try — feel there is no relation-
       hard I will be   ship between my efforts
       successful   and my success

Look at this manager's Grid (Fig. 11.1) and decide for yourself what questions you would want to ask him when feeding back the Grid, and what conclusions you might want to test in conversation with him about his motivation at work. (Element 10, by the way, was created after the construct-elicitation phase, by asking him which end of each construct he preferred in his work.)

Among the interesting points in this manager's Grid are:

1. There is a close correlation between E3, E9, E1, E10 and E5. E3 and E1 are examples of events where he felt strongly motivated; E5 is a routine event he enjoys; E9 is the most significant thing he remembers about yesterday; and E10 is the 'fantasy' element composed of the preferred end of all his constructs. It is a fair assumption, therefore, that this is a manager who is likely to be strongly motivated and to be enjoying his work. In the feedback interview he readily assented to this proposition.

2. E6 — the routine event he dislikes, in his case attending award ceremonies — seems to be quite differently construed from the rest of his job. Asked how he felt about this, the manager readily assented and waxed lyrical about how he felt his job was to keep the system going, not to waste time on ceremony.

3. The family of constructs C9R, C7, C16, C14R and C3 are all closely correlated. Written out, they look like this:

> acting on my own authority — preparing material for others
> easy to discover how well — difficult to discover how
>   I am doing   well I am doing
> feel that if I try hard I — feel there is no relationship
>   will be successful   between effort and success
> atmosphere of cooperation — atmosphere of conflict
> things happening at the — things happening at the
>   right speed   wrong speed

from which it is possible to infer that he feels confident of success and of knowledge of results only when he himself is in charge of the operation. When this interpretation was put to him the reaction was one of slightly surprised embarrassment: 'Yes, I suppose I do feel like that, but hadn't realized it was so strong. Makes me look like a bit of a martinet, doesn't it?'

The feedback discussion then moved on to discussing how particular elements were rated on particular constructs, and to attempt a subjective rating of the importance of each construct. Much of the insight into what motivated this manager was generated in the feedback discussion, but if we were to quote from it in greater depth we would be breaking confidences; we hope that we have shown enough of the picture of a well motivated man with a high need for autonomy and for personal involvement, who happened to be almost ideally suited to the senior job he was occupying.

Method 2

This involves a slightly different approach, and is more suitable for large studies of motivation. Here we did group administration of Grid, adapting the technique slightly to fit the new conditions.

Managers were taken in groups of 6 to 8, from the same function and roughly the same level. Each was given an envelope containing 10 cards and a questionnaire. The interviewer explained the purpose of the group, and then asked them as individuals to write on their cards short descriptions of events that had happened to them in the last 18 months, using exactly the same eliciting questions as in Method 1. (The tenth card was in case anyone wanted to change anything.) This procedure took about half an hour. Then the managers were asked to give their attention to the questionnaires. Each questionnaire was laid out like a semantic differential, with bipolar scales on which each event in turn was to be described. (An example is shown in Table 11.1.) These bipolar scales had in fact been derived from earlier pilot interviews using full Grid technique, and were representative of constructs that had occurred frequently and/or aroused disagreement. (In our example we have made up a form using the constructs from the manager in the previous example. In practice the constructs should come from Grid interviews on site and may look totally different from the ones we quote here.) The managers were asked to rate each event in turn on the series of scales, using one piece of paper for each event. There were some additional pages at the back of the questionnaire, asking them for their views on motivation at work, and for their experience of motivators and de-motivators in general. The questionnaire-completing stage lasted about half an hour. Finally the interviewer asked if anyone would like to start the ball rolling with a discussion on motivation; primed by their earlier efforts, most of the managers were eager to join in and some excellent discussions resulted, in which the interviewer was able to note down salient points or comments.

If you use this method you should note the following points:

1. It is not as easy in the group situation to get elements precisely refined, particularly E7 and E8. This may be a price one pays for the advantage of speed and group discussion.
2. It is surprising how many managers have no experience of semantic-differential type questionnaires. The actual mechanism of filling the forms in should be explained in detail.
3. The selection of constructs to turn into bipolar scales is important. Try not to use scales that you think will beg the question, e.g. *I was highly motivated – I was poorly motivated*, nor to use questions where the answer is bound to be

Table 11.1

In this event . . .	1	2	3	4	5	In this event . . .
There were many guidelines or rules I had to follow	—	—	—	—	✓	There were few guidelines or rules I had to follow
I was acting alone	—	✓	—	—	—	I was part of a team
Things happened at the speed I want them to	—	—	—	✓	—	Things happened at the wrong speed for me (please circle FAST or SLOW)
I had the chance to make an impression on senior management	—	✓	—	—	—	I had no chance to make any impression on senior management
I had the chance to make an impression on the public	—	—	—	✓	—	I had no chance to make any impression on the public
I had no choice about whether to get involved	—	✓	—	—	—	I could choose whether to get involved or not
It was easy to discover how well I was doing	—	—	✓	—	—	It was difficult to discover how well I was doing
I needed to use my technical or professional skills	✓	—	—	—	—	I needed to use my skills in handling people
I was preparing briefs or information for others	—	—	✓	—	—	I was acting for myself alone
Was spending or investing money	✓	—	—	—	—	I was trying to save money
I was doing something that would have quick results	—	✓	—	—	—	I was doing something where the results would not be seen for a long time
I was doing something for which I had had formal training	—	✓	—	—	—	I was doing something which I had picked up as I went along, without training
I was trying to do something new	—	✓	—	—	—	I was doing things as they had been done
The atmosphere was full of conflict	—	—	✓	—	—	The atmosphere was full of cooperation
I had all the resources I required to do the job	—	—	—	✓	—	I had none of the resources I required to do the job
I felt confident that if I tried hard success would reward my efforts	—	✓	—	—	—	I had no confidence that if I tried hard my efforts would be successful

obvious. It is worth pointing out at the time of administration that the scales derive from interviews with people like themselves.

4. This method has a useful spin-off in that it gets managers together talking about an important problem that they might otherwise not address. If you have purposes to do with team building or getting people to share points of view, then this group administration — though it sacrifices some individual detail and the opportunity for individual feedback — is worth considering.

Analysis of the group material uses two different techniques: the elements themselves can be content-analysed — what sort of things do people enjoy? dislike? dread? — and the ratings of elements on constructs can be analysed using either a Grid-analysis program or a standard questionnaire-analysis program. With a standard questionnaire-analysis program, one would look for the degree of similarity between E10 and all the other elements, for example; for the average ratings of all the other elements, so that a composite E1 can be produced, a composite E2, and so on.

11.3 Results

Several interesting findings on the subject of motivation itself have arisen in the course of these studies. One example concerns working conditions: according to Herzberg, poor working conditions are a demotivator and stand in the way of good performance. We have found in several organizations that this need not be so, particularly in industries that are obviously heavy, dirty or exposed to the elements. If you become a milkman, or join the railway or work in a steel mill, then you do not expect potted plants and fitted carpets — indeed they may well be demotivating, signifying to your peers that you have gone soft. We have uncovered pure patriotism — local and national — acting as a motivator. Perhaps the most useful insight we have gained ourselves is that in some industries it is necessary to distinguish between job interest and product interest. This is a particularly useful distinction when examining motivation in the transport industries; people here will often stay in remarkably boring jobs but be sustained by contact with a product they like (planes, trains, buses — it seems they exert a fascination all of their own). Much difficulty in understanding motivation in these industries was cleared up once we had recognized — and Grid made it very easy to recognize — that interest in the product is a separate and sustaining type of motivation, and can be quite different from interest in the job.

12. Using Repertory Grid to investigate organizational climate and managerial effectiveness

What managers think about the organization they work in influences the kind of organization it is; and the nature of the organization influences their thoughts. Several investigators have used Grid techniques to study the climate of an organization — that indefinable something which is also called culture, mores, style, flavour — or to study one specific aspect of the climate, namely the qualities required to be an effective manager in that climate.

12.1 Grid in the study of organizational culture

Joe Edwards, of the Furniture & Timber Industry Training Board, has used a very simple and economical form of Grid to reveal the culture of organizations and to get him a base from which to start organization development work (and, incidentally, a base from which to measure his success). His technique is to interview managers at all levels in the organization, using construct-elicitation techniques only, getting them to construe either their own activities at work or their own colleagues. He then content-analyses the constructs, by the various levels in the organization, into Need Achievement constructs, Need Affiliation constructs, and Need Power constructs. (The breakdown of needs is taken from McLelland's work on human motivation.)

Examples of Need Achievement constructs:

getting ahead — getting nowhere
pushing myself forward — pushing someone else forward
the sky is the limit — only limited success possible
success — failure

Examples of Need Affiliation constructs:

making enemies — making myself popular
done alone — done with others
no-one notices — I get praise for
with people I like — with people I dislike

and examples of Need Power constructs:

winning — losing
under my control — under others' control
to my standards — to others' standards
ready to compromise — insist on winning

Basically, Need Achievement constructs reflect a desire to achieve, to do things, to make a mark, to grow, or a consciousness that the organization demands these characteristics. Need Affiliation constructs reflect a desire for human company, the esteem of others, the desire to be liked and thought well of — or at least a consciousness that the organization desires these characteristics. And Need Power constructs reflect a desire to have power and control over other people and over events, or at least an awareness that the organization demands these characteristics. These three needs — which McLelland says can be used to describe much of human motivation — are often abbreviated to NAch, NAff, and NPower.

Usually Edwards is working with fairly small companies. It is therefore practicable for him to split a company into three levels — top, middle and bottom. He then looks to see which need is most predominant in each of the three levels, enabling him to present a simple picture of his findings thus:

TOP   NPower

MIDDLE   NAffil

BOTTOM   NPower

indicating a company where the top and bottom levels of management appeared to have a need for power as their strongest construct type, whereas the managers in the middle were conscious more of a need for affiliation. Readers might like to reflect on the likely long-term survival prospects for such an organization.

Edwards can also present the data in a rather more sophisticated form, showing the relative proportions of each kind of need at the various levels (see Table 12.1), which shows the pattern for the same firm, but in more detail; the top management's strongest construct type is in the area of Need Power, and their lowest scores are for Need Affiliation; the middle manager's strongest construct type is in the area of Need Affiliation, and the weakest on Need Achievement, and so on.

Table 12.1

	NAch	*NAff*	*NPower*
TOP	xx	x	xxx
MIDDLE	x	xxx	xx
BOTTOM	x	xx	xxx

One of the strengths of this method lies in its simplicity and the ease with which it starts discussion going. Often Edwards is dealing with small firms who lack the sophistication of an ICI or IBM; they have neither the time nor the resources to devote to complicated personnel research. Using this technique, the researcher can first demonstrate that the data came unaided and uncontaminated from the managers themselves; he can explain his three-way category system and even get some of the managers to help with the coding; and he has a simple yet compelling way of presenting the problem, if problem there be. For there is no obvious right distribution of contructs x levels; but the picture allows one to ask questions such as:

1. — Do the situations these people find themselves in marry harmoniously with their construing styles? Or are we (say) putting people with a high need for

affiliation into tough negotiating situations, or putting people with low need for achievement into jobs where only a man with fire in his belly can succeed?

2. — Are there strong differences in style between levels so great as to influence the performance of someone newly promoted adversely and unfairly? For example, are we growing a team of junior managers with a high need for affiliation and then promoting them into middle-manager posts where the requirement is for a high need for power and a low need for affiliation?

3. — Do the construing styles our people display harmonize with the market? Because if we have an organization of high achievers in a static or declining market, we are going to have morale problems of a high order before long.

So, the opportunity to intervene with some offers of organization development work — if it is needed — can be made to develop naturally out of the data themselves — data that are the managers' own data and not imposed by some outside criterion. It is difficult to make this process judgemental — 'The theory says you're wrong' — and easier to keep remedies, where necessary, in the hands of the line managers rather than have them delegated to Personnel. Though this use of Grid was pioneered in small companies, it has obvious applications in larger organizations and in team-building work, work to facilitate corporate mergers, etc.

12.2 Grid to investigate managerial effectiveness

People's perceptions of what makes an effective manager also vary depending on the organization they are in. We have used Grid to clarify what people mean by 'effective manager' — sometimes using Grid on its own, sometimes using Grid as a preliminary to the design of a questionnaire. In our research we have found that two types of element set are necessary, depending on whether the manager we interview has a great many colleagues and/or subordinates or only a few.

Grid technique alone, without a questionnaire

This application is used in small organizations or at the top of large organizations, where there would be too few people to answer a questionnaire. For example, we were asked to assist a firm to come to a description of the qualities required to be an effective merchant banker. Though the organization was small, they all worked under the same roof and knew each other well, so we used as elements the names of (a) three colleagues who are in your estimation effective in their job, (b) three colleagues who are in your estimation less effective in their job, (c) two colleagues about whose effectiveness your opinion varies — some days you think they are effective, other days you are in doubt, and (d) yourself. The interviewees were encouraged not to put names of real people on the element cards, but to use initials or nicknames instead, and the cards were thrown away at the end of the interview. The elements were construed 'in terms of the way they go about their job.'

This set of elements needs some skill to handle if the resulting constructs are not merely to be personality judgements — interesting though these may be, they are not particularly useful at training and appraisal time. So the interviewers often found themselves repeating questions such as: 'You say that two are confident with the client and one is nervous. Now can you tell me what the confident ones *do* that makes them different from the nervous ones? If I was a man from Mars watching these people with the client, what would you show me the confident ones doing that made them different from the nervous ones?' and so on. The interviews ended by asking the interviewee if the interview had given him the opportunity to form any further thoughts about effectiveness that had not been covered in the discussion so far. As usual when one asks that kind of question, one of two answers followed; either 'No, I've told you all I know and more,' or 'Yes, the key things are x, y and z.'

The data were then content-analysed and an overall description produced of the construct poles that people said were related to effectiveness. Obviously we cannot give the whole list here, but there were some interesting construct groups that had not emerged in studies of managers elsewhere, or had not emerged with such strength.

1. — Peer relations were stronger in this environment than we have seen them anywhere else. The effective merchant banker here must be able to rely on his colleagues, to let them rely on him (on everything from meticulous documentation to market judgement), to share the credit and the blame.
2. — Being difficult to pigeon-hole was important for client relations. Merchant banks sell money, basically. Their money is the same as anyone else's and comes from the same source. Therefore client appeal is based partly on technical competence and partly on personality. Any characteristic — unusual family background, being obviously ex-patriate, odd hobbies, accent that does not gel with appearance — that makes the banker difficult for the client to sum up quickly is an advantage, because it makes him memorable and perhaps fascinating.
3. — Tough detachment from world events and tragedies that enables the banker to view the prospect of the Iranian revolution, say, or the assassination of Lord Mountbatten, in terms of its effects on the money markets; not losing his human concern, but keeping it entirely separate.

As a result of this exercise — and after the interrogation phase that follows, and which is described in more detail on p. 114 — we were able to develop changes to the performance-appraisal and career-development patterns that better reflected the real demands for effective performance. The existing appraisal system, for instance, had no mention of peer relations, although they were probably one of the most important characteristics shown in our research.

Where managers do not know many colleagues or subordinates, a different set of elements must be used. We use a set of elements based on job activities. One set of eliciting questions is as follows:

E1 : An activity that is very important.
E2 : An activity that may or may not be important, but which takes up time or happens frequently.
E3 : A activity that is important but unplanned — e.g., a crisis activity.
E4 : As E1.

E5 : An activity that makes demands on your skills.

E6 : As E1.

E7 : As E2.

E8 : As E1.

E9 : *Ad lib* — with the cards spread before him the interviewee is asked to name an activity that will help round out the picture of his work.

Another set of eliciting questions that serves a similar purpose is as follows:

E1 : An event where you feel you performed well.

E2 : An event where you feel you failed to live up to your own expectations.

E3 : An event that was important and which you could not or did not see coming.

E4 : A routine event you enjoy.

E5 : A routine event you dislike.

E6 : An important event requiring mainly managerial skills.

E7 : An important event requiring mainly technical or professional skills.

E8 : Another event where you feel you performed well.

E9 : Any other even that helps round out the picture.

Either set of elements is construed 'in terms of the demands they make on your skills'.

The interview is probably a little more difficult with these elements than with people as elements, once the initial difficulty of using colleagues is overcome. The skill lies in getting people away from situational constructs (*in the office — out of the office*) to constructs about demands, skills and abilities. Nonetheless, once this is accomplished the construct data are as informative as when people-elements are used, and the elements are also available for analysis.

Content analysis is used to build up a picture of the skills people say managers need in order to be effective. This picture must then be interrogated — see p. 114 — and then the resulting description of effectiveness dovetailed into the management-development programme.

An example of the output for this process (characteristics for an effective merchant banker) is given below.

MARKET KNOWLEDGE AND PERFORMANCE

He will have in-depth knowledge of his own specialist field and, in addition, a working knowledge of all the other aspects of the markets in which the Bank operates. He will exhibit a wide range of interests, for example in politics, economics and clients, which will be demonstrated through his reading, travel and hobbies. He must be able to interpret the implications of world events for business, without allowing personal or political emotions to cloud his judgements. He will be able to identify new opportunities and to re-appraise existing problems to arrive at new solutions. He will exhibit a good sense of timing. He will continually strive for the highest professional standards.

CLIENT MANAGEMENT

He will know who to contact in the client organization and will aim for a Bank relationship with several people in the client organization, rather than an individual relationship, in order to broaden the initial contact. He will anticipate the client's requirements. He will look at deals from the client's point of view, and so present the benefits as the client understands them. He will tend to talk the client away from a complex idea towards a simple one that is almost as good. He will be able to tell early in the relationship the probability of an enquiry from a client turning into a deal. He will recognize when a client is unreceptive to a Bank proposal, but, conversely, will help the client make up his mind and reach a decision when the outcome seems favourable. He will be able to interact with the client on a social level, so that the relationship has a broader base than a purely commercial one. He will not become depressed or offended if a client places business elsewhere from time to time. He will act quickly once he has appraised the situation.

PERSONAL IMPACT AND APPEARANCE

He will appear lively, confident and enthusiastic, not slow and deliberate. He must however avoid extremes of over-optimism and over-confidence. He must be able to match his personal style to suit the individual client and the organization. He should exhibit no obvious nervous mannerisms. He should be a good time-keeper in connection with appointments, the duration of meetings and the production of reports. He will not be shy of initiating action or making fresh contacts. He will not react defensively to personal criticism.

PERSISTENCE

He has clear objectives and always keeps his goal in sight. He only collects the information he really needs and declines to be sidetracked. He will not easily take 'No' for an answer, but achieves this without making the client feel harried. He is not easily discouraged by failure. He will turn away unprofitable business.

ADJUSTMENT TO THE BANK

He is committed to the Bank, and works for the Bank first and the client second. He is not a follower of the crowd and is prepared to do business on his terms. He is prepared to work hard and run faster than the competition. He prefers the organization of the work to be task- or person-centred, not bureaucratically defined. He is prepared to work long hours — often at short notice. He is prepared to travel, and ensures that he stays in touch while travelling. He realizes that subordinates will have to cope with pressure on family life, gives sympathetic support, but urges the resolution of priorities at an early stage.

OPENNESS AND HONESTY

He is conscientious. He takes responsibility for his own failures. He is not secretive but keeps his colleagues informed of his contacts and of the progress of the business. He knows the advantages and disadvantages of a deal and is prepared to discuss them. He is prepared to discuss his fears and doubts about the business with his colleagues in order that a decision may result.

COPING UNDER COMPLEX DEMANDS

He can work under high pressure without becoming flustered and irritable and without taking his stresses out on other people. He can handle many different problems at once. He can think on his feet, both face-to-face and on the telephone. He is able to put problems into perspective. He is methodical, having a good bring-forward system. He has important calculations checked. He plans the day and the week in detail.

RELATIONSHIPS

A. *With superiors*

He requires little supervision. He takes ideas to his superior rather than waiting to have them requested or suggested. He is not over-deferential.

B. *With colleagues*

He enjoys teamwork. He is free and trusting with his own ideas and knowledge. He makes an effort to keep abreast of what other departments are doing. He keeps other people informed of what he is doing and whether he has useful information for them. He asks for help if he needs it. He is flexible and prepared to change his mind if convinced by others in the team. He forgives quickly and does not bear grudges. People seek his advice and feel confident about suggesting his ideas to others. He respects other people's confidences.

C. *Development of subordinates*

He is prepared to delegate. When he delegates, he keeps out of the details. If staff make a mistake, he goes through it with them rather than taking on the job himself. He does not ask people to do things he would not do himself, assuming the competence were in his possession. He rewards good work. He creates opportunities for staff to meet new people. He puts on occasional, not constant, pressure. He takes trouble to discover whether his staff are contented, and takes action if they are not.

COMMUNICATION SKILLS

He speaks and writes concisely. He writes short sentences, using correct grammar. Words are used with their proper meaning. He is never ambiguous. He writes so that little re-drafting is necessary. He prepares well and thoroughly for meetings so as to be quick and concise in presentation. He keeps a record of phone calls, makes trip notes, and has an adequate log of his activities.

COMPLEX TECHNIQUES

He is numerate. He is quick to grasp complicated financial information. He can explain complex financial or statistical information to a lay person, translating jargon where it occurs. He can see market and price patterns and correlations easily amongst apparently unrelated data. He seeks to increase his own technical knowledge.

INTELLIGENCE AND CREATIVITY

He has a good basic intelligence and can apply it. He can generate new ideas or new formulations of old ones. He can follow through an idea from inception to its final form.

Grid technique leading to the design of a questionnnaire

This application is where the position under scrutiny — the one for which we wish to obtain a description of present effective performance in post — is occupied by many people. Thus it is useful in middle- to larger-sized organizations, and at the bottom of the hierarchy rather than the top.

Suppose the organization is dissatisfied with the performance and/or supply of first-line sales managers, and wishes to undertake a concentrated effort to develop some more. Clearly it is important that we begin by learning how effective first-line sales-management performance is presently viewed by those doing and managing the post, because we need to know (a) whether people's present views have survival value for the future, and (b) if they do not, how much and what kind of effort will be needed to get them to adopt a more suitable picture of effectiveness.

The procedure here is to interview sales managers themselves, using either colleagues + self as elements, or job activities/events as elements, depending on how many colleagues they are likely to know well. The interview elicits constructs, ladders, and asks for preference questions, but does not go on to full Grid. Examples of constructs taken from one such interview, using colleagues as elements:

goes on accompaniment to — goes on accompaniment to
sell himself   coach the salesman
takes every refusal as a — accepts that he is bound to
personal insult   lose some orders
poor telephone technique — good telephone technique
can easily be talked into giving — never gives discounts
discount

Interviews with 12 or 15 sales managers are usually enough to give a large pile of different constructs, which are then content-analysed and turned into a questionnaire. The questionnaire contains items in a bipolar form, around a five-point scale, with statements expressed in behavioural form about the activities of a sales manager. Thus the first, second, and fourth constructs above give the following items:

when he goes on — — — — — when he goes on
accompaniment it   accompaniment it
is to make the sale   is to coach the
himself   salesman

he takes a refusal — — — — — he accepts that
as a personal   some lost orders
insult   are inevitable

he often offers   — — — — — he never offers
discounts   discounts

but the third construct would require laddering into behavioural terms before it would be useful, and the interviewer would not have done a proper job had he left it in its existing form.

The complete questionnaire contains between 80 and 120 items, and attempts to represent all the behavioural, job-related constructs that have been produced by the interviewees. The next stage is to distribute the questionnaire to at least two groups of people in the organization — the sales managers themselves and the sales managers' managers. In the instructions they are asked to think of the most effective sales manager they know, and to describe him, warts and all, on the questionnaire. The two important features of these instructions, which must not be omitted, are (a) they must be thinking about a real person, not an ideal type, and (b) they must describe him warts and all, good points and bad. When all the questionnaires have been returned and a gap of three weeks or so elapsed, a second copy of the questionnaire is then issued to the same managers. This time they are asked to describe the least effective sales manager they know — again a real person, good points and bad. The completed questionnaires are then analysed to discover (a) which items significantly discriminate between effective and less effective managers, (b) which items are strongly associated with effectiveness and (c) which items are strongly associated with ineffectiveness. From this analysis a pen-picture is drawn, of 'the effective manager' as he is seen by the people closest to the job. An example, the pen-picture of an effective sales manager in an office-products company, is given below.

MANAGEMENT OF HIS SALES FORCE

He encourages his salesmen to find their own solutions, even if this takes a little longer, and when they are in difficulties he helps them find their own way out rather than taking on the job himself. He discusses the salesmen's performance with them on a frequent schedule, and he is prepared to talk about their personal problems with them. He believes that they need training, and he gets them to write proposals rather than doing it himself. When he is talking about the salesmen's ideas to other people he is sure to give them the credit. If he accepts a salesman from another district he is content to let him continue as before, rather than imposing his own style on him, and he is content to let his salesmen all have different priorities. When talking to them he tries to sell unpopular decisions to them, and he tells them the good news and the bad. At the beginning of the week he knows whom he is going to accompany on field visits, and he chooses for field accompaniment the middle-of-the-road performers. He believes there is more pay-off in coaching inexperienced salesmen. He goes on field accompaniment to train the salesman, not to make sales himself.

RELATIONS WITH CUSTOMERS

If a customer and his boss were both calling for him at the same time, he would go to the customer. He gets information about the customer from the salesmen and other sources as well. He is better at dealing with high-status people in the customer's operation. He tries to sell the customer only as much as he needs.

RELATIONS WITH BOSS AND SENIOR MANAGEMENT

He tells his boss the good news and the bad news. His first loyalty is to the company, and he always accepts senior management decisions.

RELATIONS WITH ENGINEERING

He always checks with engineering before making a promise to the customer, and he lets them know if the customer is having problems.

PLANNING AND ADMINISTRATION

He prefers to work to a plan; he makes long- and short-term plans, and contingency plans, but when his plans are upset he can improvise easily. He gives more time to preventing problems than to curing them, and he prepares sales talks in advance. He is best when working on the big picture rather than the details. For him, the job of analysis is not complete until the results are being used. He believes that sometimes it is necessary to make a call without an immediate sale in view. He distinguishes accurately between fact and opinion, and he accepts that administration is a necessary part of his job.

SPEED OF ACTION

He takes immediate action on customer complaints, and if the distribution of territories is unbalanced he changes it fast. He prefers to work fast even if this brings some mistakes; under greater-than-normal pressure his performance improves. His performance is not affected by lack of fast knowledge of results.

ATTITUDE TO DIFFICULTIES

He goes out to meet difficult customers, and he gets on with unpleasant tasks. He makes some mistakes, and he admits to them. He tolerates compromise, and he will work on projects he did not start himself and will give his best efforts when in a situation not of his own choosing. When he is demotivated he manages to hide this from the salesmen and keep them motivated nonetheless. Faced with a potential loss he redoubles his efforts.

SELF-MANAGEMENT

If he gets into a rut he pulls himself out. He freely admits his own training needs, and he asks successful salesmen from other branches to come and talk about how they did it. He is selective in what he reads. He is best when using new solutions. He sees himself as a manager.

NEED FOR COMPANY

He works best in the field, and he works better with other people than alone.

A fuller explanation of the analysis and use of the data is given in *Tomorrow's Managers Today* (see Bibliography), in which we describe how this technique is used as the first stage in building a management-assessment programme.

Whether the picture has been developed through using a questionnaire, or through the construct-elicitation process alone, it needs interrogating. The picture gives us a precise detailed statement of how the people presently doing and managing the job view effective performance in that job. Before the picture is used as a basis for selection, training, assessment, etc., it must first be interrogated, line by line, with the question: 'What is the survival value of this picture for our organization in the future?' Ideally this interrogation should be done with the aid of the most senior line manager responsible if things go wrong. It is not a decision that should be confined to the Personnel or Training department; rather, they should see it as an opportunity to involve the line in strategic decisions about manpower quality. The picture as a result of the interrogation should look different in some respects from the one produced by the interviews.

Long-term validation studies of assessment programmes built on these interrogated pen-pictures indicate that considerable improvements in company performance have resulted and been sustained. These validation studies are reported in *Tomorrow's Managers Today*.

One problem with the pen-pictures of effective performance generated by this technique is that they all have high face validity until you see another one. Any description of effective performance looks appealing. Having collected well over 50 such descriptions, we can assure the reader that the differences are great – so great as to refute any theory that 'the good manager can manage anything', and so great as to make it definitely worth while to do your own investigation before designing a programme. Among the major variables that differentiate between effective performance in different firms we can number the following:

1. – Contact level: up, down and sideways, inside and out – how much of each does the manager have to do and where do his priorities lie?
2. – Time horizon: is he to pay more attention to the next six weeks or the next six years?

3. — Industrial relations: is the psychological contract with his staff coercive, calculating or cooperative, and does he have to sort out his messes himself?
4. — Risk: what kinds of risk may he take, and should he be looking for gains or to protect losses?
5. — Negotiating style: who does he negotiate with? should he confront or cooperate?
6. — Technical contribution: does he make a direct contribution, or only by coaching /buying ideas?

and many more. The history of selection and assessment methods is sadly littered by examples of firms who bought in criteria from outside, only to have the method fail through inappropriateness or lack of ownership. Using Grid techniques to derive the measures first ensures that the organization develops a method suited to its own unique requirements, and the fact that all the data have come from the people themselves is methodologically and politically a strong weapon for the researcher to use.

13. Using the Grid to evaluate training

NICKIE FONDA

An evaluation of any kind has three components: a purpose, a judgement and information on which that judgement is made. Thus, we could say that, in its most general sense, the evaluation of training is the making of a value judgement about some systematic learning activity for some purpose, based on the information available to, and used by, the person making that judgement.

Many people, particularly trainers, frequently express their concern that training is not being evaluated. Yet, in reality, the evaluation of training takes place all the time. Indeed, people in organizations are clearly making an evaluation when they ask each other, or themselves, such questions as: 'Was that a good course? Will I learn anything useful from that workshop? Should I send Joe on this course or that one? Should we run a course on that subject?

Thus, when people express concern that training is not being evaluated, what they probably mean is something more specific. For example, it may be that they feel that not enough relevant information has been gathered, or is being used, to form the basis for a sound judgement. Or, they may feel that judgements are being made using the wrong criteria. Or, they may think that other people's purposes for evaluation are irrelevant to their own purpose, or not legitimate in some way.

In fact, even when trainers talk about the evaluation of training, they may have many different organizational or personal purposes or objectives in mind, such as:

1. To decide whether resources should be devoted to training or to some other forms of investment or expenditure.
2. To decide whether new kinds of training are required.
3. To decide whether to modify or stop existing training.
4. To decide which type of learning activity is most appropriate for some purpose.
5. To decide how to 'sell' or justify training.
6. To decide whether or how training could be made more enjoyable for participants.
7. To decide trainers' training needs.
8. To reassure trainers.
9. To satisfy their curiosity about what is happening.

Any of these objectives may be a legitimate and relevant concern for some trainers in the organization at some time.

If we want to be systematic about achieving our objectives, however, we need to have, before we start, some fairly clear ideas about the kinds of information we will want, and what criteria and factors we will use to evaluate this information for our purpose. Without this, we could spend a lot of time either gathering together information we will not want to use, or deciding how we could use the information we have gathered.

The Repertory Grid can be both a help and a hindrance at this stage. Because of its flexibility, and its ability to generate detailed, structured information about individuals' ways of seeing the world, it can be used very successfully to explore a whole range of evaluation issues — the criteria we and others are using to assess the value of training; the extent to which trainees' behaviours is seen as different after a course; what people have learned during training; what training people think we should be offering; how individual behaviour is seen to relate to business achievement, and so on. Because the Grid can provide so much, and so many different kinds of, information, however, we run the risks of being swamped by data we cannot use, and of forgetting that Grids do not make decisions for us, i.e., someone still has to interpret, assess and use what we find.

Bearing these points in mind, therefore, the remainder of this chapter will be concerned with discussing several ways in which Grid methods can be used to gather relevant information, and ways in which this information can be used to achieve our evaluation purposes. Although we will give specific examples of various approaches, the reader is asked to bear in mind that these examples can only illustrate some of the possibilities. Because the Grid is so flexible, the limits to its applications lie chiefly with our imaginations.

13.1 Ways the Grid can be used for evaluation purposes

Basically, Grid methods have been used to obtain information about the following for evaluation purposes:

1. Training needs.
2. Trainees' changes during and after training.
3. Trainees' views of the success of training events.
4. Trainers' views of the success of training events.
5. Managers' views of training courses.
6. Management's views of training as a function.

Let us look at each use in turn.

Training needs

There are many reasons why the evaluator of training might want to have some idea about the perceived training needs of individuals, roles (e.g., supervisors) or functions (e.g., the Marketing Department) — for example, to decide whether new areas for training are required, to decide whether existing training is designed to meet organizational needs, to decide whether training is actually meeting these needs, or to choose the appropriate form of training for a particular situation.

Note that we have used the words 'perceived training needs' here. It is important to remember that the identification of training needs is always a subjective judgement. Sometimes there will be more agreement than disagreement about abilities needed to do a job, the extent to which these are trainable and the extent to which training should be provided to assist individuals to develop these abilities. Let us illustrate this point by thinking about the possible training needs of a production supervisor. If we talk to the supervisor, he will tell us what abilities he needs to develop, to what extent he thinks they are trainable, and how much time — if any — he would be prepared to spend to get assistance in developing these abilities. However, if we talk to the production manager, the chances are that he will see things differently. The Production Director too will see the situation somewhat differently from either the supervisor or the production manager, and any trainers who know the supervisor or the job will have yet another perspective. (If you do not believe this, try it for yourself and see.) So, whose view is 'correct' in such circumstances? It depends. Partly it will depend on the evaluator's brief. If, for example, the Board has decided to change the way the production function is organized, and the evaluator is exploring what abilities will be needed in the new organization, then perhaps the Production Director's view will be what is needed (although, even here, the evaluator might want to check what the manager and the supervisor have to say). Partly, too, the 'correct' view will depend on the evaluator's judgement of such issues as his own expertise, the political situation in the organiza- tion, where responsibility for effective performance lies, who holds the purse strings, and so on. It is not possible to give hard and fast rules — the most we can say is that the evaluator should be aware of the essentially subjective nature of identified training needs.

Having said that, let us look at the various ways in which the Grid — a very help- ful tool for exploring subjective judgements — can be used to assist in the identifi- cation of training needs.

Suppose we want to find out, as a basis for identifying training needs, what behaviour is perceived to be needed to perform effectively in a certain role. To do this, we can interview job holders in that role, their managers, their subordinates, or anybody else who has a view about that role, and we can use the Grid as the basis for the interview. Here we have two options: we can use as elements either examples of important tasks or activities in the job, or people who do the job. If we use tasks or activities as elements, we will ask our interviewees to construe them in relation to 'behaviour required to perform the task effectively', whereas if we use people as elements, our interviewees should construe them in terms of 'the ways in which they go about their work.'

Whether we use tasks or job holders as elements will to some extent depend on our circumstances. In general, using tasks has the following advantages:

1. Behaviour is directly related to job activities.
2. The interviewee only needs to know his own job, or a few job holders.
3. The interviewee does not need to talk about individuals' performance.
4. Interviewees can be asked to construe jobs that do not actually exist as yet.

On the other hand, people as elements have these advantages:

1. They are often easier to construe in terms of behaviour than tasks are.
2. It usually takes less time to generate a people element set than a task element set.

3. The constructs elicited usually have an 'effective' pole and a 'less effective' pole, which may make it easier to comprehend the nature of the behaviour elicited, and may be easier to work with subsequently.

Here is a short illustration of how we might use the Grid in this way.

EXAMPLE 1

Suppose we want to find out if our training for accounts supervisors should be modified in any way to meet the needs of that role.

Our first step would be to find out what behaviour is associated with effective performance in the role. To obtain this information, we might elicit a Grid from the Accounts Manager, and Grids from some or all the accounts supervisors.

To elicit the Accounts Manager's Grid, we would start by asking him to list his current supervisory subordinates as the basis for the element set (if he had enough subordinates). Then we might offer as additional elements THE MOST EFFECTIVE SUPERVISOR WHO HAS WORKED FOR ME and THE LEAST EFFECTIVE SUPERVISOR WHO HAS WORKED FOR ME. Once we had the element set, we would ask the Accounts Manager to construe the elements in terms of 'the way in which they go about their work'. Having obtained the constructs, we would ask the Manager to say, for each construct, which pole is more associated with effective performance by supervisors, and we would then ask him to say whether each construct was of Great Importance, Some Importance or Little Importance to the supervisor's effectiveness overall.

To analyse this Grid, we would note down the behaviours that were of Great Importance and Some Importance.

To elicit the accounts supervisors' Grids, we would ask each supervisor to look at the job description for accounts supervisors (assuming the job description is up-to-date and accurate), and to think of particular situations that involved each of the main tasks in the job description. Thus, as elements we would have several events that illustrate the tasks in the job.

We would then ask the supervisors to construe these events in terms of the behaviour required to handle these situations effectively, and we would ask each supervisor to rate his elements on this constructs. We would end by asking the supervisors to sort their construct poles into behaviours of Great Importance, Some Importance and Little Importance to effective performance in their job overall.

To analyse these Grids, we would take the behaviours seen as being of Great Importance or Some Importance and would use the element ratings to find out which behaviours were associated with which tasks. Then we would combine those constructs and elements to give us statements such as 'being firm when disciplining staff' (where 'must be firm' was the construct pole label, and 'disciplining staff' was the element category).

We would then list out all the statements for all the supervisors, and group them in some way, probably by type of behaviour. Thus, we might have categories such as 'Inter-personal Behaviour', 'Accounting Skills' and 'Organizational Understanding'. Having done this, we would next enter the Accounts Manager's constructs into these categories to see where he shared an understanding with his subordinates about the behaviours required (we might find that we need some new categories for some of his constructs).

At this point, we would turn to the training we currently offer and would note which of the behaviours listed by our Accounts staff we currently offered training in. We might also find that some of our training is designed to meet needs that have not been identified. Three questions now remain:

1. Should we be offering training in the behaviours we are not currently covering?
2. Is some of our training redundant, because all the supervisors already possess the required level of ability?
3. Are some of the objectives of our current training that have not been included in the Accounts staff's list nonetheless still relevant?

To answer these questions, we would go back to our Accounts Manager, as the man responsible for the work of his supervisors, to have a detailed discussion about these questions, on the basis of our findings.

There are several variations on this basic approach that can also give us useful information about training needs. The example we have given has involved eliciting Grids from job holders and/or their managers, but the method can equally well be applied if we have agreed that there is an 'expert' whose views we should use. Let us imagine that we have an Industrial Relations Manager who is seen to be very good at his job.

EXAMPLE 2

Suppose a manager tells us that one of his subordinates needs industrial-relations training, and we want to assess which type of industrial-relations course would be most suitable for that subordinate.

In this case, our first step would be to discover what behaviours the Industrial Relations Manager saw as contributing to effective handling of industrial relations in the subordinate's job. We would start by collecting from the subordinate and/or his manager a list of industrial-relations situations in which the subordinate had been, or could be, involved, and which represented the range of industrial-relations activities with which he was, or could be, concerned. These would be our elements. We would then go to the Industrial Relations Manager and ask him to construe these elements in terms of the behaviours needed by the subordinate. After we had turned the elements and constructs back into statements, we would go back to the manager and, as before, discuss in which areas there was a need for improvement, and which needs were most urgent (the Industrial Relations Manager might also be asked for his views on the urgency of the needs).

'Experts' can also be used in other ways to help us establish training needs, by showing us how the experienced and competent person perceives a situation, and how these perceptions relate to the actions they take. To obtain this information, we first of all need to elicit a Grid from the 'expert' in which the elements are events or situations, and the constructs are 'features of the element that are relevant to the task'. Having obtained these features, we can then ask our 'expert' to tell us, or show us, how he would use them to decide on his actions, and what those actions would be. Here is an example of how we might do this.

EXAMPLE 3

Suppose senior management has decided on a long-term investment in computer technology and, to support this decision, has decided to invest in training for middle and junior managers. Senior management want the training to boost managers' confidence and enthusiasm about computers and to help them manage the introduction and operation of computerized systems. Our task is to decide what specific training objectives we should have, so that we can design the training to meet the overall training need.

In this situation we are fortunate because some departments in the organization already have experience of the implementation of computerized systems. Further, it is agreed that some managers are more enthusiastic and competent at managing this change than others. Our first step, therefore, is to find out what distinguishes those who have been successful (our 'experts' in this case) from those who have been less successful.

To do this, we would want to elicit Grids from these two groups of managers, and we would want a common set of elements for all interviewees, if possible, in order to make our comparisons easier. For this project, therefore, we might choose as our elements some of the important steps in the process of systems design and implementation. To get a shared element set we might, on this occasion, ask our DP trainers (as another group of 'experts') to list the steps for us (e.g., deciding the objectives of the new system, programming the system, training user staff). Then we would use this element set to elicit the managers' constructs about 'the demands these make' on them, and we would ask the managers to rate the elements on their constructs.

Once we have the managers' constructs and ratings, we will explore with each manager the actions he took, or would take, to respond to the demands at points where demands were great (i.e., those elements for which the manager had given a rating of 1 or 5). Thus, for example, one of our managers may have given us the constructs *need to make sure users and computer staff understand each other — no need for computer staff to communicate with users*. This manager may also have rated 'training user staff' as 1 on this construct, i.e., this step requires, in his view, a high need for users and computer staff to understand each other. So, we would ask: 'What did you do to make sure users and computer staff understood each other when it came to training user staff?'

Having elicited both 'demands' and 'actions' from our managers, we are now in a position to consider in detail what distinguishes the successful manager from the less successful one. To do this, we would start off by listing the actions the two groups of managers took in relation to each element, and then categorize the actions in some way. Thus, we might come up with Table 13.1 as an example, for the element TRAINING USER STAFF. In this example we can see clearly that the actions of the two groups are different, and we are beginning to get some feel for what the focus of our training might be.

Table 13.1

Successful managers' actions (categories)	Less successful managers' actions (categories)
Discussions with computer staff	Deciding timing of training programme
Obtaining feedback from trainees	Notifying computer staff about timing
Examining proposed training before it is carried out	
Notifying own staff about training content/times, etc.	

But we have obtained these actions from managers' perceptions of the demands on them. We can ask ourselves whether the two groups perceive the demands in a similar way, but just act differently (in which case our training only needs to concentrate on actions), or whether the two groups act differently because they perceive the demands on them differently (in which case our training might need to focus on these perceptions as well). To find out the answer to this question we can, as before, list the construct pole names relevant to each element for the two groups and then categorize the constructs in some way. The result in this case might look as in Table 13.2.

So, in general it would appear that, in this case, different perceptions lead to different actions (and we could go on to show ourselves in what ways these perceptions lead to actions by drawing lines between the 'Action' categories and the 'Demands' categories). On second glance, however, we discover from Table 13.2 that the two groups of managers have one common category - 'Control over what specialists do'. We would therefore want to go back and look at the constructs in this category for each group, in order to decide whether this really is a common category, and if so, to decide what this implies for our training objectives.

Table 13.2

Demands on successful managers (categories)	Demands on less successful managers (categories)
Communication between specialists and users	Keeping to work schedule
Agreement between specialists and manager	Control over what specialists do
Control over what specialists do	
Planning departmental schedule	
Confidence in computer staff's judgement	

By going through this process for each of our elements in turn, and by aggregating our findings, we will arrive at a very detailed understanding of what our training objectives should be if we want to help our managers to handle the introduction of computer systems effectively. As we have seen, there are several ways in which the Grid can be used to identify training needs. In summary, to use the Grid for this purpose we need to ask ourselves:

1. — Whose perspective should we obtain?
2. — Who are the 'experts' in this situation and who will decide what needs should be addressed by the training?
3. — Will the Grid be used to decide the training needs of those from whom the Grid is elicited, or will the Grid be used to assist in the identification of training needs in others?

Trainees' changes during and after training

When many people speak about evaluating training, what they have in mind is some assessment of the extent to which training has assisted trainees to change. Sometimes this is because they want to know whether the training has 'worked' by producing outcomes they are seeking, sometimes they are interested because they want to decide whether they should modify their training methods or objectives, or the way they should 'market' the training, and sometimes because they just wonder whether the training is associated with any changes and, if so, what these changes might be.

Once again, the Grid can be used to provide us with systematic, detailed information to help us make our assessments, as it can give us not only a picture of how trainees themselves have changed, but also an understanding of the extent to which others perceive changes in those who have been trained.

Let us start with the supposition that we want to find out whether our training seems to be having some effect on the way individuals go about their work. If we have identified training needs in one of the ways discussed in the previous section, we can relatively easily find out the perceived degree of competence of individuals before and after training and see whether this has changed. We can do this in one of two ways: either we can ask someone else to rate the individual, together with some of his co-workers, on each of the behaviours required for the job, or we can ask the trainees to produce Grids for us before and after training. Which method we choose will depend on the way in which training needs were originally identified. Here are three examples.

EXAMPLE 4

Suppose we have used the approach in Example 1 to identify the training needs of accounts supervisors, and we now want to find out whether the training we are doing is have an effect on the supervisors' work performance.

Our first step would be to find out before the course how the Accounts Manager perceives the work behaviour of his supervisors. To do this we might ask the

Manager to complete a sheet that looked like Table 13.3. (Note that we have turned the original statements about relevant behaviour back into bipolar statements, and that the behaviour 'Makes relevant contributions to departmental meetings' has been divided into two, to take account of the two ideas in the statement — the relevance of the contribution and the amount of the contribution.)

Table 13.3

	Supervisor Name					
	A	B	C	D	E	F
Behaviour						
Is always firm in disciplining staff						Is never firm in disciplining staff
Always makes relevant contributions to departmental meetings						Always makes irrelevant contributions to deparmental meetings
Always makes relevant contributions to departmental meetings						Never makes contributions to departmental meetings

Although only Supervisors D, E and F are scheduled to receive training, we would ask the Manager to think about all his supervisors (A to F) so that D, E and F are placed in the context of their colleagues. We would ask the Manager to use a seven-point scale (because we want fine distinctions) to tell us to what extent each of the supervisors was like either the left-hand or right-hand statement on each line. Thus, the Manager might give the following ratings on the distinction *is always firm in discplining staff — is never firm in disciplining staff*:

A	B	C	D	E	F
4	2	1	5	6	2

This would tell us that he sees Supervisor C has 'always firm' and Supervisor E as 'almost never firm', with the other supervisors somewhere in between (incidentally, this would also tell us that Supervisor C probably does not need training in this area).

If Supervisors D, E and F then take part in our training, we can come back to the Accounts Manager sometime later — in this case, about six months later, so that the supervisors have had an opportunity to consolidate what they have learned and put it into practice — and ask our Manager to use the seven-point scale again for all his subordinates on all of his statements. This time our Manager might give his supervisors the following ratings:

	A	B	C	D	E	F	
Is always firm about disciplining staff	4	2	1	3	3	1	Is never firm about disciplining staff

We can then compare the Manager's ratings before the training with those he gave after the training, and in this case, the result looks as though the training has had an influence in the way we had hoped: Supervisors D, E and F have all moved more toward the outcome we were aiming for. However, before jumping to conclusions, it is usually worth our while checking back with our Manager by showing him where his ratings have changed and asking what reasons he might give for these changes. If we did that with our 'being firm about disciplining staff' objective, our Manager might say: 'I gave Supervisor F a score of 1 because recently he has been very firm and I put that down to your training. Likewise with Supervisor D. He could still take a firmer line on many occasions, but things have improved since your course. And, yes, Supervisor E has made a significant improvement, but I think that is because I could not stand it any longer and decided to spend a fair amount of time coaching him — I certainly did not notice any change after the training, and I was getting desperate"

Thus, on this objective we could conclude that we had had some positive results with two of the supervisors, but that our efforts are not resulting in change on every occasion, and we might want to explore further why Supervisor E had not benefited from this part of the course.

EXAMPLE 5

Suppose we have designed the training that came out of our work in Example 3, and we now want to assess to what extent we are achieving our objectives.

We know how managers who are successful in managing the introduction of computer systems see the demands this makes on them, and the actions they would take in responding to these demands. Our first step, therefore, is to find out whether our trainees are more like our 'experts' after the training than before.

To discover this, we merely need to repeat the process we went through in Example 3. Because we are looking for change, however, we would want to ask each of our participants to produce two Grids — one before, and one after, the course. Then we could firstly compare the content of the two Grids, and their associated actions, and secondly compare the after-course Grids with those from our 'experts'. We could, as in Example 3, treat all our trainees as one group and put together their results for an overall picture, or we could look at individual change by comparing each manager's Grids with our 'experts' views. The latter approach would give us more detailed information, and enable us to highlight individual difficulties, but the former approach might give us the general trend more easily. With either approach, however, we could quickly see what impact the training was having.

If we elicit our second Grid directly after the course, however, we will only know about our trainees' perceptions at that point, and this may not be the end of the story, because most of our managers will not yet have had any experience of actually introducing computer systems. Thus, we may also want to go back to our trainees after a year or two and do another Grid to see whether their views have changed again once they have some 'real' experience (although we will probably only want to do this if we are still running the course then!)

All the above examples started from the premise that we knew what constituted effective performance, and we could assess our training against those criteria. Sometimes, however, we do not have this information either because we could not obtain it, or because there is a 'development' component to the training that cannot be specified very clearly in behavioural terms. Nonetheless, by asking our trainees to produce Grids for us before and after training, we can gain a very detailed picture of the changes that have occurred in individuals' construing which we can then assess for ourselves, or show to someone else for an assessment. Example 6 is an example of the approach we could use in such a situation.

EXAMPLE 6

Suppose we sent our high-potential middle managers to a post-experience general-management programme run by a Business School, and we want to find out whether the course really has any impact on them.

In order to discover this, we need to elicit two Grids from each manager who attends the programme: one before he attends, and one when he returns to work. We then need to compare the two Grids, talk with our managers about the extent to which they are aware of any changes, and their perceptions of the reasons for the changes we have uncovered.

A relevant element set for such an exercise would be the jobs of the managers concerned. To generate our elements, we would ask each manager before the programme to list out the major activities in his job, and then to think of an event which incorporated that activity — the events would thus become the element set.

We would then ask each manager to construe his elements in any ways he thought were significant for him, and rate his elements on these constructs.

After the course, we would give back to each manager his original element set and his original constructs, with the original ratings removed, and we would ask our managers (a) to rate their elements on their constructs again, and take out any elements or constructs that were no longer significant, and (b) to add any new elements or constructs that seemed significant, and to rate them.

At this point a computer can make life easier and give us useful insights. If we use the FOCUS program, we might get the results shown in Figs. 13.1 and 13.2 for Manager A. In comparing these two Grids, we will look for the following changes.

1. Have new elements or constructs been added? (Yes)
2. Do the new elements and/or constructs elaborate pre-course clusters, and thus appear in the middle of the Grid, *or* are they new and distinct ideas, in which case they will appear at the periphery of the Grid? (New elements 7 and 8 are

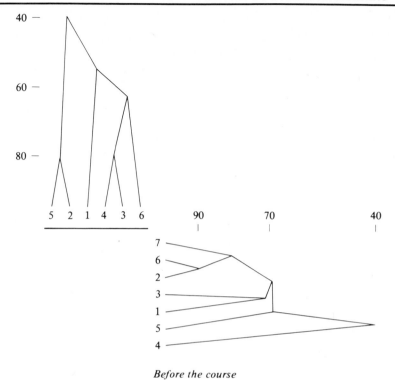

Before the course

Figure 13.1

embedded in the Grid, so they are elaborating the original element set. New construct 8 is also an elaboration, whereas new construct 9 is distinct.)

3. Have the ratings of any elements and/or constructs altered? (Yes. There has been a marked change in the rating of element 3 and in the rating of construct 2. In addition, there has been some change in elements 4 and 5, and in constructs 5 and 6.)

4. Have the pre-course patterns of elements and/or constructs changed, i.e., are elements and/or constructs clustered together differently after the course? (Yes. Before the course the elements were clustered in two groups: one formed by 4, 3 and 6; the other formed by 5 and 2. Element 1 was somewhat distinct. After the course, the clusters 6, 7 and 4 and 8, 3 and 5, with elements 1 and 2 distinct. Before the course, constructs 2, 6 and 7 formed a cluster, as did constructs 1 and 3. Constructs 4 and 5 were distinct. After the course, there are clusters formed by 9 and 7, and by 2, 5 and 6, and a cluster formed from two sub-clusters made up from 4 and 8, and from 1 and 3.)

5. Are there more clusters than there were before the course? (Yes. With the elements, there were two clusters plus element 1 on its own, before the course. Now there are two clusters, plus two elements on their own. The constructs

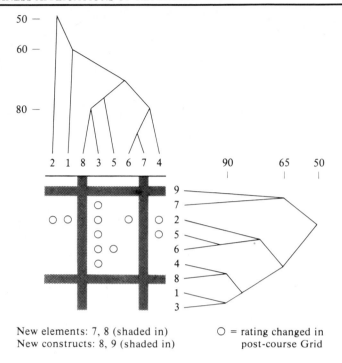

New elements: 7, 8 (shaded in)   ○ = rating changed in
New constructs: 8, 9 (shaded in)   post-course Grid

After the course

Figure 13.2

before the course formed two clusters, with two distinct constructs. Now there are two clusters, plus a third cluster made up of two sub-clusters.)

6. Has the degree of relationship between the elements altered? (Yes. On the whole relationships are higher, e.g., there is now a 90 per cent match between elements 6 and 7, and element 2 is matched with the other elements at 50 per cent. Before the course the highest match was 80 per cent, and element clusters related together at 40 per cent.)

7. Has the degree of relationship between the constructs altered? (Yes. On the whole relationships are higher, e.g., there are now four matches at 80 per cent or above, and the constructs now relate together at about 50 per cent. Before the course, there were only two construct matches at 80 per cent or above, and construct 4 was only matched in at 40 per cent.)

In this case, we would therefore conclude that some very significant and dramatic changes had resulted from the manager's participation in the Business School programme. If we were to ask him he would undoubtedly say something like 'it has transformed my understanding of my work' but would probably be unable to say precisely how. By talking him through the changes in his Grids, however, we could help both of us to understand these changes more fully, and we could also learn something of the events on the programme that he associated with his changes.

This method of using the Grid can be applied in a wide variety of circumstances. Let us give one more illustration, which also incorporates an 'expert' view.

EXAMPLE 7

Suppose we are running a course designed to develop inter-personal skills needed by supervisors. We know what skills are needed because we have conducted a training-needs analysis, and we plan to do an evaluation along the lines of Example 4, but we want to know what happens to our trainees during the course so that we can understand more clearly the information we get from supervisors' managers, and because we want to find out to what extent our trainees incorporate our understanding of inter-personal behaviour (as the 'expert') into their own way of looking at things.

In this case, we would begin by asking our course participants to do a Grid for themselves at the start of the course. We would obtain a common element set for the group by asking the group to draw up and agree a common list of situations in their work in which interaction was important (e.g., attending meetings, disciplinary interviews, talking to one's manager). After explaining how to complete a Grid, we would ask participants to construe the elements in terms of 'their important features from an interaction point of view.' Participants would also be allowed to add additional elements personal to their own situations. When participants had rated their elements on their constructs, we would collect them and begin the course.

At the end of the course, we would hand back to each participant his original Grid, with the original ratings removed. Then we would ask participants firstly to think whether they wanted to add or delete any elements or constructs, and, secondly, to rate their elements on their constructs.

Our analysis of these Grids would take place in two stages. The first stage would be for us to compare our construing with that of the participants, to see where we agreed and disagreed at the start and the end of the course. To do this, we would first compile a set of all the participants' constructs and use these constructs to rate the common element set. Then, we would compare our ratings with those given by the participants. As an example, Participant 1 might have had the following construct with the following ratings after the course:

Situations

	A	B	C	D	E	F	G	
Interaction is necessary	2	4	5	1	3	2	4	Interaction is voluntary

And we might have given the elements the following ratings:

A	B	C	D	E	F	G
1	2	5	1	1	2	1

Thus, there is significant agreement between us in 4 cases out of 7 (on A, C, D and F).

We can do this for each construct in each Grid and build up an overall set of ratios for each participant, both before and after the course.

The second stage would consist of an analysis of each participant's Grids using the FOCUS program, to explore changes in construing during the course. For participant 1 we might get Fig. 13.3, and for Participant 2 we might get Fig. 13.4.

By seeking answers to the questions posed in Example 6 we can pinpoint the changes in construing that have occurred, and we will undoubtedly conclude that Participant 2 experienced less change than Participant 1.

Whether we assess this to be a positive outcome in either case will to some extent depend on what our participants' managers tell us when we talk with them, but we can draw some preliminary conclusions by returning to the first stage of our analysis. Thus, if we agreed with Participant 1 on 15 out of 35 ratings before the course, and on 30 out of 63 ratings after the course, we can conclude that the changes in Participant 1's construing did not lead him to become markedly more 'like us' (although by examining the changes and additions to his individual ratings we might conclude that some of these changes had been in our direction). On the other hand, if 35 out of Participant 2's 48 pre-course ratings were like ours, and 40 of his 56 post-course ratings were also the same or similar, we can say that Participant 2 was much more 'like us' to begin with than Participant 1, and that his new construct, added after the course, increased our degree of similarity.

Up to this point we have been assuming that we must have a 'before' and 'after' measure in order to explore individual change, but this need not always be the case.

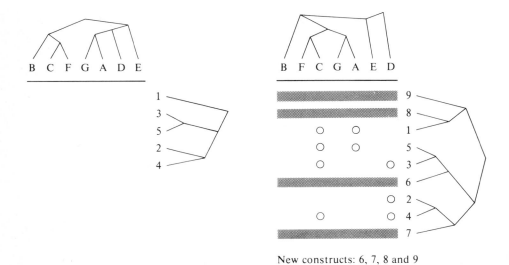

New constructs: 6, 7, 8 and 9

Before the course   *After the course*

Figure 13.3

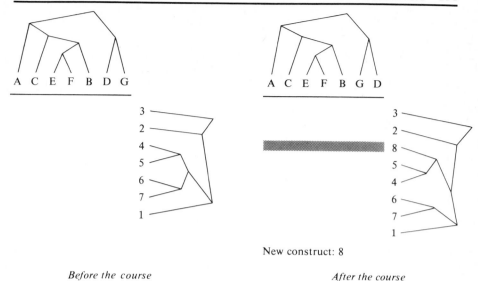

New construct: 8

Before the course   *After the course*

Figure 13.4

In some situations, we may want to use the Grid to ask individuals for their own assessment of what they have learned, or how they have changed, as a result of some experience. To do this, we do not need a pre-course Grid from trainees, as we can ask our participants to use course sessions or course events as elements, and to construe them in terms of what they 'got out of these sessions', or what they 'have learned from these experiences'.

EXAMPLE 8

Suppose we are running one-day workshops on unfair dismissal and want to find out what, if anything, people feel they have gained from these workshops, so that we can discuss the day's programme with the tutor and 'market' the workshops to other potential participants more effectively.

In this case we want to explore what participants feel they have learned from the workshop, so we will want our element set to be components of the workshop programme. This we can obtain by sitting in on the workshop and noting down the programme events (e.g., talk about the law's wording, question and answer session about the law, individual work on case study about Mr X).

Then we can go to some or all of the workshop participants shortly after the event and ask them to construe the programme's events in terms of what they 'learned from these parts of the workshop'.

For marketing purposes, we can devise categories for the constructs by looking at the words used by the participants and grouping the construct labels in some way. Thus, we might end up with categories such as ORGANIZATIONAL IMPLI – CATIONS, PERSONAL RESPONSIBILITIES, LEGAL COMPLEXITIES and

CONFIDENCE ABOUT DISMISSALS. We can then use these categories to tell potential participants that these are the kinds of understanding they are likely to gain from attending the programme.

In preparation for our discussion with the tutor, we can list out the major components of the day's programme (the element), and enter the construct categories that came up for each element, together with the number of participants who said they learned something in that category. So, for example, if we had interviewed 10 participants, we might have:

Workshop Component: *Talk about Law's Wording*

LEGAL COMPLEXITIES – 5
CONFIDENCE ABOUT DISMISSAL – 7

When we have done this for each of the workshop components, we can review the outcome and ask ourselves and/or our industrial-relations specialists (a) whether there are other outcomes we might expect to see (that is, other categories), (b) whether there are any inappropriate outcomes and (c) whether we should be trying to increase the number of participants who say they have learned certain things from certain sessions. Having made these decisions, we are in a position to review the workshop with the tutor.

In summary, then, we can use the Grid, and information from the Grid, in various ways to explore how trainees change during and after training. If we want to collect such information for our evaluation purposes, therefore, we should ask ourselves these questions:

1. What, and whose, criteria will we use to assess change?
2. From whom will we elicit Grids – participants and/or others?
3. Do we need 'before' and 'after' measures, or can we just collect our information after the training?
4. Do we need to interview participants individually, or can we elicit Grids from individuals in a group setting?
5. What elements and types of constructs will give us relevant information?
6. At what time(s) will we elicit our Grids and collect our data?

Trainees' views of the success of training events

The most common type of evaluation is the assessment of the extent to which participants are satisfied with the training they have experienced. Usually this is carried out, in effect, by asking trainees to use our constructs to rate sessions or speakers or the training as a whole: we ask participants to say how relevant or new the course content was, how interesting the sessions were, how satisfied they were overall, and so on.

Despite the fact that this type of evaluation is relatively common, trainers often express dissatisfaction with the outcomes of these assessments by participants, particularly when the results are not highly positive. This expressed dissatisfaction probably has several sources, but one likely reason may be that trainers do not know what to do about negative ratings. Part of the reason for this may be that we do not have enough detailed information about what participants mean when they say, for example, that a session is not very relevant to them. Here again, the Grid can assist us by helping us to understand what factors contribute to participants' overall assessments. To use the Grid for this purpose, we will probably want as elements course session or course speakers, and we will want to ask our participants to construe the elements in terms of their relevance, or sources of satisfaction, or whatever global term we are interested in.

EXAMPLE 9

Suppose we are running an inter-personal skills course for supervisors that we believe will have most impact if it is seen by the supervisors as being relevant to their work. We therefore want to know what parts of the course our supervisors see as relevant and irrelevant, and what makes these sessions relevant or irrelevant, from their point of view, so that we can re-design the course to make it appear more relevant (we have done a training-needs analysis with some of the supervisors and their managers, so we know that we are offering assistance that should be important for their work).

To find out this information, we would elicit Grids from participants at the end of the course. Our elements will be the course sessions, plus the course overall, and we will ask our supervisors to construe and rate these in terms of their relevance. We will also offer the construct *overall, was highly relevant to my work — overall, was largely irrelevant to my work*. Suppose we obtain a Grid from Supervisor E which looks like Fig. 13.5 after it has been put through the FOCUS computer

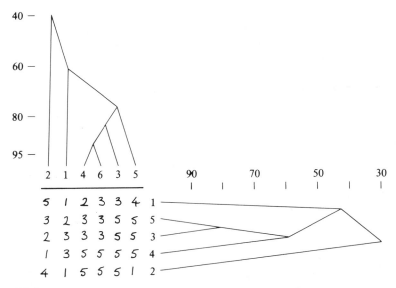

Figure 13.5

program (as in all our examples, this Grid has been simplified for purposes of illustration). In this example, the elements were:

E1 : Session: 'Why We Behave the Way We Do' (Talk)
E2 : Session: 'Listening' (Exercise)
E3 : Session: 'Components of Effective Communication' (Talk)
E4 : Session: 'Asking for What You Want' (Exercise)
E5 : Session: 'Saying How You Feel' (Exercise)
E6 : The Course Overall

and the constructs were:

C1 : did not understand what was being   — understood clearly
said
C2 : do not need to know about that in   — do not need to know about that
my job   for my work
C3 : I could do what the tutor told us   — I could not do what was shown
C4 : you need confidence to do that   — anybody can do it
C5 : overall, highly relevant   — overall, largely irrelevant

Without the computer analysis, and just by looking at the constructs, we can see in what ways Supervisor E thinks about whether or not sessions are relevant. However, the computer analysis gives us additional, valuable and possibly surprising information: it shows us that for Supervisor E 'overall relevance' is most closely associated with being able to do something, and with confidence, and by looking at the ratings of the elements, we can see that this supervisor felt he 'could not do' and 'needed confidence to do' several of the course sessions.

If these kinds of ideas (or any other ideas) were closely associated with 'relevance overall' in several supervisors' Grids, we would then have a clear picture of what we need to do in order to increase the perceived relevance of the course to supervisors.

The above example illustrated how we could use the Grid to elaborate one issue, in this case 'relevance', which we think is important. The same approach can also be used to allow participants to show us the ideas they are using to think about the overall success of the training from their point of view.

EXAMPLE 10

Suppose we are running the course described in Example 9 and want to design a standard form that participants can use to give us feedback about their satisfaction with the programme. If we can find some ideas commonly used by our participants, we can design part of our form using these ideas, and then include a space on the form for additional, personal ideas.

To find out in what terms participants think about satisfaction, we can ask our participants at the end of the course to construe the course sessions (the elements) in terms of their 'sources of satisfaction'. We would also ask them to rate the elements on the constructs, and would offer them the construct *very satisfied overall — very dissatisfied overall*.

We would then use the FOCUS analysis in the same way as in the previous example, in order to extract the constructs most closely associated with 'overall satisfaction'. These constructs would be reviewed for common terminology between Grids, and those that came up regularly (in more than 50 per cent of the Grids) would become the basis for our 'evaluation form'.

It is just possible that no constructs will come up regularly, in which case, we will probably want to abandon our objective of designing a standard form.

One construct that often appears in a Grid of the kind described above is *met my expectations – did not meet expectations*. If trainers have reason to believe that participant expectations affect overall satisfaction at the end of the course, they might want to find out about these expectations before the training, so they can try either to modify the expectations or the training. The Grid can be used in the same way as illustrated in Examples 9 and 10 to explore these expectations before, or at the start of, the course. The elements would be course sessions (plus the course overall) and the participants would be asked to construe these in terms of their expectations. In this case, the computer analysis would be used to make it easier for the trainers to review whether participants' expectations could be met for each session (e.g., will our session on 'Argument' on the Negotiating Skills course show the participant how to 'put the union in its place'?). We will not give a specific example here, as the approach is so similar to our other illustrations.

In conclusion, then, the important issues to be considered when thinking about using the Grid to explore trainees' views of the success of a training programme, could be summarized as follows:

1. What aspect(s) of satisfaction or success do we want to explore?
2. Can we get access to a computer, or will we rely on manual analysis?
3. Do we need to interview participants individually, or can we elicit Grids from individuals in a group setting?
4. At what point(s) will we elicit our Grids?

Trainers' views of the success of training

Trainers usually have opinions about the way their training programmes and sessions have gone, about course design, about what types of course are suitable for what people, and about many other aspects of the training with which they have been involved. In other words, trainers evaluate training.

Frequently these evaluations are neither systematic, nor made explicit, so that the full benefit of these assessments for future action is lost. The Grid, however, can help us to be systematic and explicit about our own evaluations.

Several of the examples earlier in this chapter have illustrated ways in which Grids elicited from trainees, or potential trainees or their managers can provide information that trainers can use to make their own views explicit, but in this section we propose to consider two ways in which trainers might elicit Grids from themselves.

EXAMPLE 11

Suppose, as trainers, we run a training programme that participants like, but which leaves us unsatisfied in some way we find difficult to be specific about, but ideally would like to tackle. We can elicit a Grid from ourselves in which the elements are the course sessions, or events, construed in terms of 'their sources of success and failure'. This process can make somewhat clearer the factors we have in our minds when we think about 'success' and 'failure' in this context.

If we then go on to rate the elements on the constructs, we can FOCUS our Grid (manually or by computer). This will clearly highlight those course sessions we are happy about, those we are unhappy about and those about which we have mixed feelings. By looking again at our constructs, and our ratings of the elements on the constructs, we can hold a counselling session with ourselves (or with the help of a colleague) in which we think about ways of overcoming the specific difficulties we have highlighted.

The second way in which trainers can use Grids with themselves concerns situations in which they are making choices between options. In such circumstances, it can often be helpful to make the options the element set, and to construe the elements in terms of the features, their likely outcomes, or some other important quality.

EXAMPLE 12

Suppose the trainer is seeking an inter-personal skills course for a manager in his organization. The trainer has some idea of his manager's needs, and be knows something about the various methods used by different training organizations. What the trainer wants to decide is which course is most likely to be appropriate.

As his element set, the trainer would select the courses that could be appropriate. He would then construe them in terms of their 'likely outcomes' for his manager and rate his elements on his constructs. Before FOCUS-ing his Grid, he would also select his preferred pole for each construct, bearing his particular manager's needs and concerns in mind.

On looking at the FOCUS-ed Grid, it might be immediately clear which course to select, because one course has come out at the preferred end of all the trainer's constructs. However, and more likely, no course may be entirely positive and several courses may come out as having one or two drawbacks, which will mean that an immediate decision is not possible. But this outcome also means that the trainer can now concentrate his attention on these drawbacks and decide their relative importance, from his point of view. Having done this, he can then choose the most appropriate course, or search for another course that overcomes the drawbacks he has identified.

Managers' views of training courses

If we want to 'market' training, or if we want a manager to help us to select a training programme that he sees as appropriate for one of his subordinates, it is important that we know in what terms our managers think about training of various kinds.

We can use the Grid to discover something of the ways managers think about training by offering, or eliciting, training events as elements and by asking our managers to think about these elements either in general terms, or in relation to something specific – a subordinate, himself, outcomes or whatever is relevant to the issue at hand. Often we will not even need to have the elements rated on the constructs, because 'preferred poles' and some indication of the relative importance of different constructs will suffice. The example below illustrates how the Grid can be used without rating all the elements on the constructs. See Example 12 for an approach that uses ratings.

EXAMPLE 13

Suppose we have been running a training course which we and our participants think is successful, and which is designed to meet an identified need. Yet registrations have been low and we want to find out why, so we can see if we do do something.

In this case, we would select for interview several managers who are in a position to nominate subordinates for the course, but who have not in fact done so.

As our elements we would elicit from the managers the titles of several courses known to them (preferably several they thought highly of and several they thought less highly of), and we would also include the course we are interested in as one of the elements (we might also offer one or two other course titles to hide our true purpose somewhat).

Then we would ask our managers to construe their elements in relation to their relevance to his subordinates, and to say which pole of each construct was more relevant for the subordinate. We might also do some laddering up to find out why they were making the choices they were. Then we would ask which of their constructs our managers would think of as most important in determining what training they suggested to their subordinates. Having done this, we would ask our managers to consider the course we were interested in, and to tell us at which end of each construct the course appeared to be.

To analyse these Grids, we would first look for distinctions between the important 'preferred poles' for subordinates and the perceived characteristics of our course (for example, suppose one manager had the construct *long – short* and said he preferred a short course, but saw ours as a long course). Next, we would look to see whether any of these distinctions had come up in several Grids – if so, they represent a common source of difficulty that we might want to work on. Finally, we would look at the distinctions that had not come up regularly and see whether they were opposed in other managers' Grids (another manager might see our course as long and might prefer long courses for his subordinates. This view would be opposed to that expressed by our manager above). If managers' views did not cancel each other out, we would have some other sources of difficulty to which we could direct our attention.

Management's views of training as a function

Sometimes the most important evaluation of training – in terms of its impact on resources or activities – takes place not at the level of individual courses or

individual needs, but rather at the level of an assessment of the function as a whole.
The criteria that go to make up these assessments, and their outcomes, can of
course be seen — depending on one's point of view — as either indicating a training
need in those who are doing the assessing, or as providing a sound basis for management action. However, for the trainer who wants to improve or maintain the image
and value of his function in the organization, an understanding of these assessments
and their bases can prove a valuable starting point.

To gather this information, one useful type of element set would consist of
various functions or departments within the organization (e.g., Marketing, Production, Purchasing), including Training or Management Development, or whatever the
relevant department is called. Managers whose views are sought would then be
asked to construe these elements in some terms, such as 'their contribution to the
organization', 'the impression they give' or just 'their important features for you.'
The direction in which we would choose to guide our managers' thoughts would, as
always, depend upon our purpose for doing the Grid.

EXAMPLE 14

Suppose our management-development function, which reports to the Personnel
Director, has existed as a separate function with its own staff for the past three
years. We are now planning how the function will develop over the next three years
and want to do our best to be seen to be contributing a useful service to the organization. In order to develop our plans, we would like to know in what ways managers
see various functions as 'contributing a useful service' and we want to know how we
currently measure up.

To obtain this information we would arrange to elicit Grids from middle and
senior managers in several other departments. Our element set would consist of
various functions in the organization, including management development, and
would have two special features: the elements would contain several aspects of the
work of the personnel function generally (so we can see to what extent our managers
see us as distinct from other parts of the personnel function), and it would always
contain the function in which the manager we were interviewing worked (so we can
see how he views his function in relation to ours). We would ask our managers to
construe the elements in terms of 'their contribution to the organization' and to
rate the elements on their constructs. We would also ask for the 'preferred pole' for
each construct, and we would want to know whether our managers saw some types
of contribution as more important than others.

To analyse the Grids, we would first of all FOCUS them manually or by computer, and we would then build up a picture of (a) the ways in which we were
currently seen to be making a positive contribution to the organization, (b) the ways
in which we were not currently seen to be making a positive contribution and (c) the
extent to which we were seen as similar and different to other aspects of the personnel function and to the manager's own function. As an illustration, suppose that

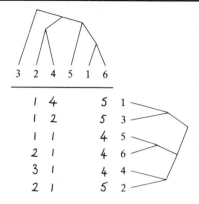

Figure 13.6

the Marketing Director's Grid looked like Fig. 13.6, which the elements are:

E1 : Finance
E2 : Recruitment
E3 : Operations
E4 : Management Development
E5 : R & D
E6 : Marketing

and the constructs are:

C1 : does not contribute   – does[P]
new ideas to the
organization
C2 : has little to do with my   – contributes significantly to
function   my function[P]
C3 : tactical[P]   – strategic[P]
C4 : inward-looking[P]   – looks outside the organization[P]
C5 : not income-producing   – income-producing[P]
C6 : contributes to people's   – contributes to organization's
welfare   welfare[P]

(P = preferred pole)

From this, we can conclude that the Marketing Director sees us as making a positive contribution by 'contributing new ideas', being 'tactical' and by being 'inward-looking'. On the other hand, we are not seen as making a positive contribution because we 'have little to do with his function', are 'not income-producing' and 'contribute to people's welfare, not the organization's'. Further, because of this we are seen as very similar to Recruitment (another personnel function) and very dissimilar to his own function. From this analysis, however, we can undoubtedly think of several steps we could take that could increase our perceived contribution, from the Marketing Director's point of view. If we did this analysis for all the Grids, we would then have a detailed picture from which we could work.

A second type of element set that can also be useful for exploring perceptions of the training function consists of components of training. These components could either be things such as operator training, supervisory training and sales training, or they could be activities such as courses, workshops, projects and coaching, depending on the purposes of the Grid. Then, as above, these elements could be construed in some particular terms. This type of Grid may be particularly appropriate when we want to obtain information that can assist us to make choices between various aspects of the training function.

EXAMPLE 15

Suppose all departments are being asked to cut back their budgets by 10 per cent. In the Training Department we have some idea about where the cuts should be, but we would also like to find out the views of some of our client managers before making our decision, as we would expect that many managers would have a vested interest in certain of our training activities (e.g., Production might be expected to be particularly concerned about apprentice training). We would therefore be seeking to discover whether there is any consensus about priorities.

In this case, our element set might consist of the types of training in which we are currently engaged — induction training, clerical training, apprentice training, sales training, etc. We would ask the managers of the 'interested' departments to construe these elements in terms of 'their contribution to the success of the organization as a whole' and we would ask managers to say for each of their constructs which pole contributed more to organizational success.

Then we would FOCUS the Grids and look to see whether there was any consensus about the ordering of the elements, i.e., whether any aspect(s) of our training consistently came out as contributing relatively little overall. If there was no consensus, we would still have to take a decision, but we might be able to use the information we had obtained to come up with some lower-cost alternative way of maintaining some of the perceived benefits that the activities we had reduced had provided for some parts of the organization.

In the final three sections of this chapter, we have been discussing ways of making explicit the criteria we and other managers use to judge the effectiveness or success of what we are doing. In such situations we usually do not have a 'captive' audience (as we have on a training course) nor do we necessarily have people who are particularly interested in being systematic and explicit about their criteria. Thus, although some of the issues that have been important for other uses of the Grid are also relevant here — particularly the questions of what elements are appropriate and whose perspective we should obtain — the most important issue to which we probably need to address ourselves if we want to use the Grid in this way is: How can we obtain our own commitment to produce a Grid, and how can we obtain the commitment of others to do likewise?

As we said earlier, and as the reader is no doubt by now aware, the Grid is a highly flexible tool. For this reason we would encourage readers to look through the whole of this chapter for ideas about how they might use the Grid for their own evaluation purposes. Although certain approaches appear under certain headings, this has been done primarily for illustrative reasons and does not mean that they are inappropriate in other circumstances.

After reading this chapter, readers may well be fired with enthusiasm to go out and use the Grid to collect all sorts of information in order to evaluate their training from several perspectives. They may want to conduct a training-needs analysis, explore trainees' learning during the training, discover in what ways trainees are satisfied or dissatisfied with the training, review their own judgements and check to see what impact all this has had on managers' perceptions of the training function. All of this can be assisted by using the Grid but — as we said at the beginning of this chapter — evaluation has a purpose and we really should be clear before we start as to why we are collecting information, how we are going to use it and whether the result is likely to justify the effort. Readers are therefore strongly encouraged to think carefully before setting out to consider where, in reality, their efforts are likely to produce the greatest benefit in their own organizations.

14. Using Repertory Grid in counselling

In this part of the book we assume that the reader has a high level of skill in the use of Grid and also in counselling in general. If you have no previous experience of Grid, and happen to open the volume at this point, please do not try to operate the procedures here without going back over the earlier teach-yourself applications, nor without trying some of the more superficial uses of Grid given there and in this part of the book. If you have no experience of counselling, try to get a brief introduction from a course, by working alongside an experienced counsellor for a while, or by listening to the BBC programmes on the subject. You should know something about how to negotiate a counselling contract, what active listening means, when and when not to suggest solutions.

With this warning we are not trying to say: 'The only people who should attempt to learn counselling Grids are those who are already skilled enough not to need them.' What we are saying is that before you tackle a counselling Grid you should be sufficiently familiar with the technology of Grid not to let the cards and pieces of paper get in your way, and to be able to choose the part or parts of Grid procedure that will bring the most benefit; and you should have enough experience of counselling to be able to think several moves ahead, and to be able to subordinate your own needs to those of the interviewee.

In this chapter we treat counselling Grids in detail, beginning with issues of negotiating the contract and looking for the real problem, and going on to consider your decision as counsellor about where the main burden of the interview shall lie, from the viewpoint of Grid technology — in the elicitation of elements, the elicitation of constructs, the application of constructs to elements, the contrasts of particular elements or constructs, the full Grid, the use of offered elements or constructs, etc. We have arranged the chapter this way rather than by (say) subject-matter for counselling, because one of the first things people worry about when they start using Grid for counselling is: 'Shall I be able to do a good job if I don't have a computer/three hours available/ready prepared forms, etc?' If you know something about how to match the interview you do to the resources you have available you should find that you can meet most counselling purposes with the resources you happen to have available at the time. First, though, let us consider two important preliminary issues: negotiating the contract and initial probing.

14.1 Negotiating the contract

You may be working inside the same firm as the interviewee, or you may be an outsider called in to do the counselling job or another job. The interviewee may come to you with his problem, or you may believe that he has a problem and try to open a discussion with him. These and other factors may influence the early stages of the counselling relationship, and affect your strategy in getting his trust.

Insiders have the problem of knowing where the bodies are buried – if not before the interview, then afterwards. They may also have a technical problem when it comes to probing the issues – the interviewee may feel there is no need to explain himself fully if the interviewer shares the same perspective on the organization. Against this, the insider has the advantage of some familiarity with the situation; he also has the benefit of continuity of contact, and can plan a series of interviews or follow-ups without much difficulty.

Outsiders have the problem of unfamiliarity with the situation, which may lead to wrong decisions about where to press further and where to let matters lie. They are also more likely to be pressed for time, or to need specific appointments made – factors that can detract from the spontaneity of the interview. However an outsider can use his unfamiliarity, turning it into professional naivety that insists on further explanation, or using it to give new perspectives on affairs. The outsider is more likely to be viewed as politically neutral, and a better recipient of confidences about the boss and other close working relationships.

When the client comes to you you have the advantage of not having to work with him to convince him there is a problem, and you have some *prima facie* evidence that he sees you as a worthy recipient of his confidences. Timing can be a problem, though; sometimes it takes a lot of resolution to admit that you have a problem you need to talk about, and if the counsellor's immediate reaction is to get his secretary to make an appointment for two weeks' time the momentum may have been lost.

When you go to the client you have more control over the time and place, the resources available, etc. Going to the client may also be a message of concern or support in itself, irrespective of the outcome of the Grid interview. Conversely, the client may not realize that he has a problem, may ask you why has been singled out, etc.

In an ideal world these issues would represent choices to be made before embarking on a given counselling project. Most often they represent considerations faced by a counsellor who has little choice about when and where from he meets the client. There are some guidelines:

1. Relationships. Counselling interviews done by someone in a direct line relationship with the client, or with a strong influence over the client, need handling with special care. Recognize that it may not actually be possible for a boss to get a Grid from his subordinate that includes elements such as MY BOSS and MY IDEAL BOSS – a good climate of trust will allow it, a poor climate may not stand it. Also, if there is one person with total responsibility for management development, he may find that he needs to do counselling interviews from time to time; he should make it clear which 'hat' he is wearing when he does the interview, so as to make it clear to the interviewee whether the results of the interview will have a direct influence on his management-development prospects.

2. Confidentiality. It should be clear from the start who owns the data. In most counselling interviews the data belong to the interviewee. Much can be done

to convince the interviewee that this is so, by allowing him to fill in forms himself, write his own cards, draw up his own comparisons, etc. After the event a good way of reinforcing this belief is to leave the interview records with the interviewee himself.

3. Low profile. With many counselling operations it is best if people know that there is a counsellor around, but it is up to them to knock on his door. For the counsellor to go around drumming up trade, to have a line of clients queueing up outside his office like children waiting to see the headmaster, is not a good thing. When there is a special effort to see everybody — as part of a training-needs analysis programme, or as part of a team-building or organization-development activity — then the counsellor can be seen to make an effort to see people, but where there is only a routine counselling service, the counsellor should try to make himself generally visible, but waiting to be approached.

4. Clear purpose. A counselling interview should feel to the interviewee as if it is being done mainly or exclusively for his benefit, by a disinterested outsider. So if the outsider is doing other jobs besides the counselling job he should make sure they are clearly separated in the eyes of the client. Outside counsellors, and people paying short visits to sites away from Head Office, are particularly vulnerable here; it is easy to schedule a business meeting with the senior manager in the morning, have lunch with the top management group, and try to fit in a counselling interview with a supervisor in the afternoon, but the supervisor may wonder whether you come to the interview with clean hands.

So, at the beginning of each counselling interview, and perhaps at the end also, you should be careful to make it clear who you are, why you are both there, what each of you can expect to get out of the interview, who owns the results from the interview, who else will hear about the interview, and with whom the initiative for any action will lie. If you announce your presence on site with a circular letter or notice on the board you should cover these points, but should go over them again in the interview itself.

14.2 Problem identification

People do not always bring to the counselling interview the real problem they have. Once, in a programme of counselling interviews we asked people to let us have a brief note of the subject of their problems beforehand. What we actually talked about in the Grid bore little relationship to the advertised billing: 'Consequential Loss Insurance' turned out to be a problem with negotiation techniques, 'How to motivate older staff' turned out to be the problem of a specialist turned manager regretting the loss of his professional skills, and 'How to Innovate' turned into 'How do I sell my ideas to other people?' Experienced counsellors know that they often have to discuss the presented problem before discovering the real one; people give their problems 'safe' labels, labels that make them seem other people's fault (salesmen ask for training in product knowledge, not in sales skills), labels that make them seem other people's problems.

The initial discussion with the client to get closer to the real problem should give you a lead about the kinds of elements to include in the Grid. In many counselling Grids you want to contrast areas of certainty with uncertainty, or good with bad, or routine with extraordinary, or happiness with sadness. Other Grids may explore networks of relationships between people at work, customers, etc. So while you may open the discussion with questions such as 'Can you tell me a bit more about the problem/situation as you see it?' early follow-up questions might be: 'What are some of the particular things that give you cause for concern?' or 'What areas are you happy with? less happy with?', trying to estimate the class of element that will define the Grid interview.

Remember, too, that you can only address the problems of the person who actually come to you for counselling. A boss who arrives complaining about his subordinate's being work-shy can have a Grid that explores his notions about being work-shy and being hard-working, or a Grid that explores his notions about how to get people to change their behaviour; but he cannot have an interview that will directly change his subordinate's attitude to work. This is one of the most difficult things to convey to the client, because it depends so much on a sense of timing; to say to the client early in the interview 'We can only talk about things that are *your* concern, not concerns that you think other people should take action about,' is a necessary step, but if it is performed too early, before the problem has been properly defined, you risk sending away someone who really does have a problem of his own to talk about. Conversely, reluctance to admit this may lead the counsellor into forcing the client to have a problem because the agenda says he should have one.

Do not feel that you have to identify the problem, and the appropriate set of elements, right first time. The Grid procedure gives you several bites at the cherry; you could start counselling with a sales manager using customers as elements, for example, and, when it becomes apparent that the problem is not with the customers but with the salesmen, switch to an element set of salesmen or mixed salesmen and customers. You can involve the interviewee in defining the element set, with questions such as: 'I'd like to compare and contrast your feelings in this area in a rather more structured fashion now. Would it be useful if we were to explore further your feelings about your sales team?'

14.3 Your choice within the Grid conversation

Looking back over around 150 Grid interviews performed for counselling purposes, we see that different parts of the Grid interview are useful for different purposes. You may have had this feeling as you went through the exercises and examples in the rest of this book. In some interviews, most of the work is done when you have elicited the elements — if you ask someone to tell you six or eight events in the last two years where on reflection he feels he has learned something, you are asking him a question he has probably never asked himself before and in arriving at the answers he may have gained new insights into himself. In other interviews the client gains most benefit when he sees the number of constructs he is able to produce, or can compare the kind of constructs he produces with the range he has available. Or you may find that for some purposes you are interested in getting a comparison of just two or three elements – how does SELF compare with IDEAL SELF, for example, or MY IDEAL NEGOTIATING SITUATION compare with THE NEGOTIATION I CONDUCTED LAST WEEK? You use a full set of elements, so as to get a full range of constructs, but in reality you are only interested in looking at the differences between a few of these. Yet again, for other purposes you may want to look at the whole Grid, analysed by computer program probably; you might want to examine how the client views all his subordinates as a working group, or how he views the totality of his job. And you may be interested in seeing how the client can work with elements or constructs you offer him, either because you would like to test them yourself or because other people in similar situations have offered them.

The 'weight' of the interview – where most of the work gets done – shifts depending on the purpose and on the counsellor's skill in matching the interview to fit the resources available and the atmosphere. Different counsellors have different approaches; in the next few sections we shall give examples of Grid interviews to illustrate how the burden of the interview is located in different places, but if after trying these approaches you find yourself comfortable with a different strategy and you are still reaching your counselling objectives, do not worry in the least.

14.4 The elements for a counselling interview

In the first part of this book we stated that most elements can be classified as people, objects, events or activities. We also reviewed the three strategies for getting elements onto cards: interviewer supplies elements, interviewer names class of elements and asks for free response, and interviewer elicits elements through questioning. The element set should be selected bearing in mind the statement: 'You can only understand what I mean by *good* if you also know what I mean by *bad*.' So if in the initial questioning the client indicates that there are areas he is unhappy, unsure or worried about, then elements should be selected representative of these areas but also including some areas that he is happy, certain or confident about.

EXAMPLE 1

A. *Client problem*

I am worried about teaching a course on adapting to a foreign culture. I have never done anything like this before.

B. *Element-elicitation questions*

Three courses you have taught that were successful.
Three courses you have taught that were failures.
One course that proved easier than you had anticipated.

One course that proved more difficult than you had anticipated.
The Foreign Culture course.

This assortment of elements allows us to examine the characteristics of courses he is unhappy about teaching, in the context of courses he is happy about.

EXAMPLE 2

A. *Client problem*

I am worried about teaching apprentices; I do not think they take to the classroom situation as well as foremen.

B. *Element-elicitation questions*

Three people (one older, one younger, and one in the middle) you have enjoyed teaching — *not* apprentices.
Three people (one older, etc.) you have disliked teaching — *not* apprentices.
Two apprentices you have liked teaching.
Two apprentices you have disliked teaching.

Here the person had actually had experience of teaching apprentices and could name some he liked and disliked teaching. The first teacher was worried about the subject matter, the second about the pupils; in both cases the element set needed to run the gamut from comfort/confidence to discomfort/worry. The inclusion of one or two questions designed to elicit elements the client is doubtful about (e.g., 'One course that proved easier than you anticipated') makes for more subtle triads at the start of the interview. If the elements are all black or white with no shades of grey you can find one or two superordinate constructs emerging very early on (e.g., *I like — I dislike*) which the interviewee then gets stuck on.

   Another likely element set is the group of people whose relationship to the interviewee is causing problems. The first step here is to find out how many there are and if they are a coherent group (e.g., my subordinates, my customers — in some industries — the members of the Consultative Committee). If they do form a coherent group and the numbers are less than about 15 it is probably worth using them all as elements. Above 15, or with a varied group of people, the interviewer should look for a selection of people to use as elements.

EXAMPLE 3

A. *Client problem*

At the end of a long day I feel as if another customer were to ask another stupid question I would bite his head off.

B. *Element-elicitation questions*

Two customers whose heads you did bite off recently.
Two where you felt like it, but did not.

Two customers you enjoyed serving.
Two run-of-the-mill customers — you neither enjoyed nor disliked serving them.
Your ideal customer.

Here, a salesman in a retail organization with a large throughput of customers is giving vent to a cry of despair. He was asked to think of particular customers — he had to identify them on the cards as events rather than people, e.g., LADY WITH BAD BREATH WHO BOUGHT A HOTPOINT, or MAN BOUGHT MAGIMIX 3 MINUTES PAID CASH, but he was thinking of specific people and events so they were good, useable elements. The last one — 'My ideal customer' — was not identified as a particular person, but left on the card as MY IDEAL CUSTOMER. Later in this chapter we treat the use of MY IDEAL . . . as an element in more detail.

In counselling interviews the elements are usually people or events/activities. Things like school subjects creep in from time to time, for purposes like career counselling. A useful distinction to think about is whether the element set is likely to be well rehearsed in the mind of the interviewee; with an unrehearsed element set and a good range of eliciting questions, the weight of the interview may well lie in the element-elicitation stage.

What do we mean by well rehearsed element set? If you were asked to name your colleagues at work, you could probably do so without much trouble; or your favourite books or television programmes; things you like and dislike doing on holiday; things your boss does which annoy or please you. On the other hand, suppose you were asked to think of events at work in the last two years where you felt highly motivated; or events which in retrospect you felt you learned something from; or people who legitimately and unlegitimately have expectations about you: or the ten days in history you would like to be able to alter in retrospect. Chances are that you will have to think quite some time before even giving answers to these questions. A well rehearsed element set is one where you have little or no trouble producing the elements themselves, and often the constructs that describe the elements; with a less well rehearsed element set the eliciting question is itself novel, the elements do not spring immediately to mind, and constructs to describe the elements may likewise take longer to produce. If your client has a well rehearsed element set — his subordinates, for example — then the weight of the Grid interview will lie at the point where you jointly examine the kind of constructs he produces, or the way they interrelate on a full Grid. But where the client must think hard for the elements before writing them down the element elicitation process can be the most self-revelatory part of the interview. The chapter on Motivation gives examples of element-elicitation schedules which produce unrehearsed element sets.

EXAMPLE 4

A client complained of chronic indecisiveness and inability to please everyone, leading to his doing nothing at all — 'and even that causes problems.' Preliminary questioning indicated that he was trying to please everybody, was distressed when anybody expressed disappointment with him, and at the same time felt resentful of being 'pulled every which way.'

A. *Element-elicitation questions*

Three people you interact with at work who have expectations of you that are legitimate in your eyes.
Three people you interact with at work who have expectations of you that are not legitimate in your eyes.
One person you interact with at work who has no expectations of you. (Could not answer).
One person you interact with at home who has legitimate expectations of you.
One person you interact with at home who has unlegitimate expectations of you.
Yourself.

B. *Stimulus question*

In what way are two of these people alike and different from the third in terms of the demands they make on you?

C. *Examples of constructs*

make instant demands — give me time to think
assign responsibility clearly — leave me in the dark
say thank you — never say thank you

D. *Preference question*

Under which condition do you find it easiest to act? (e.g., do you find it easiest to act when instant demands are made on you, or when you have time to think?)

You may like to try this Grid on yourself. It is fairly easy to do, and the results are often surprising. Probably the actual elicitation of the elements will tell you something about yourself you did not know before.

EXAMPLE 5

As part of a regular management-development activity, a manager had been to a course that included a discussion of stress at work and how to control one's reactions to it. The manager maintained before the course that she led a healthy life, had no difficulty switching off when she needed to, and therefore did not need to be told how to manage stress. After the course she said that it had been interesting, but stuck to her view that the course had been unnecessary for her. She was invited to a Grid interview, as part of post-course follow-up, and asked to name as elements 9 to 12 things which she did to her subordinates which they found stressful.

An example, this, of an element set that is well rehearsed in one context but not in another!

EXAMPLE 6

As part of a career review with an employee who was thought to be talented but difficult to place, a Grid interview was conducted. The interviewer asked the interviewee to fantasize about a perfect day, in 15 years' time — what would the interviewee be doing then? As the interviewee fantasized the interviewer wrote down the events as they were described, thus:

GET INTO WORK REFRESHED INSTEAD OF SWEATY
FIND AN EMPTY IN-TRAY, i.e., NOTHING LEFT FROM YESTERDAY
NOTE OF PRAISE FROM MY BOSS
SHORT PRODUCT-DEVELOPMENT MEETING AT WHICH MY IDEA FOR THE TX50 IS ACCEPTED
etc., etc.

This process gave about 25 elements on cards, which were then spread out in front of the client. He was invited to choose the 9–12 elements that were most important and most different from today's situation. The Grid then proceeded.

A. *Stimulus question*

In what way are two of these elements like each other and different from the third, in terms of how you feel about them?

B. *Examples of constructs*

> sense of achievement — frustrating
> manager's role — specialist job
> only I could do — anyone in my position could do

C. *Preference questions*

1. Which sort of situation do you feel most useful in?
2. Which sort of situation is most like your present job?

The two preference questions allowed us to identify constructs where he felt most useful in activities that fell at one end of the construct (e.g., specialist job) but where his present job pushed him towards the other end of the construct (e.g., manager's role)

Again, an extraordinary amount of productive work came from elicitation of the elements — just asking someone to fantasize about a perfect day 15 years' hence is enough to start some serious self-questioning.

From these examples it is clear that in some Grid interviews the elicitation of elements is not merely a preliminary to the interview, but a valuable part of the interview itself. Knowing this will not only help you manage the passage of time better, but will also help if you need to establish your credibility as someone who asks wise questions.

14.5 The nature of the constructs in a counselling interview

For certain counselling applications, most value is obtained during the construct-elicitation stage. The counsellor may find that there is no need to go to a full Grid of elements on constructs if he can elicit constructs and ladder them. There are two major ways of analysing constructs: by number, and by quality. Let us look at each in turn.

Counting constructs

The rationale here is that you do not have many constructs about an area in which you are ignorant. (Most readers would not have many constructs about the moons of Jupiter or about old Shetland knitting patterns.) So a construct-elicitation interview that pays attention wholly or partly to the sheer number of constructs produced is, in effect, defining an area of ignorance. This can be useful; it can also be very tricky, and much depends on the degree of trust the client has and the counsellor's ability to make the delineation of ignorance helpful rather than condemnatory.

EXAMPLE 7

The client was a young schoolgirl asking for careers advice. She was given a programme of tests of ability to see what she would best be capable of; she was also given a construct-elicitation interview.

A. *Element-elicitation question*

Write down six jobs or careers that you might like to do, and three that you think you would dislike.

B. *Stimulus questions*

In what way are two of these jobs different from the third in terms of (a) how you feel about them, (b) the special skills you might need, (c) what you know about them generally . . . .

C. *Examples of constructs*

The client produced eight constructs in all:

exciting — dull
man's job — woman's job
sitting down — standing up
working with figures — working with people
local employer — national employer
routine — not so routine
dirty job — clean job
always going on strike — never hear about strikes

This application is typical of those where you are interested in the number of constructs produced. It was interesting to see the client trying to ladder; asked for example about the construct *local employer – national employer* ('what are the differences between working for a local employer and working for a national employer?', 'Can you think of anything that might happen differently?', 'If you were working for a national employer instead of a local employer would your life be any different?') she got stuck, could not think of anything other than admitted irrelevancies (national employers were more likely to have well known trade marks, but she was certain that did not affect her attitude to working for them). A more experienced person might well see a lot of differences, in terms of career prospects, mobility, being part of a local community. Our client could not see any. Similarly when she was asked to ladder to the construct *working with figures – working with people* ('Do you need different skills for dealing with figures as opposed to dealing with people?', 'What might you need to do differently?', 'Be good at in one but not in the other?') she could not analyse further. And she saw the identifying characteristic of man's job as the fact that it had always been thought of as a man's job, and a woman's job had always been viewed as a woman's.

By this stage the client was getting a little worried. 'I have not thought about this very much,' she said, and 'Perhaps I ought to go away and come back when I know a bit more.' The counsellor responded that the interview was not a test she had to pass, more a device to help her find out more about what she didn't know. He asked her if she knew anyone doing the jobs she had named as elements; where she did know someone, the counsellor worked with her drawing up a list of questions she could ask the person, trying to tie the questions into her original constructs:

INTERVIEWER   You said that Mary is a receptionist and that receptionists have to be good at dealing with people. So you'll go and see Mary and ask her if she thinks that you have to be good with people in her job. Ask her what she thinks it means – what she enjoys about dealing with people and what she dislikes about it, what advice she'd want to give someone who wanted to be good at dealing with people. OK?

And you said that Jill's Dad works for a national employer – talk to him about his job, what he has to be good at, what he enjoys and doesn't enjoy, and ask him specially if he thinks it makes any difference working for a national employer.

And your Uncle Bill works with figures . . . .

Two weeks later the client returned for a further interview at which she was able to say a lot more about these jobs in particular, and about jobs in general. Besides having more constructs available, she had had the experience of questioning people about their jobs and found this useful.

This example of a construct-elicitation interview where construct count is important contains nearly all the lessons that the interviewer must have learned before he can tackle this sort of assignment. The points to note are:

1. Vary the stimulus question. You must be sure that the production of a small number of constructs indicates a genuinely small number of dimensions to judge the elements, and not merely that the interviewee is 'stuck' on a particular class of construct. So the client should be asked to view each triad from several points of view – in our Example 7 we quote three separate stimulus questions.

2. Ladder well and thoroughly. You need to know whether a construct implies other constructs of a higher or lower order. Is the construct just 'there', as in *man's job – woman's job* in Example 7, or does it relate to subordinate constructs? Again, you should not make a judgement about the number of constructs available until you are sure you have exhausted the laddering process; and the laddering process is often remarkably educational for the client.

3. Link the interview to action. When the client has failed to produce many constructs he may feel that he has failed. It is important that he should leave the interview with a positive statement of what he will do next. About halfway through the interview, when the construct-elicitation stage has finished, the interviewer should say something like this: 'Well, it seems as if you have not got very much to say about these particular topics, but do not worry, nobody could have expected you to at this early stage. What we have done so far is to define what you already perceive about these things; now let us work out a plan to expand that knowledge. Has anything we have talked about so far triggered any thoughts about what you might do to learn more?'

4. Follow-up if at all possible. A second interview, conducted when the client has had a chance to take some action, is a great morale booster. The counsellor must be careful not to be seduced himself into thinking that sheer numbers of constructs is a good thing, but there is no harm in his congratulating the client on having doubled or trebled the number of distinctions he can see. Later on, if they get to the point where the number of constructs becomes embarrassingly large or the counsellor suspects that some may be trivial, he can work with the client to pick out the most important ones. In our Example 7, this would have led to a 'shopping list' of 20 vital questions for the client to ask about any job.

When counting constructs you may begin with the full-context method to make things easy. With the full-context method you spread out all the element cards in front of the interviewee and ask him to choose which two are most alike. Pick these up and pair them together, and then ask him to choose the one most different from these two. Then ask him to name what it is that the pair have in common that makes the singleton different, and record this as a construct. Return the three cards to the element set and ask him to choose two more that are similar, and then a third which is different. Gradually you can introduce the notion of construct elicitation and if necessary after a few tries with the full context you can revert to the three-card administration. This is a useful technique to use where you believe that the available constructs are very few in number, or where the client is having difficulty grasping the procedure.

When would you use a construct count in counselling? Career counselling is one good example; not just with teenagers, but also in redundancy and redeployment counselling. Someone who has been doing the same job for years may well have lost what little he knew about other jobs before this one. In some forms of training evaluation, too, it can help the teacher to measure what has been taught; better still, it can help the student plan his learning more efficiently. One of our most productive such counselling interviews was with a student of politics, where we used as elements various national governments. He had very few constructs available; all about international relationships and most of those about relationships with the USA. It did not take him long on reflection to realize that he needed to know more, and to develop some constructs about the domestic policies of these governments. Here we move from looking at the sheer quantity of constructs through to the quality, almost inevitably.

We stated above that the reader should not be seduced into thinking that large numbers of constructs are desirable. The two constructs:

has few constructs — has many constructs

ignorant — knowledgeable

are imperfectly correlated. Someone who can produce few construct labels and has difficulty laddering and difficulty when the stimulus question is asked does not have many perceptions about the area under discussion. However if you found someone who had a lot of construct labels you would have to look at the full Grid to see whether the differently labelled constructs discriminated differently between the elements: he could have a lot of labels, but the labels could mean only a few separate things in action. This is why when someone produces a lot of constructs and you are not going on to do a full Grid you may want to ask him to select the constructs that are most important to the purpose.

Content analysis of constructs

The sheer number of constructs someone has may be less useful in the counselling situation than the quality of his constructs. Interviewer or client or both may, at various stages in the counselling process, stand back from the list of constructs and try to assign them to different categories, gaining as they do so insights into the pattern of the client's thinking.

EXAMPLE 8

The client was a shop manager who expressed dislike of having to do interviews — selection interviews in particular. The dislike was getting so strong that she contemplated moving to a different kind of job. Early questioning elicited the information that appraisal interviews were less of a problem because a plan existed for the way to carry them out; she would like some way of formulating a plan for selection interviewing in a logical manner.

A. *Elements*

Five selection interviews the client had done recently.
One appraisal interview.
One offered element: THE GOOD INTERVIEW.
    Triads always included THE GOOD INTERVIEW element

B. *Stimulus question*

Tell me something that two of these have in common that makes them different
from the third, in terms of what you did or would do.
    The client had difficulty producing constructs — the cards needed to be physi-
cally manipulated and a lot of help given.

C. *Constructs obtained*

I am not certain I put over the idea — I put over the idea of the job well
of the job well

painted a very general idea of the job — go through the job item by item

making the job sound interesting — interviewee more interested in
while mention the drawbacks   time off, etc.

communicating well with interviewee — not communicating well

relaxed (self) — tense

making interviewee more relaxed — interviewee tense

talking more generally about — talking entirely about practical
interviewee's interest   considerations of job

put herself over without my — trying to think of how I could
having to draw her out   relate to her as a person

felt I was getting to know her — felt I was not getting to know her

asking questions because I wanted — asking questions out of a sense of
to know the answer   duty

getting to the bottom of how the — undecided as to how the person
person would be as an employee   would behave once employed

ask the right questions — questions asked in the wrong way
                          — did not get as full an answer as
                          I needed

know what information you want — not enough information — trying
                                to make decisions on too little
                                information

draw somebody out, not to say just — could have got more information
'yes' or 'no'

aware of sensitive, personal side — could have questioned more
of things   tactfully

jumped in and started talking — setting the scene with a proper
to interviewee before telling my   introduction — who everybody is,
side of the story.   what job requirements are

The counsellor felt that many of the constructs were expressing objectives for the interview, rather than what the client actually did in the interview (bear in mind the stimulus question 'in terms of what you did or would do'). The counsellor pointed this out to the client, stressing the positive side: clearly, she knew what she wanted to achieve in selection interviews. The counsellor took each of the constructs that related to interview objectives in turn and asked what the client had done or would do to achieve those objectives. Often the counsellor related this back to specific interviews, but few constructs were forthcoming. The counsellor shared her feelings that the client had a fair number of constructs about ends, but few about means — did the client agree? The client did agree, and asked where she could find out about developing her skills in this area. At this point the counsellor, who had some skill in selection interviewing and had trained other interviewers, began to recommend specific practices and also talked about helpful books and courses.

This example illustrates many of the skills required to perform a counselling interview where constructs are content analysed. One needs to be certain about the appropriate stimulus question for the purpose (suppose in Example 8 the question had been ' . . . in terms of what you were trying to achieve in these interviews.' The interview would then have been specifically about ends and not means, and the low level of constructs about means would have to be interpreted quite differently). One also needs the ability to ladder. It helps, too, to have some experience with the kind of problem under discussion; the counsellor need not be an expert, but he should be familiar enough with the topic of discussion to be able to analyse as the interview progresses and get some feeling for the relative importance òf different quantities of constructs.

EXAMPLE 9

The client was a junior management trainer in a large organization. He was given responsibility for organizing and running training courses, without having been given proper induction training himself. As a result he was doubtful of his ability to pick the right course for particular needs, and found that reading the brochures was unhelpful and he did not know what questions to ask when he had tried ringing up course organizers to question them.

A. *Element-elicitation questions*

Name nine courses you have had to deal with in this new job, some that you feel fairly confident about and others that you feel less confident about.

B. *Stimulus question*

' . . . . in terms of what they do for the participants.'

C. *Examples of constructs*

Most of the constructs were of the form:

> run on site — run in a hotel
> expensive to run — cheaper to run
> by a well-known organization — by a less well known body

etc., etc., and only a few of the form:

> technical skills taught — man-management skills taught
> for young people — for people any age

As the interview progressed, the client began to show signs of realizing that his constructs were falling into two camps, with the first predominating. The counsellor invited him to write the constructs onto cards and sort them into the two piles. Asked to name the two piles, he struggled a little and then said that the larger pile was about course *context*, and the smaller about course *content*. Immediately then he saw that 'I'd been asking the wrong questions when I rang people up — and letting myself be fobbed off with the information about menus and dates and fees when what I really want to know is what goes on in there.'

He and the counsellor agreed that the next step should be drawing up a list of questions about course content that he could ask prospective course runners and also use to question participants on previous courses. At the next interview he said that the list had been useful, but there ought to be more there. The counsellor then suggested a second interview, this time using the 'Events I have learned from' elements. This released a good number of new constructs about the learning process as the client had experienced it — constructs that he was then able to incorporate into his list of questions to ask about what went on on training courses.

Note the use of a second construct-elicitation interview with different elements and a different purpose. In the first interview, we were asking the question 'What do you perceive about these training courses?' and in the second interview the question 'What do you perceive about the way you learn?' From reflecting on the conditions necessary for him to learn to reflecting on the conditions necessary for other people to learn was a short step; another short step led him to formulate a series of questions that he could ask course runners about the learning climate they provided. Two or more interviews as part of one counselling project is not uncommon; changing the elements or the stimulus question may be very helpful. Where the client is wary, or you sense that there is a big problem here, but that trust must be established before it is fully defined, it is often useful to start with an 'outward-looking' Grid (e.g., tell me about your subordinates . . . these training courses . . . industrial disputes on your plant . . .) and use the material emerging from these interviews before going on to more 'inward-looking' interviews (e.g., tell me about what you do in your job . . . events that you have learned from . . . times when you have been caught up in a quarrel).

To do a content analysis of constructs as they emerge may be difficult until you have practised a few times and know what kinds of construct to expect and how finely to categorize them. It is difficult for us to suggest categories without tying them to particular purposes; many category systems nonetheless fall into one or more of the following patterns:

1. Propositional–sensory–evaluative.
2. Past–present–future.
3. Ends versus means to an end.
4. People issues versus technical issues.
5. Content versus context.
6. Reacting versus taking the initiative.
7. Alone versus with other people.
8. My problem versus someone else's problem.

You may also find that the client himself is capable of categorizing constructs – perhaps not as he produces them, but if you break for a cup of coffee, return afresh and ask him if he can see any 'families' of constructs he may be able to.

If you know in advance that a major part of the counselling interview will be devoted to construct elicitation and categorization, it helps to write the constructs down on individual cards. They can then be shuffled about at will. Comments made during laddering can be written on the back of the card, or the laddering process may generate new constructs needing their own cards. Colour-coding helps; buff cards for the elements and white for the constructs, or different coloured inks.

14.6 Laddering and core constructs

One of the ways in which you as counsellor and the client can categorize constructs is in order of importance to the client. Present the client with his constructs and ask him to pick out the two or three that are most important, bearing in mind the purpose of the Grid; and then ask him why they are important. There is probably no quicker way to reach core constructs.

In the earlier part of this book we warned against experimenting with core constructs too freely; they can take you into issues that neither you nor the client wanted to uncover. But if you are counselling you need to know how to uncover core constructs and how to manage them once there.

You arrive at core constructs by one of two procedures. Either you ask about the construct: 'Why is that an important distinction to make about . . . ' or you ask for a preference for one end of the construct over the other, and then ask why that pole was preferred. You then carry on the questioning process, as in the example below, taken from an interview about motivating situations at work.

INTERVIEWER   So, with two of these situations you took the initiative and with the third one you found it forced on you. Why is that an important distinction to make about situations at work?

INTERVIEWEE   In the first two, I said how things would proceed, but in the third someone else laid down the timetable.

INTERVIEWER   And why should this be important?

INTERVIEWEE   I feel it's important for me to be able to have things under control.

INTERVIEWER   Having things under control is important is it?

INTERVIEWEE   Very important.

INTERVIEWER   Why is it important to you to have things under control?

INTERVIEWEE   I like to know where things are, where things are going.

INTERVIEWER   Why should that be important to you?

INTERVIEWEE   I can't afford to have things happen to my part of the organization that aren't under my control.

INTERVIEWER   Why not? What would happen if they got out of your control?

INTERVIEWEE   They'd get taken over by somebody else, and I'd lose control myself.

INTERVIEWER   And you'd dislike that?

INTERVIEWEE   Yes. I've got to keep control myself otherwise things get out of hand. I'm surprised you can't see that.

Here the interviewer is testing to see whether the interviewee can explain his need for control in terms of any other concept, or does he see control as a good end in itself? The fact that the interviewee cannot, that he keeps presenting a circular argument — control is important because it is important to have control — indicates that *control* is a core construct for this interviewee.

A good counsellor knows how and when to elicit core constructs. Try the exercise in the first half of this book if you are not sure. Good counsellors also (a) watch the body language and (b) learn not to show surprise at the extraordinary diversity of core constructs people exhibit. Body language is usually a very good tell-tale; most people when approaching core constructs start to make circular or inclusive gestures, open gestures with the hands out, as if to say 'I'm doing my best, but it's all one, I can't analyse it any further, that's it because that's the way it is.' Occasionally when people feel threatened by having their core constructs revealed they make protective gestures; the gentleman whose interview is abstracted above, a director in a very large organization who would not let anything happen without his having started it (which led to great intertia in the system) put his hands tight between his crossed thighs whenever he was questioned about the importance of having control.

Not showing surprise when you discover someone else's core constructs is a much more difficult art. The key skill in learning to watch body language is the recognition that your instincts are good — they are one reason why the human species has survived much longer than it has had speech — and if you can accept that what you think body language is telling you is probably true, you have won the battle. Even experienced counsellors can get caught off guard when they meet core constructs that are outside their own previous experience.

For example, most of the people reading this book would probably have *control* as a core construct, because the book is written for people in industry and academics who have an interest in finding out and taking action about issues and problems. You may not express your need for control in the same way as the interviewee above did, but you probably know how he feels. But would you expect to find *control* as a core construct in: a nun, a teenager, a retired bank manager, your local postman? Perhaps not.

Allied with the ability not to show surprise when you uncover someone's core constructs is the ability to estimate how long it will take the two of you to resolve any problems that might emerge from so doing. This would be a problem only with a few people; most people's construct systems have got survival value for them and get them around the world well enough, so you must not expect problems every time you work with core constructs. But there are occasions where the revelation of the core constructs causes problems, and you must have the skill to guess how much time you must both devote to issues arising. Experienced counsellors should not have too much trouble in this respect, but if you find yourself constantly running out of time in other interviews you conduct — selection, appraisal, etc. — you should perhaps look for advice here.

Laddering and core constructs were discussed here in the context of interviews where a construct count or content analysis were used. The comments apply equally to all the other kinds of interview we discuss below, as you should not think of eliciting constructs without also laddering. Now we move onto interviews where a full Grid is elicited, in various formats.

14.7 Full Grid with comparison of limited elements

Sometimes it is useful to be able to compare within a full Grid the way one or two elements are rated. One or two examples may make the point.

EXAMPLE 10

The client was a salesman in a chemical manufacturing firm. The problem as he stated it was 'My boss keeps telling me I'm not the right kind of person to be a salesman.' We discussed his ideas of successful and unsuccessful salesmen for a while, and then elicited constructs around the following elements.

A. *Element-elicitation questions*

Three successful salesmen you know and work with.
Three less successful salesmen you know and work with.
MYSELF.
MY BOSS.
MYSELF AS I WOULD LIKE TO BE.
N.B. The element MYSELF AS I WOULD LIKE TO BE is often shortened to IDEAL SELF when reporting Grid interviews.

B. *Stimulus question*

' . . . in terms of the way they behave at work'.
    Construct elicitation was relatively easy and the client quickly relaxed and saw

the point of the procedure. After producing about 20 constructs he was asked to select the most important of these. The interviewer next asked him to rate each of three elements on these constructs, taking one element at a time: SELF, BOSS and IDEAL SELF. The interviewer then drew up the picture shown in Fig. 14.1, and put it to the client that this was how he had described in his own words the important characteristics of himself, his boss and his ideal self. The counsellor gave the picture some time to sink in, and then asked whether the client saw any pattern in the picture.

INTERVIEWEE The obvious one — that I've talked about myself as I would like to be in almost exactly the same way as I've described my boss.

INTERVIEWER Did you realize that the similarity was so close?

INTERVIEWEE No, I didn't.

INTERVIEWER Can you think of any more constructs where you and yourself as you would like to be are the same, and different from your boss?

INTERVIEWEE Give me time to think about that — no, I'm not sure that I can.

INTERVIEWER You remember that I asked you to look at these people in terms of how they behaved at work. Do you think that the descriptions you gave me are mostly about behaviour, or are they about something else?

✓	SELF	IDEAL SELF	BOSS	✗
Extravert	✗	✓	✓	Introvert
Gets lots out of other people	✗	✓	✓	Gets little out of people
Ruthless	✓	✗	✓	Devious
Good at selling ideas	✗	✓	✓	Poor at selling ideas
Confident	✗	✓	✓	Diffident
Live-wire	✗	✓	✓	Not a live-wire
Takes people at their face value	✓	✗	✗	Looks for people's hidden motives
Trusting	✓	✓	✗	Suspicious

Figure 14.1

INTERVIEWEE   Some of them are about behaviour, some are about personality, now I look at it.

INTERVIEWER   Does that make it easier for you to think of ways in which you and yourself as you would like to be — these two cards here — are like each other and different from this one here — your boss?

INTERVIEWEE   I see what you mean, but it's still a bit difficult. My boss is always banging on about personality being the thing that matters, and my not being enough of a raving extravert.

INTERVIEWER   OK. Let's look at the thing from a different angle. Suppose that I ask you to have a fantasy about a perfect day five years' hence — a day when everything happens the way you want it to happen. What would that day look like?

INTERVIEWEE   I'd get in to find that my boss had put me up for the Golden Key Award, that he's asked me to give a presentation at the next team meeting because we'd beaten ICI to the big order we'd been after. Then he takes me off for a drink. . . . '

At this point the counsellor had a strong hunch that the client was taking too much of his opinions from his boss, and was maybe too dependent on him. The counsellor was also impressed by the fact that none of the important constructs selected related to work output — they were all about personality. So she offered some additional constructs herself, to be written into the Grid, relating to performance at work, output and happiness. This caused the client to volunteer some more constructs himself, so that the picture came to look like Fig. 14.2. The last construct ('*sweetie salesman*' — *chemical salesman*) was offered by the client after the counsellor had shown him the new Grid with the question: 'Whose problem is this anyway? Yours or your boss's? If you're happy, make good decisions, get the business, and are respected by your peers, do you really have a problem? Or are you taking over your boss's problem for him?

INTERVIEWEE   Maybe I am. I hadn't looked at it like that. The real things are OK, it's just these peripherals like him wanting all his team to be live-wire heavy-drinking politicians. He's never really forgotten his days on the road staying at awful commercial hotels with the lads.

INTERVIEWER   Go on about that, will you?

INTERVIEWEE   Well, he used to work for what he calls fast-moving consumer goods, and the rest of us call sweeties, and he's never really made the transition from selling out of the back of your car to selling to industry out of an office. I suppose you had to be ruthless and extraverted and a live-wire if you spent all your time in small shops and supermarkets.

INTERVIEWER   And do you think he's applying the same standards now?

INTERVIEWEE   I think he probably is. I think that's why I've rated him as unhappy. I thought he was unhappy with his sales team but I think he must be more unhappy with his own job.

INTERVIEWER   And if you think that, would you want to make any changes to this picture, where you've got yourself so different from your boss and yourself

✓	SELF	IDEAL SELF	BOSS	✗
Extravert	X	✓	✓	Introvert
Gets lots out of other people	X	✓	✓	Gets little out of people
Ruthless	✓	X	✓	Devious
Good at selling ideas	X	✓	✓	Poor at selling ideas
Confident	X	✓	✓	Diffident
Live-wire	X	✓	✓	Not a live-wire
Takes people at their face value	✓	X	X	Looks for people's hidden motives
Trusting	✓	✓	X	Suspicious
Happy	✓	✓	X	Unhappy
Gets the business	✓	✓	✓	Fails to get business
Makes good decisions	✓	✓	✓	Makes poor decisions
Respected by peers	✓	✓	✓	Not respected
Co-operative	✓	✓	✓	Unco-operative
Good strategist	✓	✓	✓	Poor strategist
'Sweetie salesman'	X	X	✓	Chemical salesman

Figure 14.2

as you would like to be? Let's take them one by one. Do you really want to be an extravert?

INTERVIEWEE   I don't suppose I do, no. He'd like me to be an extravert because he's happiest with extraverts around him, but . . . that's his problem?

INTERVIEWER   That's *his* problem. Does it make any difference to the sales or the customer whether you're an extravert?

INTERVIEWEE   Customers? Not a bit, as long as you know your stuff and know their needs.

INTERVIEWER   Then it's his problem. Go on, say it.

INTERVIEWEE   That's his problem.

INTERVIEWER   Good. Are there any more in this list that we can label as his problem?

INTERVIEWEE   Yes . . . confident/diffident . . . live wire . . . looking for hidden motives . . . .

Eventually the conversation came to the remaining discrepancies between SELF and IDEAL SELF which the client could not label as his boss's problem, and the two discussed ways in which he could set about getting more out of people and being good at selling ideas.

Follow-up interview six months later — not a Grid interview, just a short conversation — elicited comments like: 'I feel much happier — got the problem into perspective. I put the customer first and if the boss starts nagging at me I just ask myself whether he's doing it for my sake, the firm's sake or his sake. I'm probably selling better now I don't feel that he's sitting like a monkey on my back.'

This example illustrates the main points in a counselling interview where a limited number of elements are to be compared. A full set of elements is necessary to begin with, to get a rich variety of constructs. The interviewer chooses the elements with an eye to performing a limited comparison later, after the initial talk to define the problem. Here, hearing the statement 'I'm not the kind of salesman my boss wants me to be,' the counsellor obviously thinks that one element must be SELF, one must be BOSS and one must be MYSELF AS I WOULD LIKE TO BE. Having elicted some constructs, the counsellor draws up, or gets the client to draw up, a table of comparisons between the important elements and presents it for reflection. Then they talk to discover (a) whether the table represents the whole picture or whether other constructs should be included, and (b) what should be done about any important discrepancies as the client sees them.

EXAMPLE 11

The client was a bookshop manager working for a shop that recently been acquired by a large chain. Concern about the merger had caused her to wonder whether she was pursuing the right occupation or should she change before it was too late.

A. *Element-elicitation questions*

Three jobs you have done in the past
Three jobs you feel would be attractive to you
Three jobs you feel would be unattractive to you
Your present job
Your ideal job (not defined — just MY IDEAL JOB)

B. *Stimulus question*

' . . . . in terms of their appeal to you.'

The client produced 42 constructs, not all of which are given in this book. She was then asked to rate her current job and her ideal job on the constructs she had provided (see Table 14.1).

These were the constructs on which her ideal job differed from her current job. There were more constructs on which her ideal job resembled her current job (see Table 14.2).

When this comparison table had been drawn up, the counsellor asked the client to review it and see what it told her. After looking for a while she said: 'If I'm successful, I'm tempted to carry on no matter what I'm doing, and I'm reasonably successful here. I'm not keen on doing further training — I'm basically a lazy person and prefer to keep the skills I've got. Really I want to have my cake and eat it.' Further musing, to the effect that the differences between the ideal job and the

Table 14.1

√	Ideal	Current	x
Cog in a large firm	x	√	Working for yourself
'Taught' skill	x	√	Intuitive skill
Free to be creative	√	x	Little scope for creativity
End product	√	x	Administrative
System to follow	x	√	No system to follow
Wouldn't care about how many hours done	√	x	Work flexible hours up to a point
Requires imagination	√	x	Cannot allow imagination
Necessary job	√	x	Dispensible
Dealing with people	x	√	Solitary job

Table 14.2

√	Ideal	Current	x
Responsible for other people	√	√	Will not affect people directly
Secure job	√	√	Precarious
Mixed sex job	√	√	One sex only
Not violent or dirty	√	√	Nasty, dirty job
Some freedom to act	√	√	Little freedom to act
Cerebral occupations	√	√	Doing things
Variety	√	√	Not a broad scope
Career	√	√	Job

current job were real, but perhaps not worth the effort of overcoming them, led her to conclude that she was probably better off staying where she was.

The chief point emerging from this example is the importance of letting the client draw his or her own conclusions from the comparison of elements; this is helped if the client actually draws up the comparison table himself. Many counsellors who use Grid say that they have had to learn to hold themselves back at this point; as you elicit the constructs you often get a very clear idea of what the comparison table will look like, and what the problem will turn out to be. Drawing up the comparison table may be no more than a confirmation of what the counsellor has already learned during the elicitation process. But the counsellor has to realise that the comparison table presents new information in a new way to the client, and he must give the client plenty of time to absorb it. It is quite common for the client not to need any further counselling help after the table has been drawn up: 'I see what the problem is,' they say, and do the rest of the work themselves. Many wise men have pointed out that people already know the solutions, but cannot see the problem.

The two examples above have used MY IDEAL . . . as an element. Now follows an example of a counselling interview using limited comparisons of elements, but in a slightly different way.

EXAMPLE 12

The client was a systems analyst who had been given an assignment to examine and report on whether his firm could profit by installing a manpower-planning system. He had done the work, and concluded that there would be much to be gained by putting in manpower planning, but he could not bring himself to write the actual report. He felt that it was dishonest to write a report that was supposed to be about a dispassionate analysis of a situation but which was intended to persuade the reader to adopt a certain point of view.

A. *Element-elicitation questions*

One written report by someone else which you class as honest.
One written report by someone else which you class as dishonest.
One verbal presentation by someone else which you class as honest.
One verbal presentation by someone else which you class as dishonest.
One past report of your own which you were pleased with.
One past report of your own which you were displeased with.

B. *Stimulus question*

' . . . . in terms of how you feel about their honesty.'

C. *Constructs produced*

Construct elicitation produced the following list of constructs:

'clever' — factual
ego-trip — hard work
dishonest — honest
distorted scales — didn't distort
manipulative — straight
objective — subjective
factual — opinions
number-based — not number-based
logical progression — difficult to shape
based on experiment — no experiments
opinions testable — opinions untestable
conclusions obvious — conclusions dragged up
ulterior motive — no ulterior motive

The counsellor then drew three columns down a sheet of paper and asked him to give the ratings on each construct for (a) my preferred style of report, (b) the 'persuasive' report — 'persuasive' being the word he used to stigmatize bad reports — and (c) the report on manpower planning he was presently battling with. The picture looked like Fig. 14.3.

✓	PREFERRED REPORT	PERSUASIVE REPORT	PRESENT REPORT	✗
Clever	X	✓	X	Factual
Ego-trip	X	✓	X	Hard work
Dishonest	X	✓	X	Honest
Distorted scales	X	✓	X	Did not distort
Manipulative	X	✓	?	Straight
Objective	✓	X	X	Subjective
Factual	✓	X	?	Opinions
Number-based	✓	X	✓	Not number-based
Logical progression	✓	X	?	Difficult to shape
Based on experiment	✓	X	?	No experiment
Opinions testable	✓	X	?	Opinions dragged out
Ulterior motive	X	✓	?	No ulterior motive

Figure 14.3

In discussion, the counsellor adopted the approach of first looking for the good news. The client had come believing that there was nothing good he could say or believe about the report he had to write; now he could see that on a number of important constructs his rating of the present report corresponded to the rating of the preferred report.

The counsellor then suggested that they take each of the remaining constructs — constructs on which the present report differed from the preferred style and more closely resembled the 'persuasive' report — and see under whose control the issue was and whether it mattered. Counsellor and client reached the conclusion that whether the report was manipulative or straight was under the client's control to some extent. The client was convinced that the report would be subjective, because it contained only one point of view, and this amounted to subjectivity as he saw it. He thought that he could try to make the report discuss facts rather than opinions, and he was happy that the report would be number-based. A counselling breakthrough came when the counsellor asked what he meant by *logical progression – difficult to shape*:

INTERVIEWEE   I mean that a good report should have its own natural order.

INTERVIEWER   Could you tell me what that means?

INTERVIEWEE   A proper scientific report starts by setting out the hypothesis, describes the experiments you've done to test the hypothesis, asks whether the hypothesis has been upheld, modifies it where necessary, and reports conclusions and suggestions.

INTERVIEWER   I see. And you say that this report on manpower planning doesn't conform to this sequence?

INTERVIEWEE   It can't. I haven't got any hypothesis and I didn't do any experiments. So the thing doesn't have a shape.

INTERVIEWER   Could you think of any other way of presenting your conclusions so they'd still have a shape?

INTERVIEWEE   No, I can't. That's the way I've always been taught to do it.

INTERVIEWER   OK. Can I ask you some more questions about what you mean here, because it seems to be important – you've already said that without the shape you can't start work. If you wanted to write a report or do a talk about the life cycle of the mosquito, say, could you see a logical order to how you'd go about that?

(The counsellor wanted to get the client talking about 'narrative' reports as opposed to hypothetico-deductive ones.)

INTERVIEWEE   Oh yes. You'd start with the egg in the bloodstream, go on from its being hatched through to maturity, mating, the fertilized eggs, and death.

INTERVIEWER   You had no trouble thinking of that?

INTERVIEWEE   None at all, it's obvious.

INTERVIEWER   But you haven't recounted a hypothesis and an experiment et cetera, have you?

INTERVIEWEE   No.

INTERVIEWER   Yet it would be a good presentation, scientific, conform to your standards?

INTERVIEWEE   Oh yes.

INTERVIEWER   Does that tell you anything about your present report? Could you still make it a scientific report with relating hypotheses and experiments?

INTERVIEWEE   I see what you're getting at, but I'm still unhappy.

INTERVIEWER   OK, let's stick with the report on the mosquito for a moment. You said that you'd start with the egg, and go on until death, right? Can you tell me what assumptions you've made about your audience here?

INTERVIEWEE   Assumptions?

INTERVIEWER   Who did you assume the audience would be?

INTERVIEWEE   An audience of doctors, of course.

INTERVIEWER   Suppose you were giving a talk not to an audience of doctors, but to an audience of Red Cross workers who were collecting money for malaria relief. Would you set about your talk in exactly the same way?

INTERVIEWEE   I don't suppose so, no.

INTERVIEWER   What changes would you make?

INTERVIEWEE   I suppose I'd have to start by telling them about why they ought to listen.

INTERVIEWER   And what would happen if you didn't do that?

INTERVIEWEE   I suppose they wouldn't know why they should be listening. They wouldn't know that it was a matter that concerned them.

INTERVIEWER   So you might start by telling them something about the damage mosquitos do, the diseases they spread, that sort of thing. Would you be un-scientific or dishonest or acting with an ulterior motive if you did so?

INTERVIEWEE   No, I'd just be telling them why it was important that they listen.

INTERVIEWER   Can we go back to the report on manpower planning and ask what assumptions you've made about your audience there?

INTERVIEWEE   Got it! I'm writing for the Chairman and I'm assuming that he knows about the problem and already has some views about it. I can write a straight report but I've got to begin by telling him what the problem is and why he should be interested in it. I was getting hung up about not having done any experiments, but the problem is that I haven't set the scene and explained what the problems are before I start to talk about solutions.

There are two technical notes about this example. The first concerns the range of convenience of the constructs, an important issue that will be treated further when we look at full Grid in counselling. The interviewer examines whether a par-ticular construct discriminates between all possible elements in the set consistently – in this case is the construct *logical progression – difficult to shape* the same for reports in narrative style as for reports in hypothetico-deductive form? The counsellor produced an example of a narrative report to see how it fell on the construct, and a new area of useful discussion began.

The second note concerns the creation of new elements part-way through the Grid. In Example 12 we began with 6 reports as elements, and from the constructs elicited about those reports developed three new elements – MY PREFERRED REPORT, THE PERSUASIVE REPORT and THE PRESENT REPORT. Not only is this a perfectly legitimate action, it is very useful where you suspect that the client has a stereotype at the back of his mind (e.g., THE PERSUASIVE REPORT) but it is not sufficiently clearly defined to be used as an element at the beginning of the interview.

When you make comparisons of a limited number of elements very often one of them is an 'IDEAL' element – 'MYSELF AS I WOULD LIKE TO BE,' 'MY IDEAL JOB,' 'MY IDEAL BOSS' or 'THE WORST POSSIBLE SELECTION INTERVIEW,' 'MY LEAST FAVOURITE SHOP STEWARD,' and so on. The use of 'IDEAL' ele-ments here and in full Grid interviews presents the counsellor with choices.

14.8   Using 'IDEAL' elements

The major choice in using 'IDEAL' elements is when to introduce them into the interview – at the very beginning as one of the original set of elements, or after some constructs have been elicited and the Grid is being drawn up? Good rules of thumb seem to be:

1. If you suspect that the client has a well developed stereotype of what the 'IDEAL' means to him (e.g., 'I'm not the kind of salesman my boss thinks I should be,' or 'This isn't the job I was expecting when I accepted it'), then use the 'IDEAL' element from the start. If, however, you believe that the client has vague feelings about his likes and dislikes, but no clear picture in his own mind, then it is best to wait until some constructs have been elicited and then derive the 'IDEAL' by asking for the preferred poles of the constructs.
2. If you suspect that early confrontation with the very notion of the 'IDEAL' element would upset the client, leave it for a while and then introduce it. Some people actually have difficulty coping with the notion that MYSELF AS I WOULD LIKE TO BE is a legitimate question. If they are faced with that question too early in the interview they may never settle down.

You have also to think about how to describe the 'IDEAL' element. MYSELF AS I WOULD LIKE TO BE is nearly always better than MY IDEAL SELF. THE BOSS I WOULD MOST LIKE TO HAVE is probably better than MY IDEAL BOSS. THE GOOD INTERVIEW is probably better than MY BEST INTERVIEW. The art is to shape the phrase so to elicit an abstract ideal rather than a present or past reality which approaches the ideal, but is not the best imaginable. You may also want an element representing the best boss the client has had so far, or the best interview he has ever done, but when you ask for the 'IDEAL' element you should make it clear to the interviewee that he has to fantasize — he can if necessary imagine that a good fairy has given him one wish, or that a witch has put a curse on him.

In one or two of the interviews quoted from above we have used the 'fantasize about a perfect day five years hence' device. This is another useful way of getting 'IDEAL' elements elicited, particularly if you want the conversation to be about event elements. A good way to do this is to note down the various stages of the perfect day as the client mentions them and turn them into element cards; then ask the client to make a selection of these elements on the basis of how crucial they are to 'the perfect day' and/or how different they are from his present experience. You are then well set up for comparing some of these elements with some events taken from the present time, with the question: 'What are the barriers to getting there from here?' You will often find that the question 'fantasize about a perfect day' itself prompts the client to consider issues he had not thought of before, and puts him in a better frame of mind for counselling.

14.9 Full Grid with statistical analysis

In this kind of counselling interview a full Grid is elicited, processed by hand or by machine, and fed back to the client. Microtechnology is very much on the counsellor's side here; at the time of writing, a firm deciding to start an in-house counselling service could buy, for less than £1000, a terminal using a telephone coupled to a computer storing Grid-analysis programs which would process a Grid on the spot for a cost of less than £5. There is now no need to ask a client to wait while his Grid gets processed, and to come back in a fortnight, assuming no postal delays. Small desk-top computers involve a rather greater capital outlay, but have the advantage of low cost once bought and you are not dependent on finding a clean telephone line. Soon the options will be greater and the costs probably smaller; it should be possible to get Grid analysis by hand-held calculator before too long.

Many people will not have regular access to microprocessors; you could find yourself doing a Grid in a stranger's office, or you may do only a few Grids for counselling purposes. If you are in this position you need to ask (a) whether you have to do a full Grid to achieve the purpose of this interview, or whether you could be content with some of the earlier steps alone, and (b) if it is going to be appropriate, from the counselling and from the timing viewpoint, to break the interview into two parts, an elicitation stage and a feedback stage? Do not forget, too, that the conversation you have while the Grid is elicited can be as valuable as the Grid itself.

In the rest of this section we assume that you have access to a computer to analyse your Grid.

Under what circumstances would you use a full Grid? The following guidelines may be helpful.

1. When you need to look at the whole of a problem, or a large-scale problem that does not seem to revolve around the relationships between one or two elements alone. 'I'm having difficulty managing my subordinates . . . making decisions . . . doing my job . . . sorting things out . . . ' are the kinds of problems that probably need a full Grid, whereas 'I don't know whether to take this job . . . how to manage Jim . . . where to start writing this report . . . ' will probably require less than full Grid interview.

2. When you need to look at the interrelationships between constructs. You might believe that there are important stereotypes or prejudices that need examining: 'Women aren't suitable for promotion', 'I can make up my mind within three minutes of starting the interview', 'It's management's fault.' Even when the preliminary interviewing has not given you a hint that certain constructs may go together in a way that needs examining closely, you may find that where there are well rehearsed elements *and* well rehearsed constructs it is the interrelationships between the elements and the constructs that tell the client something about his perceptions of the world that he did not know before.

EXAMPLE 13

The client was a senior personnel manager in a large organization who had come for counselling because he was experiencing various personal and work problems. He knew that the rest of his colleagues treated him and his function with contempt; he had attended one of the Institute of Personnel Management conferences in the last five years and had 'been horrified by all the fancy things people get up to nowadays.'

These horrifying things included manpower planning, incentive schemes, training-needs analysis and appraisal systems! This was a difficult counselling assignment because it rapidly became clear that the organization would be better off without him, and he would probably survive longer if he were to leave. Only an excerpt is given below.

A. *Element-elicitation questions*

Two events where you have felt highly motivated.
Two events where you have felt like giving up.
A routine event you enjoy.
A routine event you dislike.
The nicest thing that could happen with you involved.
The worst thing that could happen with you involved.
The most significant thing that happened yesterday.

B. *Examples of constructs*

Getting attention from above — they do not notice
I enjoy doing — I dislike doing
I am confident of success — I am not confident how it will work
Getting people together — technical work

In the FOCUS-ed Grid it became apparent that there was a high degree of correlation between these four constructs. An excerpt from this Grid is shown in Table 14.3. Visual inspection reveals how closely correlated these constructs are. As part of the feedback process this correlation was put to him.

Table 14.3

Getting attention from above	5	4	2	3	1	2	4	5	They do not notice
I enjoy doing	4	4	2	2	1	2	4	5	I dislike doing
I am confident of success	4	5	2	2	2	2	4	4	I am not confident how it will work
Getting people together	5	5	3	3	1	1	5	5	Technical work

INTERVIEWER   It seems as if you say that you're most likely to enjoy doing something when you're getting people together, and getting attention from above, and you feel confident of success; and conversely you're most likely to dislike things that you class as technical work, that don't come to the notice of senior management, and that don't give you any feeling of being confident of success. Does that make sense to you?

INTERVIEWEE   Put so starkly like that it doesn't look very good, does it?

INTERVIEWER   What do you mean, not very good?

INTERVIEWEE   Makes me come across in a very poor light, I think.

INTERVIEWER   Well, that's not necessarily the full story, there's lots of other events in your work that we didn't put on these cards. Can I ask you if you can think of any technical jobs that you enjoy, or feel confident of success in, or bring you attention from above?'

INTERVIEWEE   Technical jobs? I quite like interviewing candidates for the management college.

INTERVIEWER   This is interviewing people who are nominated for the pre-middle-management course?

INTERVIEWEE   That's right.

INTERVIEWER   Let's make a new card, then, and see how you describe it on some of the other dimensions. You say you enjoy interviewing candidates for the management college, and you describe it as technical work — would you say that you're confident of success here?

INTERVIEWEE   I'm very experienced at it, yes.

INTERVIEWER   Is experience an automatic guarantee of success in this area, as you see it?

INTERVIEWEE   What other method have you got?

INTERVIEWER   Well, you tell me: as you get more experienced do you automatically do better interviews?

INTERVIEWEE   Not automatically, no.

INTERVIEWER   But you said when I asked you whether you were confident of success here that you were very experienced at it, as if experience automatically led to success. Perhaps you can think of another reason why you're confident of success here?

INTERVIEWEE   No . . . . put like that, I'm not sure I can.

INTERVIEWER   What exactly do you mean by success when you interview candidates for the middle-management course, anyway?

INTERVIEWEE   Successful interview? Keeping to time, making him feel at ease, making him relax, getting him talking, getting some candidates at the end to fill the places we've got with none over.

INTERVIEWER   Ah-ha. Just let me write that down here. Any other ideas of what success in interviewing candidates would be measured by?

(Detailed probing at this point failed to elicit any mention of success related to the improvement in performance of management or the business. The interviewer finally brought this subject up himself.)

INTERVIEWER   Can you measure your success in this area by anything to do with the quality of management who come out of this programme?

INTERVIEWEE   Oh, that's much too difficult. Very difficult to measure management quality like that.

INTERVIEWER   You can't look at your interview records and see whether you've done well this year or less well in selecting people who benefit from the course by becoming better managers?

INTERVIEWEE   No point. It'd only be a post-mortem.

INTERVIEWER   I see. Well, we may come back later and talk about this some more, but I wonder if we can go back to the computer print-out here. We were talking about the likelihood that you would enjoy something if it involved getting people together and getting attention from above, and you'd feel confident of success here; whereas you dislike things that you classify as technical work, that don't come to the notice of senior management, and you don't feel confident of success here. Does that pattern make any sense to you, in terms of your own experience?

INTERVIEWEE   I suppose it does, really, I see myself as much more of a coordinator than anything else.

INTERVIEWER   Are you happy about this?

INTERVIEWEE   Yes and no. I think it's the function I perform best, but I think perhaps I'm being asked to do things outside this function.

INTERVIEWER   Such as?

INTERVIEWEE   Such as the technical work we talked about, the manpower planning and job evaluation and that sort of stuff.

INTERVIEWER   And these are the areas where with one or two exceptions like the interviewing assignments we've just talked about, you're not confident of success.

INTERVIEWEE   That's right.

INTERVIEWER   What would have to happen to make you confident of success here, in these technical areas?

INTERVIEWEE   I'd have to go back to school, I suppose.

INTERVIEWER   You sound as if you don't like the sound of that.

INTERVIEWEE   No, I don't.

INTERVIEWER   Is there any other way you could be more confident of success in these areas?

INTERVIEWEE   I've got by so far with getting consultants in and hiring some of them on the payroll, but things are getting out of date now, and you look a fool when you go into a meeting with your own people and you haven't the foggiest idea what they're on about half the time.

INTERVIEWER   So you can cope with some of your difficulties by hiring people, but you're still left with a gap in your own feeling of confidence?

INTERVIEWEE   That's right.

INTERVIEWER   And the only other way of filling that gap that you can see is by going back to school, as you put it.

INTERVIEWEE   Right.

INTERVIEWER   What's wrong with going to school again? Seriously, I'd like you to tell me.

INTERVIEWEE   Well, how am I going to look at the next Board meeting when the Engineering Director and the Administration Director and the Finance Director and the Managing Director and all the other directors are there except me, and they say: 'Where is he?' and the answer's that he's gone back to school to learn his job a bit.

INTERVIEWER   That's important, is it? Is that what you meant when you talked about getting the attention of senior management?

INTERVIEWEE   Yes, I've only been on the Board for four months and it's still on sufferance. There's plenty who'd welcome a chance to kick Personnel off the Board again.

INTERVIEWER   What job do the Board want you to do? Is it a getting-people-together function they want from you, or are they looking to you for technical tasks as you've described them?'

INTERVIEWEE   If I stay at the getting-people-together level I'll become no more than a glorified administrative assistant to the Chairman. No, they want to hear how we're progressing with job evaluation, and the Administration Director has just sent me this clipping about a new American method of job evaluation that he would like my critical comments on, and some bright spark's done a confidential study showing that you're twice as likely to get promoted if you're a white male in this organization and the paper's come to me for comment and I can't pass it to anyone else.

INTERVIEWER   You seem to be telling me that you're stuck.

INTERVIEWEE   Not now, but give it another four weeks or so.

INTERVIEWER   Could you see this coming when you accepted the promotion to the job you're in now?

INTERVIEWEE   I suppose I could, but I didn't realize how lonely it was going to be, I thought I could cover up somehow.

INTERVIEWER   What do you mean, lonely?

INTERVIEWEE   I suppose I mean not being able to talk things over with someone else, and not being able to conceal my ignorance of these technical matters that have suddenly become so important.

INTERVIEWER   Do you feel bad about being lonely now?

INTERVIEWEE   Yes, I do. Lonely and cheated.

INTERVIEWER   Cheated?

INTERVIEWEE   Nobody told me what the job was going to be about, just like nobody did with all the other jobs I've been pitchforked into doing. Did I tell you I started here as a clerical officer? I got moved into personnel because my job disappeared in a reorganization and we have a no-redundancy policy here. So I found myself as a personnel officer trying to sort out a set of new work rosters that somebody in Head Office had put together without thinking what the effect would be in Scotland, where I was at the time. I got no training for that — nor for any of the other things I was supposed to do. It was just one job after another landing on Personnel's desk because nobody else could be browbeaten into doing something about it. If you stay long enough you get promoted because they can't think of anything else to do with you. I've just been around a long time and I can choose a decent wine and hold my drink properly, so I'm safe to be let out on the really important men.

The interview went on for a good deal longer, exploring his feelings about his job, whether he could brief himself sufficiently on the areas where he felt vulnerable without attracting unwelcome attention, what other sources of help he had, etc. By any outside criterion the personnel function in that organization was badly organized, and there were one or two reasonably competent people (the outsiders our client had brought in from time to time) who could have coped with extra responsibility, but were prevented from doing so by our client's defensiveness and his superior position. The counsellor here was in a difficult position; employed as a counsellor by the organization as a whole, he felt that this particular client (who had volunteered to come and see him) was personally unhappy and doing the organization harm. When, part-way through the series of counselling interviews, the client was offered the opportunity to take early retirement he took it, saying to the counsellor that the counselling interviews had made him realize just how big a gap there was between what he felt competent at and what he was being asked to do; and some months afterwards the organization and the client both look in better shape.

There are several methodological points illustrated in this counselling interview:

1. Testing the range of convenience of the constructs. You may find in your Grid two constructs that appear to sort the elements in exactly the same way, for instance:

| good | 1 | 3 | 4 | 2 | 3 | 5 | 3 | 4 | 2 | 1 | 5 | bad |
| Christian | 1 | 3 | 4 | 2 | 3 | 5 | 3 | 4 | 2 | 1 | 5 | heathen |

It appears on the surface, therefore, as if these two constructs mean exactly the same thing to the interviewee, as he has used them in exactly the same way; whenever someone is judged as *Christian* they are judged as *good*, and whenever someone is judged as *heathen* they are judged as *bad*. This is important information to share with the client, but first you should test to see whether the apparent identity is due to a mishap in the selection of element. So you think back to the purpose for which this set of elements was selected, and ask the interviewee whether he can name any more elements of this set which are rated differently on one construct from the other. The interviewee giving the pair of constructs above, where the element set was composed of people he would or would not take advice from, was asked: 'Can you think of anyone about whose advice you feel strongly one way or the other, someone we haven't mentioned so far, who you think of as good but heathen; or Christian but bad?'

Often people are surprised when you uncover an apparent identity between constructs, but the real counselling work — in the sense of holding up a mirror to the person's perceptions — does not start until you have asked for examples of elements that sort the constructs differently, or constructs that sort identical elements differently.

In Example 13 there were four constructs that went together in a closely correlated group. The earlier part of the counselling interview consisted of the interviewer testing to see whether these constructs did in fact occupy the same range of convenience and mean the same thing to the interviewee.

2. Picking out new constructs from the conversation. When the counsellor asked

for an example of an activity that the client classed as technical work but felt he did well, the client suggested interviewing candidates for the middle-management school; and he said that he felt confident of success here because he was very experienced at it. This is part of a new construct (*experienced in – less experienced in*) that the interviewer should write into the Grid, and later on get ratings of all the elements on this construct. The counselling interview took its next natural step, however, when the client appeared to be equating experience with success and could not, despite probing, give much further information about what he meant by success here.

3. Offering constructs. The interviewer here went on to offer some of his own constructs about what made a successful interview to the client to see if he could use them, but they were rejected. Constructs should be offered with care: they can give the impression that only this kind of construct is required and make the interviewee censor others. They may also present the interviewee with a feeling that the interviewer knows all the answers and is just waiting to catch him out. Good interviewers will often introduce offered constructs with phrases such as 'Some people might say that . . . ' or 'In your position another person might want to add . . . ' instead of phrases that directly imply 'You've missed some constructs, try mine.'

4. Counselling skill and style. An excerpt from a counselling interview with a stranger may not hold the reader's attention as much as if it were your own interview, but perhaps some of the pure counselling skill needed to do such an interview comes across in Example 13. A typical Grid counselling style may appear to be more interventionist than a purely reflective/active listening style, but most of the interventions are client-centred, in the sense that the interviewer is testing the range of convenience of the client's constructs. It is important to remember that the conversation you have with the client while the Grid is elicited may be more important than the Grid itself.

5. The contract. In Example 13 we had the difficult task of counselling someone who was unhappy in his job and was probably doing his organization harm. This is a nice illustration of the problems implicit in any counselling interview, though a full Grid interview is more likely to produce these problems simply because it generates a written or printed record that must be safeguarded. Example 13, therefore, besides illustrating the necessity of getting a good contract established and knowing for whom one is working, also shows the ethical dilemma that may arise when one is working for two masters – an organization and a person in that organization. Difficult though it may be at the time, it should be an unbroken rule that one person's Grid is not shown to another, and certainly never used in evidence against him.

In the next example we do not quote from the interview itself. Instead we take a FOCUS-ed Grid that was given to an experienced counsellor and record the thoughts the counsellor had as he looked over it. This is done to illustrate the way the counsellor looks over the Grid before feeding it back to the client, and we have a slightly artificial situation in that it is unlikely that the counsellor would not have been present during the elicitation stage.

EXAMPLE 14

The client was the manager of a management services department in a large firm. He complained of not being able to get on with or understand his subordinates. The Grid elicited used as elements his seven subordinates (E1–E7) plus himself, E8. He was asked to construe them in terms of how they behaved at work. The constructs elicted were:

C1	: theoretical	– practical
C2	: over the hill	– not over the hill
C3	: follows through well	– does not follow through
C4	: presentations are clear	– presentations are messy
C5	: career contracting	– career expanding
C6	: younger	– older
C7	: meets deadlines	– does not meet deadlines
C8	: unacceptable to clients	– acceptable to clients
C9	: rigid	– adaptable
C10	: female	– male
C11	: good judgement	– bad judgement
C12	: thinker	– doer
C13	: insider	– outsider
C14	: writes clearly	– needs editing

The constructs C6 and C13 were reversed by the FOCUS program. The completed Grid (Fig. 14.4) was then given – for the sake of this Example – to an experienced Grid counsellor who had been briefed on the purposes of the interview, but who had not been present during elicitation. Here are his thoughts as he looked over the Grid, deciding what his strategy should be for the feedback interview:

'Looking at the elements first, I can see that E7 is out on a limb – and so to a slightly less extent is E3. He obviously sees these two people as quite different from the rest of the team – altogether the correlation of E7 with the rest is still 71 per cent, so I must be careful not to over-interpret this. He sees himself as very like E6, I notice – they are correlated at the 96 per cent level – let's look for the constructs on which E6 and E8 are different. The only one on which they are different is C12 – he sees himself as more of a thinker, in fact halfway between being a thinker and a doer, while E6 is seen purely as a doer. I must ask him about that – I must ask him for some constructs that separate himself and E6, or ask him whether he really does see E6 as very like him and what implications this has got for the rest of the management team's relationship with him.

'Equally, he sees E5 and E2 as very like each other – they are correlated at the 98 per cent level. I must ask him for constructs that separate these two as well. It is a bit early to be speculating about this, but I wonder if he is only comfortable with people around him who are very much like him, and that is why he is experiencing some problems. Let's look to see if there are any clues by examining E7 – the element that is so different from the rest.

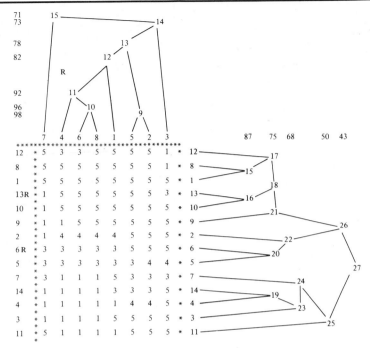

Figure 14.4

'E7 — well, on C10 E7 scores 1 and the rest score 5, so let's look for C10 — *female — male*. Looks like we might have a clue here — all except E7 are male. Must try to test to see if he has got a thing about career women.

'Let's have a look at how the constructs go together. We have got two distinct families of constructs, or three perhaps — C12 down to C9 or C5, and then C7 to C11. Two groups here that do not correlate until the 43 per cent level. Let's have a look at that group at the top. If I write it out, reversing C13, it becomes:

thinkers — doers

unacceptable to clients — acceptable to clients

theoretical — practical

outsider — insider

female — male

rigid — adaptable

'So in his thinking the ideas thinker–rigid–theoretical–outsider–unacceptable to clients go together, and are linked with the idea of female, though it would not be fair to judge him on this as he has only got one female working for him. Must ask him if other females he knows at work show this group of tendencies. At the same time if you are going to be acceptable to a client as far as he is concerned you must be a doer, practical, adaptable and an insider. If he is running a management-services department . . . I must ask him whether he is happy that they should go together, or can he think of occasions when it would be more acceptable to the client to be more of a thinker, more theoretical. I can see that he has rated himself as like the right-hand side of this group of constructs.

'The other thing that strikes me as I look at this group of constructs is that they are all evaluative — they do not say very much about how the people actually behave. Yet he appears to have very strong views in this area — all the ratings are 1 or 5, with very few 3s, no 4s, or 2s. If he is so definite in assigning ratings, does this mean that he does not give people much of a chance to show themselves before he assigns them to categories? I want to know, too, what behaviour he would want to show me to identify that someone as rigid or adaptable, theoretical or practical, a thinker or a doer. He was asked to construe these people in terms of behaviour, and he has given me a lot of evaluation. Perhaps if we look at the next group of constructs:

over the hill — not over the hill
older — younger
career contracting — career expanding

'The interesting thing here is that while he has given these constructs, he has rated everybody as younger or with expanding careers — no-one in his group is older, over the hill, with a contracting career. Of course, I do not know anything about his group, and if they are made up of sprightly 25-year-olds that could be true, but I would have liked to have been at the interview to watch how he behaved when he was asked to do those ratings — are the ratings really properties of the people or properties of himself, does he have hang-ups about age?

'OK, let's look at the last group of constructs, all associated around the 75—65 per cent level and quite strongly not associated with the rest of the constructs. We have got:

meets deadlines — does not meet deadlines
writes clearly — needs editing
presents clearly — presentations messy
follows through — does not follow through
good judgement — bad judgement

'These are getting to be more behavioural. Isn't it interesting that his behavioural judgements do not link in with his evaluative judgements? Must be careful about how I feed back that to him — this is important and he could see it as threatening.

'That's enough for starters. So when I feed back to him I will probably start with the similarity between himself and E6, and between E2 and E5, then go on to ask about E7 — concentrate there because she's different because female; then show him the two major construct groupings and ask if he can see the difference between the evaluative and the behavioural group himself, see if he asks himself the questions — if not, try to get the evaluative statements turned into behavioural ones. Then I need to get him to talk about client acceptability, I think, as the way into understanding the knot at the top of the Grid.'

This is an artificial situation, of course, because it breaks all kinds of rules about counselling Grids. But it does allow several principles to be illustrated about the inspection of FOCUS-ed Grid.

14.10 Points to note when inspecting a full Grid analysed by cluster analysis

1. Look for closely associated elements or constructs. These are used similarly by the client so *prima facie* they mean similar things. Ask:
   (a) is he happy that they mean similar things, or can he give you constructs that split similar elements, or elements that split similar constructs?
   (b) can he put some overall label onto each cluster?
2. Look for elements or constructs that are not well correlated into the rest of the Grid. These are seen as different from the rest of the elements or constructs. Inspect the body of the Grid to see where the major differences in ratings lie. Ask:
   (a) does this element or construct seem to the client not to belong to the same family as the rest, as he sees it?
   (b) is he happy to have things so?
   (c) if not, can he give some constructs on which a wandering element resembles the rest, or some elements which the wandering construct sorts similarly to the other constructs?
3. Look at the overall shape of the Grid. Does it look as if someone has sat on the construct trees and squashed them (i.e., are most of the correlations greater than about 75 per cent)? Or does it look as if someone has elongated the construct tree (i.e., are most of the correlations less than about 50 per cent)? In the first case you have a very tightly construed Grid, i.e., a change in one element or construct is likely to lead to a similar change in the others. In the second case you have a very loosely construed Grid, i.e., a change in one element or construct is unlikely to lead to changes in the rest of the Grid. Ask if this accords with the client's own views of his perceptual style, i.e., does he see things as all of a piece, or does he see things as not having much impact one on another?
4. Also look where appropriate for:
   (a) content analysis of elements and constructs.
   (b) rating of specific elements on specific constructs.
   (c) extremity of ratings used.

Summarizing the various ways Grid can be used in counselling, Table 14.4 covers the major issues and will serve as a guide to the counsellor on where to allocate effort if time is pressing, and on how to plan a programme of interviews so that issues are given a chance of being aired naturally. Of course, the Table is a guide that the experienced Grid counsellor may leave behind him; some of it undoubtedly reflects our own feelings about what we ourselves are comfortable with as counsellors. We asked some other counsellors who use Grid in industrial counselling to pass on their advice, and here are some of their comments.

Table 14.4

Stage of Grid procedure	Circumstances when this stage makes a major contribution to the counselling
Element elicitation	When the element set is unrehearsed, i.e., the client is asked to reflect over issues he does not normally reflect over or systematize
Counting the constructs	When the purpose of the interview is to define an area of ignorance. N.B. Present the stimulus question in several ways to ensure the client is not temporarily 'stuck'.
Content analysis of constructs	When the client needs to confront his own pre-dispositions to perceive along certain dimensions and not along others.
Full Grid with limited comparison of elements	When the problem hinges on a relationship between two or three elements and the other elements in the set have been used as fillers or distractors
Use of 'IDEAL' element	As a comparator to examine the client's perceptions of the differences between the real and the ideal, and as a basis for discussing what needs to change and how. Well rehearsed 'ideal' stereotypes can be brought into the original element set; less well rehearsed ones can be created part way through using elicted constructs.
Full Grid	Where the problem is one of the client's perceptions of or relationships with the whole or a large part of his environment; or when the counsellor needs to examine the interrelationships between constructs, e.g., when stereotyped judgements are being made.
Offered elements or constructs	When the counsellor needs to compare use of an offered element or construct with some already in the Grid.
General	(a) Be sure to look and listen; the conversation around the Grid elicitation may be just as useful as the Grid record itself. (b) In feedback, beware of construing another's construing. (c) Before any interview is begun, ensure contract, ownership, relationship and purpose have been decided.

'At first, I was surprised by the speed with which Grid revealed the problem to me, especially when I was using 'IDEAL' elements. I had to really rein myself in, first to make sure that I wasn't just seeing the problem as I saw it and not as it was for him, and secondly to make sure that we uncovered the problem at the right pace for him. After that I found that going through a comparison of (say) MYSELF AS I AM NOW and MY IDEAL SELF construct by construct, asking him whether the differences mattered and what he could do about them, was super because we could take the discrepancies one at a time and he could control the pace.'

'It's important to remember that the Grid you extract first time round is only the first take on what he thinks. You must feed it back, give him the opportunity to say: "Do I really believe that?", and change his mind.'

'The conversation that goes on around the Grid elicitation may be more important than the actual Grid record, especially if you are talking about areas that he hasn't examined openly before.'

'I find as an internal consultant that Grid is sometimes difficult to use in counselling because you ask questions which they think you should know the answers to. (Though in practice you often don't.) Under those circumstances I find it useful to wave my record sheets about and say: "OK, well you think I already know the answer, but for the sake of the record forms I have to ask you what it is . . . " and this way I have a licensed naivety which allows me to probe quite important beliefs and superstitions.

15. Counselling using shared Grids

A further use of Grid in counselling is to get people to counsel each other, using the Grid as a prompt. There are three basic approaches possible here: group construct elicitation, shared grids with 'right' answers; and shared grids about opinions and feelings. Each of the approaches uses a counsellor or facilitator to elicit the Grid or part of the Grid, from two or more people who are construing the same set of elements. The counsellor then arranges that the people shall share their constructs or their ratings of elements on constructs.

15.1 Group construct elicitation

In group construct elicitation, a group of people who have some reason for exchanging or negotiating their views with one another are assembled together in a room. Usually they gather around a large table, with the interviewer at the top of the table and able to use one or other of two flip-charts situated on either side of him. A typical use of group construct elicitation is as part of performance-appraisal training, where there is concern that managers may not be rating people on similar standards. In this case, each manager is given two piles of cards — a buff-coloured pile and a larger pile of plain cards.

The first stage is to elicit the elements. There are two ways of doing this; either the interviewer can ask each person individually to write on cards the names, nicknames, or initials of eight people he appraises plus himself (trying to cover the range of effectiveness). Or the group can be asked to call out the names of people at work — these names are written on one flip-chart — and then from the large number of names a smaller group is selected on the criterion that each member of that group is known to all or most of the people there.

Elements having been elicted and written on cards, the interviewer then introduces the notion of constructs elicitation by writing on one flip-chart the names of three well known people, and asking the question: 'In what way are two of these people alike and different from the third?'. The resulting constructs are written on the other flip-chart; this gives the interviewer the opportunity to point out that constructs should be bipolar, they can take different forms (propositional, evaluative, behavioural, etc.), they should be written down with the pair to the left and the singleton to the right, etc. This procedure should be carried on until everyone has got the idea of construct elicitation.

They are then told to do exactly the same thing with the people they have written on their buff cards, taking them three at a time with the question: 'In what way are two of these people like each other and different from the third in terms of how they go about their work?'. They are to write each construct on a clean white card.

The interviewer writes up the sequence in which triads are to be administered,

184

and leaves them to work through until they are obviously running out of things to say. He encourages a range of constructs, and new constructs, where appropriate.

When the construct-elicitation phase has been completed, the element cards are destroyed. There are then two choices open – either the interviewer can ask each person to mark the preferred end of each construct, or he can wait until the next stage.

At the next stage all the construct cards are gathered to the top of the table and shuffled. The interviewer randomly picks out a card and asks which end of the construct is more associated with effective performance (for an appraisal project; for a management-team building project he might ask which end of the construct is more associated with being good to manage, or acceptable, etc.). The interviewer behaves in a way that indicates that open discussion is now required and people are to question each other about their constructs. Usually this is all that is required of the interviewer, and people will spontaneously start to counsel each other, give more information about their own feelings, extract information from each other, etc.

Group construct elicitation serves two possible purposes, and very economically may be made to serve them at the same time. One purpose is data collection; in the first part of this book we cited an example of the use of group construct elicitation for collecting data about how people view their colleagues and subordinates so that we could check the relevance of the appraisal system. The second purpose is that of team building, because people see the different ways other people have of viewing the world and come to share constructs and/or evaluations in a controlled way.

Some of the uses of group construct elicitation for team-building purposes include:

1. – With customers as elements, for team building in a sales team.
2. – With clients as elements, for team building in a consultancy team.
3. – With schoolchildren as elements, for team building among their teachers.
4. – With trainees as elements, for team building among the training staff.
5. – With 'cases' as elements, for team building among social workers.
6. – With products as elements, for team building in the design team.
7. – With faults as elements, for team building among the inspectors.
8. – With projects as elements, for team building among the service staff.

The advantages of group construct elicitation lie in the control it gives over the pace of the meeting. Everyone's constructs are in the pile waiting to be discussed, so there is much more evenness of contribution than in some other meetings where the high contributors can take over early; the anonymity of the contributions is obvious and people will find it helpful if there is a second round of data collection; and the fact that constructs are taken out one by one gives a thoroughness of coverage, and also gives an opportunity to take disagreements singly and in the context of previous agreements. All these advantages must, of course, be added to the natural advantages of Grid technique, and make it an excellent way of handling group discussions over matters of common interest.

To perform group construct elicitation, the only requirement is that all the elements must be of a similar class. For some purposes a common list of elements is agreed; for other purposes the interviewer specifies the class of elements — e.g. 'people you work with' — but leaves the actual names to the individual participants. However, we have found that noun elements are a great deal easier to use than verb elements, because it is usually easier to get noun elements as precise as necessary with little guidance. Where verb elements (events, activities) are used, and one or two people produce elements that are too abstract to be useful, it is difficult to refine the elements with the rest of the group looking on.

Physical manipulation of the cards is also important. Some people have been tempted to ask for the elements to be written as a list, with the group asked to 'think of elements 1, 4 and 7 on that list . . .'. Even a very bright and analytical group who are practised in the art of Grid will find this much more difficult than if they have the cards in front of them to move around.

15.2 Shared Grid with 'Right' answers

In this instance a full Grid is elicited from one person; the elements and constructs are left in place, but the ratings of the elements on the constructs are obscured. The Grid is then given to a second person to fill in, and the first and second Grids are superimposed on one another in a way that makes areas of agreement easily apparent.

In Figs 15.1–15.3, a Grid was elicited from a teacher of statistics, using as elements various statistical tests. The constructs are all propositional constructs, describing the characteristics of the tests and when they are appropriate.

Statistics Teacher's Grid	2-Sample chi-square	Student's t-test	Mann-Whitney u-test	Wilcoxon test	k-Sample Chi-square	Spearman's rho	Kendall's tau	
nominal measure								higher than nominal
ordinal measure	?				?			higher than ordinal
interval measure	?		?	?	?	?	?	higher than interval
parametric test								non-parametric test
two-sample test								k-sample test
related samples						?	?	independent samples

Figure 15.1

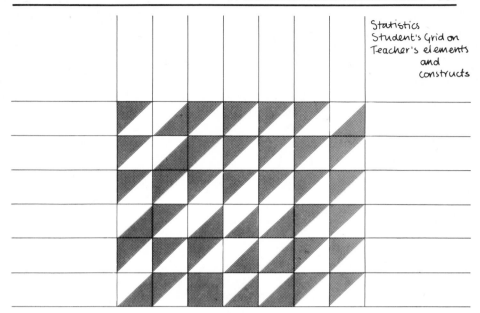

Figure 15.2

Statistics Teacher's Grid	2-Sample chi-square	Student's t-test	Mann–Whitney u-test	Wilcoxon test	k-Sample Chi-square	Spearman's rho	Kendall's tau	Statistics Student's Grid on Teacher's elements and constructs
nominal measure						?		higher than nominal
ordinal measure	?				?			higher than ordinal
interval measure	?		?	?	?	?	?	higher than interval
parametric test								non-parametric test
two-sample test								k-sample test
related samples						?	?	independent samples

Figure 15.3

For ease of presentation the tick-cross scale has been replaced with partial blocking-out of each cell in the Grid, according to the key at the top of each example. In Fig. 15.1 we have the ratings given by the teacher to the elements. These are 'right answers', in the sense that statistical tests represent a body of knowledge about which there is unanimous expert opinion; no expert on statistics would rate those elements any other way. The question mark is used to indicate Not Applicable — where the element cannot be rated on that particular construct.

In Fig. 15.2 we see what happens when the teacher's elements and constructs are left in place, and the student is asked to rate the elements using the teacher's constructs. Figure 15.2 gives the student's ratings. In Fig. 15.3 we see what happens when one rating is laid over the other; ideally this is done on an overhead projector, because the patterns then become very obvious indeed. Where there is a full black square, or where there is a partially filled square which also contains a question mark, the teacher and the student are in disagreement.

When looking at the results of a shared Grid it is important to inspect for lines and columns that are in disagreement; rarely is it for the case that the black squares are randomly distributed; much more often particular elements or constructs are causing difficulty. In this example, for instance, the two are obviously in disagreement about the last construct (*related samples — independent samples*), and the first and third constructs. Spearman's rho is giving problems, but the *t*-test is all right.

Using the procedure tells you different things at different times. The teacher could use it at the beginning of term, to test what the student already knew, so as to know where to concentrate her experience. Or she could use it at the end, in which case it would be more of a measure of her success as a teacher. In this case she used it part-way through the teaching term, and it gave her good guidance for the content of some revision lessons.

15.3 Shared Grids about opinions and feelings

This use of Grid in counselling begins in the same way as the previous example — a Grid is elicited from one person and then the second person is asked to fill it in using the first person's elements and constructs. Whereas in the previous example there were right answers, and we were mapping a learner's Grid onto an expert's Grid, here there are no right answers, only feelings.

Figure 15.4 is a Grid elicited from a trainer, A, in a medium-sized firm. He and the second trainer, B, were at loggerheads, and the managers in the firm were using this to their advantage ('If you want such-and-such, go to A . . . if you want so-and-so, go to B . . .) or were puzzled by the lack of coherence from the training department. The elements used were eight types of training course that they had been using. As before, Trainer A's responses were recorded by diagonally blocking off part of each square.

Trainer A's elements and constructs were left in place, and Trainer B was asked to rate the elements on Trainer A's constructs. Figure 15.5 shows the results here,

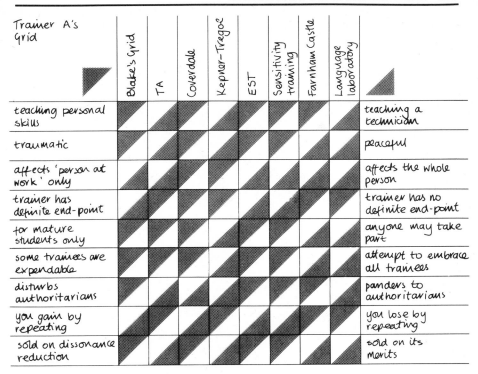

Figure 15.4

and Figure 15.6 shows the picture when the two Grids are laid one over the other. Again, the rule is to inspect for lines and columns.

The counsellor's role at this point, having laid the two Grids one on top of the other, is first to point to the good news — the number of white spaces on the picture, showing where they are in agreement. These two people were almost not speaking to each other, and would have had great difficulty volunteering any areas where they thought they agreed; yet here is a picture that limits and specifies the amount of disagreement, and puts it in the context of a fair degree of agreement.

The counsellor then indicates that the strategy is to inspect for rows and columns where there are disagreements, and to talk about them one by one. Obviously they are in disagreement about the construct *disturbs authoritarians — pander to authoritarians*, and about *some trainees are expendable — attempt to embrace all trainees*. They have different views about Blake's Grid, Coverdale, EST and Sensitivity training.

The counsellor can usually withdraw from active participation at this point; he may serve to keep them talking about one issue at a time, and he may record decisions taken, but usually the sight of the two Grids laid on one another is enough to get people asking question of each other.

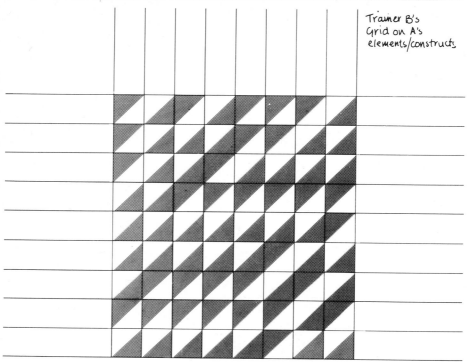

Trainer B's Grid on A's elements/constructs

Figure 15.5

In the case of our two trainers, they finished by trading actions; A agreed to have a fresh look at Coverdale and Blake's Grid, which he had formed adverse opinions about some years previously and had not kept in touch with; and B agreed to look at some of the more analytical and sceptical literature about training in interpersonal skills.

Some points to note about administering shared Grids:

1. The elements must be known to both parties. In practice this means that elements are people, objects or public events, but not personal activities or experiences. Part of the counselling purposes may be served by getting the two parties to agree on the elements to be construed.

2. A Grid can be elicited from A, and then given to B; or Grids can be elicited from both parties and swapped. Where A and B are peers it is better to elicit Grids from both; where B is a novice or newcomer it may be better just to elicit from A.

3. B can be asked to fill in the Grid using A's constructs as B believes reality to be for him, or as B believes reality to be for A. Either course of action is permissible, but of course they serve different purposes. Team building and co-counselling are likely to require the first method; negotiation training and advanced team building may require the second method.

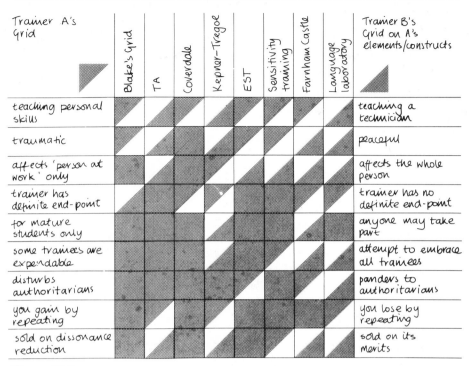

Figure 15.6

4. It is important to pay attention to how much B learns just by trying to operate with A's constructs, particularly when they are about feelings and emotions. So a brief talk with B about his experiences operating with A's constructs before proceeding to lay one Grid over the other is wise.

We have illustrated here the simplest technology for conducting shared Grids; lay one Grid over the other using shape- or colour-coding on acetate foil. Both the principal-components and cluster-analysis methods of computer analysis of Grid data offer programs where one Grid can be mapped onto another, in a way that allows much more subtlety of measurement than the simple visual presentation given here. The user must decide whether he is prepared to sacrifice immediacy for detail depending on the particular use he has in mind.

16. Some self-administered Grids

Finally, we offer the reader six ready-prepared Grid forms that have been designed for self-administration, or administration with minimum guidance from an interviewer. The topics vary from skill improvement to team building, and they are arranged roughly in order of difficulty. You might like to try these on yourself or a colleague, paying particular attention to the way the questions are framed and developed. This will help you increase your own skill as an interviewer in other situations.

16.1 Your customers and their needs

Good salesmen know what their customers needs are. It is no good knowing about your product, or knowing lots of fancy ways to close the sale, unless you know what your customer's needs are and can tell the customer how your product or products meets the customer's needs. This is an exercise designed to get you thinking about your customers and what their needs are.

How to do it

Begin by getting some 3 x 5 inch cards — 9 to 12 is a good number — or pieces of paper. Number each card in the top right-hand corner. Now think of some customers you have met lately and write down their names (or a brief physical description that will enable you to remember them), one name per card. Try to cover the range of your customers as you do this — have some that you were successful with and some you were less successful with, some routine ones and some unusual ones, some you liked dealing with and some you didn't.

Now take the customers 1, 2 and 3. Put their cards in front of you on a desk or table. Of those three customers, which two are most like each other, in terms of their needs? Write down on the record sheet what that need was, and what the third customer's need was that made that customer different.

For example, the customers might be Mrs Smith, Mrs Jones, and Miss Brown. The saleswoman works in a clothing store. She thinks that Miss Brown and Mrs Smith are most like each other because they both wanted clothing that would make them look slim, whereas Mrs Jones was different because she did not have to worry about her weight. The saleswoman writes down:

1, 3   needed to look slim — 2   did not have to worry about weight

Record the numbers of the customers who had similar needs on the left, and the number of the third on the right. Be sure to write down not only what the two had in common, but what made the third different.

You may be able to see more than one way in which two of your customers have similar needs and differ from the third. If you can, write it down in the same way.

You may be able to see different ways of pairing customers within the triad. Again, if you can, write it down but be sure to record the numbers of the new pair and odd-man-out.

Now take cards 4, 5 and 6 and do the same, trying to think of new needs for these customers. Record your answers in the same way. Then take 7, 8 and 9; 10, 11 and 12 if you have them; then shuffle the cards and take out more triads at random until you have between 20 to 30 distinctions or you are exhausted.

For example the saleswoman in the clothing store has a list of distinctions that begin:

1, 3	needed to look slim	− 2	did not have to worry about weight
4, 5	needed something that would wear well	− 6	needed something more frivolous
4, 6	needed something that would pack easily	− 5	was not worried about packing the garment
7, 8	did not care about fashion	− 9	wanted to be right up to date
1, 7	wanted bright colours	− 4	preferred dark colours
		etc., etc.	

Now take each of these distinctions in turn and ask yourself the following questions about each description:

1. How did I know that this was what the customer needed? What was I looking at, or listening to, that told me this was what the customer needed?
2. If the customer bought my product, what did I tell him or her about how the product fitted the customer's needs?
3. If the customer did not buy my product, could I have selected a better product to meet the customer's needs? Or could I have said something different about the way the product met the customer's needs?
4. What questions would you ask a new customer to find out if he/she has this need?

If you are training as a salesman or woman, or if you are a member of a sales team who have customers in common, you may find it useful to exchange views and see how other salesmen view customers' needs.

16.2 Your products − and your customers' needs

Good salesmen and saleswomen know that in order to make a sale they must know their products. But product knowledge is not enough; to make the sale you must relate product knowledge to customer needs. In a successful sale, the salesman questions the customer to find out what the customer needs, and then describes the key features of his products in terms that make clear how they fill the customer's needs.

In other words, a good salesman knows the *features* of his products; he knows how to describe those features in terms of *advantages* (things that are good about the product); and he knows how to relate the advantages to different client needs and turn them into *benefit* statements.

This self-administered exercise is designed to help you to identify what you know (and maybe what you do not know) about the products you sell. Then it goes on to help you turn this knowledge into statements of *advantages* and *benefits*. Doing this exercise when you have a moment to spare will help you when you have to sell to a customer.

How to do it

Begin by getting some 3 x 5 inch cards or pieces of paper — 9 to 12 should be enough. Number each card in the top right-hand corner. Then write on each card the name of one of your products or services.

Now pick out three cards at random. Put them in front of you on the desk or table, and see if you can think of a way in which two of these products are like each other and different from the third. Write down the feature that the two products have in common on the left-hand side of Box A on the recording sheet shown in Fig. 16.1, and the feature that makes the third product different on the right-hand side. In each case; use the line labelled 'F'.

Now take out three more cards and do exactly the same thing — think of a feature which two of them have in common but the third does not share. Write down your answer in line 'F' of Box B (see Fig. 16.1).

Go on pulling out groups of three cards at random until you have completed 12 to 20 comparisons. You may find that you can derive more than one distinction from any one triad — this is good, but please write additional distinctions in new boxes. You may also find that you can pair your products in different ways within the same triad — again this is good, but please write new distinctions in new boxes.

When you have finished this stage, check that you have written down your distinctions as in Fig. 16.2 (Example 1), in which the products are UK holiday resorts. You now have a set of product features as you see them, and you may want to check your list with a colleague's list to see if you describe products in the same way.

For the next stage of the task, write in the names or codes for each of the products you were using in the first stage, across the top of each box (see Fig. 16.2, Example 2). Now decide for each product whether it is more like the left-hand side of your description or the right-hand side. If it is very like the left-hand side, give a score of 1. If it is very like the right-hand side give it a score of 5. If it is quite like the left-hand side give it a score 2; if it is quite like the right-hand side give it a score 4. If it falls equally between left and right, score 3 (see Fig. 16.2, Example 3).

Has this told you anything about your product you did not realize you knew?

Until this stage you have been describing your products in terms of their features, because that was what you were asked to do. In the second line of each box — the line labelled A for Advantage — write the *advantage* that this feature gives a product. Sometimes both sides of your distinction can be viewed as advantages, sometimes only one side. Make sure you write down something for both sides.

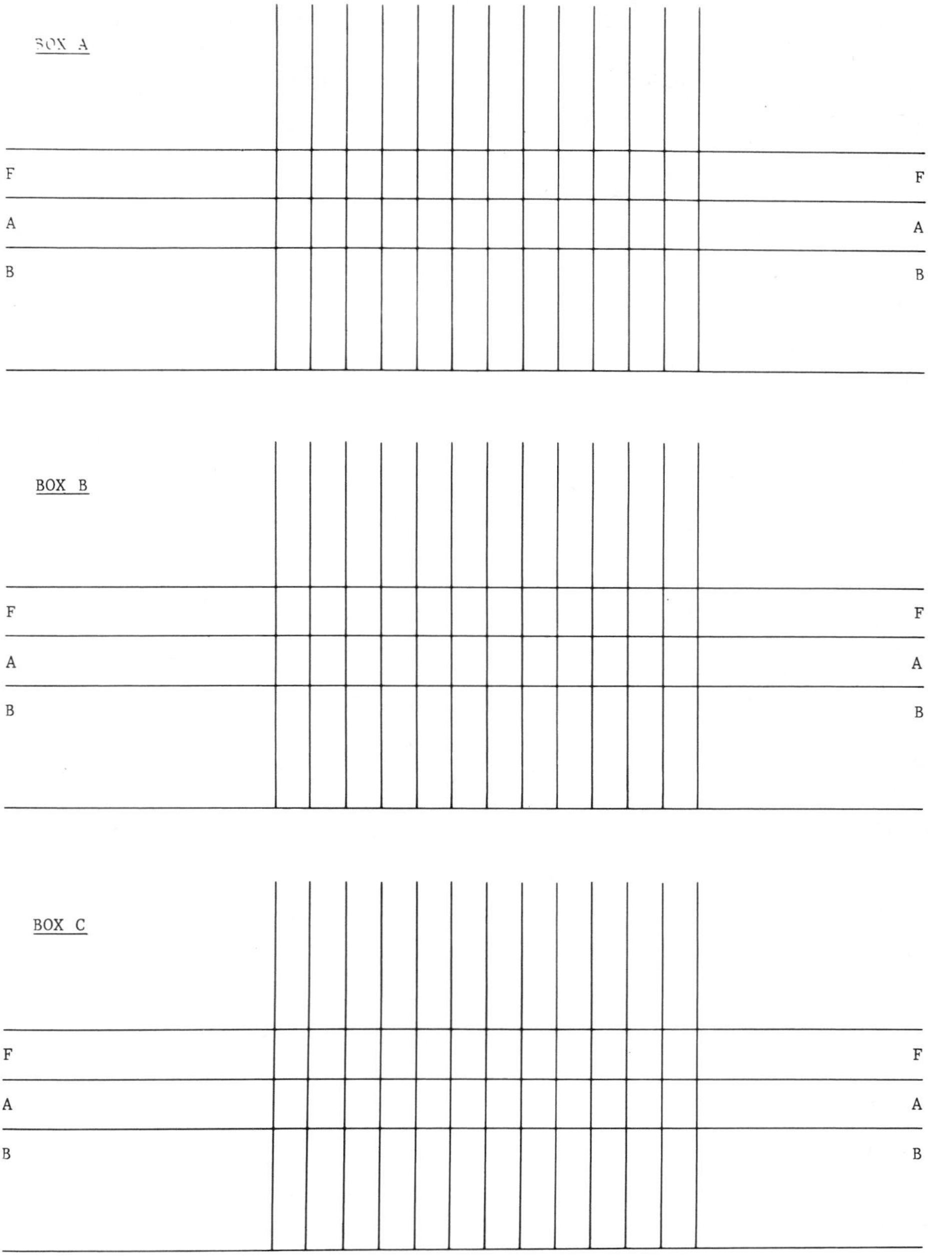

Figure 16.1

Example 1

BOX A

F Seaside													Inland	F
A														A
B														B

Example 2

BOX B

	London	Brighton	Margate	Edinburgh	Norwich	Yarmouth	Southend	Aviemore	Penzance	Skye	Mablethorpe	Bognor		
F Seaside													Inland	F
A														A
B														B

Example 3

BOX C

1	London	Brighton	Margate	Edinburgh	Norwich	Yarmouth	Southend	Aviemore	Penzance	Skye	Mablethorpe	Bognor	5	
F Seaside	5	1	1	4	5	1	1	1	1	3	1	1	Inland	F
A														A
B														B

Figure 16.2

BOX A

	1	London	Brighton	Margate	Edinburgh	Norwich	Yarmouth	Southend	Aviemore	Penzance	Skye	Mablethorpe	Bognor	5	
F	Seaside	5	1	1	4	5	1	1	1	1	3	1	1	Inland	F
A	You can sunbathe & swim	4	2	1	5	4	1	1	1	2	3	1	1	You can go sightseeing	A
B	Families. People who spend time indoors													Young couples without children. People who live at the seaside already.	B

BOX B

	1													5	
F	Quiet	5	4	3	4	2	4	4	4	2	1	2	3	Noisy and busy	F
A	You can relax, sleep, doze	5	5	2	3	2	5	4	4	2	1	3	3	Dancing, discos	A
B	Older people. People who've been ill. People wanting to get away													Younger people. Athletic types	B

BOX C

	1													5	
F	Sports places	3	3	4	3	4	4	3	1	3	5	4	4	No sports facilities	F
A	Games and sports	3	3	4	3	4	4	3	1	3	5	4	4	No games & sports	A
B	Keep-fit enthusiasts. Sporty types													People who want somewhere quiet	B

Figure 16.3

You have rated the products from 1 to 5 in terms of each feature statement. Do the ratings stay the same when you rate the products in terms of their advantages? If not, does this make you change the way you think about product features or advantages?

Finally, remember that a product advantage has to be turned into a *benefit* before the customer will buy. You should do more than say what is good about your product; you should what is good about your product for the particular customer you are seeing. To help you turn advantage-statements into benefit-statements, look at each advantage-statement you have made, and think of a customer who would find that advantage a benefit. You should work at both the left-hand and the right-hand side of the advantage statements. So you will write about one type of customer on the left, and a different one on the right. Customers are different, and what one customer finds appealing another finds off-putting. You should find that your sensitivity to different customer needs increases as you try to think of different customers' evaluations of the features of your products. You can write down specific customer names, or you can write about types of customer. Fig. 16.3 shows completed boxes for three different constructs.

If you are still training to be a salesman you may want to show your results to a sales trainer. If you are a part of a sales team selling similar products to similar customers you may find it useful to share your results and discuss them with your colleagues. You may also wish to keep this exercise as a record and repeat it in a few months' time.

16.3 How much do you know?

This is a test of professional knowledge — with a difference. Instead of setting you lots of questions to answer, this exercise makes you think of *everything* you know about the subject-matter. There's no question-master, and no score card — just yourself to compete against.

How to do it

Take nine 3 x 5 inch cards or pieces of paper. Now you have to think of the kind of topic you are going to quiz yourself about. It should be of direct personal relevance to you and something you have to know about to do your job. For example:

1. If you were a safety officer, the topic might be ACCIDENTS.
2. If you were a salesman, the topic might be PRODUCTS.
3. If you were an industrial-relations expert, the topic might be UNIONS.
4. If you were a store buyer, the topic might be PRODUCTS I AM OFFERED.
5. If you were a teacher, the topic might be METHODS OF INSTRUCTION.
6. If you were a travel agent, the topic might be HOLIDAY RESORTS.

Think first of the class of topic; then think of nine examples within that class of topic, and write their names one to a card. (The travel agent, for example, might write down: **PARIS, MAJORCA, SEYCHELLES, LONDON, MEXICO, TENERIFE,**

PRAGUE, ICELAND, TANGIERS). Make sure that you have a homogeneous set — do not mix topics from different classes.

Now take the first three cards. Think about the elements that they represent. Can you think of something that two of them have in common that makes them different from the third? (The travel agent might think that MAJORCA and SEYCHELLES are similar because they are both open-air holidays, whereas PARIS is a city holiday). Write down your answer on a record sheet, such as that shown in Fig. 16.4. Think of as many ways in which two are like each other and different from the third as you can. This may mean that you choose different pairs within the same triad — fine.

THESE TOPICS ARE SIMILAR BECAUSE:	AND THIS ONE IS DIFFERENT BECAUSE:

Figure 16.4

When you have exhausted the first triad, go on until you have completed the following sequence:

$$123 \quad 456 \quad 789 \quad 147 \quad 258 \quad 369$$
$$159 \quad 267 \quad 348 \quad 169 \quad 248 \quad 357$$

Your object is to think of as many differences as you can between the topics, using this structure to help you. Go on until you can think of nothing further.

When you have paused a while, look over your answers. Can you group your differentiations into subject areas? so some subject areas seem to predominate? How do your answers compare with your colleagues when they try to beat you? Can you or your colleagues look at your answers and point to areas where your knowledge is deficient?

Try this exercise several times. It is especially useful when you are part way through studying a new topic area and want to test what you have learned so far before going further.

16.4 Reflections on selection

Selection interviewing is not easy. Good selection interviewers know what they are looking for and how to control the progress of the interview so that they discover the right things. Often it is difficult to reflect on what you did and how you did it. If you spend some time doing the exercise outlined below you may gain new insights into your views on selection interviewing. This is particularly useful if you are at the start of interview training, though you must have had some previous experience for the exercise to work.

How to do it

Begin by getting nine 3 x 5 inch cards or small pieces of paper. Number them from 1 to 9, in the top right-hand corner.

For the next stage you must think back to selection interviews you have conducted. Think of three that you believe you handled well, three that you believe you did not handle well, and three that you believe you handled fairly well. On each card write a short phrase that will enable you to identify the interview. You should have nine cards, each with a name or phrase referring to a specific interview.

For example, Bob recruits salesmen for a big organization. He writes on his cards the name of the interviewee when he can remember it, if not a brief phrase to remind him:

> 1 — Alan Jones
> 2 — Dorothy Francis
> 3 — Man from Plymouth with red hair
> 4 — Man with feet on desk
> 5 — Jenny
> 6 — Agency woman last Monday
> 7 — Derek Brown
> 8 — Howard
> 9 — Steve who bit his nails

It does not matter what phrase you use to remind you of the interview, as nobody but you yourself will see your cards. You should however make sure that you have specific interviews in mind, not just general descriptions.

Now take the first three cards and put them in front of you on a desk or table. Think about the interviews and what you were trying to achieve in them; think about how you set about achieving these ends. Then ask yourself if you can see something that two of these interviews have in common that makes them different from the third. Write down what the two have in common, and what makes the third different, on a sheet of paper ruled up as in Fig. 16.5.

For example, Bob thinks that interviews 1 and 3 have in common the fact that he was interviewing experienced salesmen, whereas in interview 2 he was interviewing someone with no sales experience. So he writes:

1,3   interviewee had sales experience — 2   interviewee had no sales experience

THESE TWO INTERVIEWS WERE ALIKE BECAUSE:	AND THIS ONE WAS DIFFERENT BECAUSE:

Figure 16.5

You should try to write the feature common to the pair of interviews on the left and the feature which makes the *odd one* different on the right. You may see more than one way in which your pair of interviews are similar and different from the third.

Bob also thinks that interviews 1 and 3 have in common the fact that he felt in control of the interview, whereas in interview 2 he felt he had less control. So he writes:

1, 3   I felt I had control − 2   I felt less in control

You may also find that within your group of three you can see different pairs. If you can do this, write the distinctions down in the same way.

For example, Bob thinks that 1 and 2 have in common the fact that the interviewee was very relaxed to begin with, whereas in 3 he had to work to get the interviewee relaxed. So he writes:

1, 2   interviewee was relaxed − 3   I had to make him relax

When you cannot think of any more differences and similarities within the first three interviews, go on to look at the next three, recording your answers in the same way. You will find that sometimes the answers are the same as before, but you should be able to find out something new about each group of three. Go on until you have been through the following list of triads:

123   456   789   147   258   369
159   267   348   169   248   357

Now look at your list of paired statements. Forget about the interviews they came from for the moment. Ask yourself questions about the paired statements:

1. Most people find that the differentiations they make can be classified as 'means', 'ends', or 'environment'. (A 'means' differentiation describes the way the interview was conducted, e.g., *I asked open questions − I asked closed questions*. An

'ends' differentiation described what the interviewer was trying to achieve in the interview, e.g., *trying to make him relax — no need to relax him*. And an 'environment' differentiation described the external circumstances relating to the interview, e.g., *in the office — out of the office*.) Can you classify your differentiations in the same way?

2. Look at your 'means' differentiations. You may find it helpful to re-write them on a sheet of paper (see Fig. 16.6). Take each side of each differentiation in turn and write underneath it as many purposes as you can think of for doing this in an interview.

For example, one of Bob's 'means' differentiations is:

I started at the Application Form   — I started by asking him to tell me about himself

and he writes underneath:

— when I want to control the flow   — when he looks nervous and I want him to relax

— when I disbelieve the form
etc., etc.

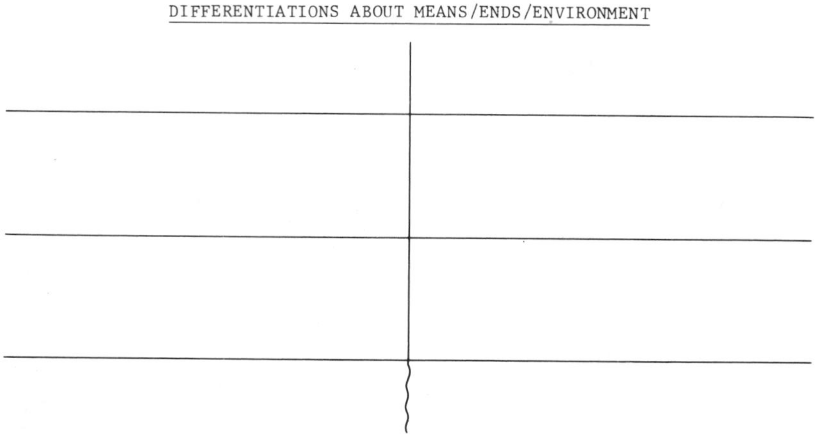

DIFFERENTIATIONS ABOUT MEANS/ENDS/ENVIRONMENT

Figure 16.6

3. Look at your 'ends' differentiations. You may find it helpful to re-write them on a sheet of paper (see Fig. 16.6). Take each side of the differentiation in turn and write down underneath it as many ways as you can think of for achieving this end in an interview.

For example, one of Bob's 'ends' differentiations is:

Trying to entice him on board   — Trying to put him off joining us and he writes underneath:

— tell him the good points about the job	— make the job sound difficult
— tell him how the job meets his skills	— do not commit myself at the interview
— make a date for the second interview now	
etc., etc.	

Think hard about this part of the exercise. Most selection interviewers know what they want to achieve but have not often written down or thought hard about how they achieve these ends. Trying to look at ends and means together may help you clarify what you already know, or detect some training needs.

4. Look at your 'environment' differentiations. You may find it helpful to re-write them on a sheet of paper (see Fig. 16.6). Take each side of each differentiation in turn and write underneath what difference it makes to the way you do the interview.

For example, one of Bob's ENVIRONMENT differentiations is:

Looking to fill a specific vacancy	— Looking for people in general

and he writes underneath:

— must work to the manager's specification	— work to a general man specification
— working under time pressure	— less time pressure
etc., etc.	

As you get more experienced at interviewing you should find that you have more differentiations about 'means' available, and more ways of getting to particular 'ends'. You can do this exercise again in the future, or you can use it as part of a training course.

16.5 Understanding motivation at work

Motivation is a very individual thing. What is motivating for you may be demotivating for one of your colleagues, whereas a third colleague may not notice it at all. Understanding what motivates *yourself*, rather than understanding motivation in the abstract, can be very useful. This exercise is designed to get you thinking about your own motivation. It may help you arrange and plan your work better; or you can use it to prompt a discussion with your boss or one of your subordinates.

How to do it

Take nine 3 x 5 inch cards or pieces of paper. To begin with, you are going to think back to events in the last year or so, and write very brief descriptions of these events on the cards — the time, place, person or purpose involved — not a long essay but enough to allow you to identify each card with a specific situation.

On Card 1, identify an event where you felt strongly motivated to do the best you could.

On Card 2, identify an event where you felt disillusioned, dispirited, demotivated.

On Card 3, identify another event like Card 1.

On Card 4, identify another event like Card 2.

On Card 5, identify a routine or regular event which you enjoy being part of.

On Card 6, identify a routine of regular event which you dislike being part of.

On Card 7, think of the nicest possible event that could happen to you, if you could have a wish from a good fairy prepared to grant your desires.

On Card 8, think of the worst possible event which could happen to you, if you were unlucky enough to be cursed by an ill-wisher.

On Card 9, identify the most significant thing that happened to you last week — not necessarily from the point of view of motivation, just the thing that stands out most in your mind.

Go back and look over your selection of events. They should all be events that involved you personally, rather than things done by other people that did not have you as an active participant.

For example, Ian thinks back over his last year at work and writes:

1 — introduction of TP 7 new product line.
2 — Performance-appraisal interview.
3 — Sales conference — presenting our results.
4 — Losing the UniMax order.
5 — Briefing myself on new product range.
6 — Filling in time sheets.
7 — Elected to the 100% club.
8 — Getting moved anywhere out of sales.
9 — Breakthrough with Jones Ltd.

Now, take the first three cards. Think about the situations they represent. Can you think of something that two of the situations have in common that they do not share with the third? Write down the feature they have in common, and the difference. Use a record sheet like that shown in Fig. 16.7.

For example, Ian looks at the first three of his situations and realizes that two of them had himself in the driving seat, whereas in the odd one out his boss was in the driving seat as he saw it. So he writes:

1, 3　self in the driving seat — 2　boss in the driving seat

You may be able to think of more than one way in which the pair of situations are like each other and different from the third. For example, Ian also realizes that in the pair of events he has put together he had planned his own part in the proceedings, whereas he had not prepared for his appraisal interview. So he writes:

1, 3　I had prepared — 2　I had not prepared

THESE EVENTS WERE LIKE EACH OTHER BECAUSE:	AND THIS ONE WAS DIFFERENT BECAUSE:

Figure 16.7

You may also be able to see different pairs within the same triad of situations. For example, Ian also realizes that events 2 and 3 involved things that had happened in the past, whereas he saw the first event as relating to the future. So he writes:

2, 3   past events — 1   future events

Record all your differentiations this way. Try to think about the circumstances of the events, and about your own feelings and actions at the time.

When you have run out of things to say about the first three situations, go on to the next triad. You will probably find that some of the differentiations you can make within the second triad are the same as the first; but you should be able to think of some new ones. Go on until you have done twelve triads, as follows:

123   456   789   147   258   369
159   267   348   169   248   357

For the next part of the exercise you need to concentrate on your list of differentiations. Forget for the moment the actual situations you were thinking about at the time — just look at your list of paired statements. Think about each statement in turn and ask yourself: 'In which kind of situation do I feel more motivated, situations that are like the left-hand description or situations like the right-hand description?' Mark your preferred side with a clear tick. Work your way through all the differentiations in the same way, but take it slowly — each time ask yourself why you prefer things this way. The harder you work at this bit the better you will come to understand something of your own motivation at work.

Now you have a map of your preferences, you can use it in several ways. For instance, you could look back at the last occasion on which you felt really demotivated and see how it matches with your preferences, using a cross this time to describe the demotivating event. Where the tick and the cross fall on different sides, reflect whether you could have had things arranged differently, and whether this gives you any guides for next time.

Or you could use it to rate your next assignment or project, looking to see whether there are any important features of the coming project that you believe will be demotivating, and asking how you can minimize their effect; and what you can do to maximise the effect of those features you find motivating.

You could also ask your subordinates or colleagues to do this exercise with you, and compare notes. Do you all find the same things motivating? (It is unlikely). Does the experience tell you anything about the style to adopt with different people, or the kinds of assignments they should have?

16.6 Looking at your colleagues

Few people enjoy working alone all the time and have the opportunity to do so. For most people working as part of a team is a regular demand their job makes on them. Yet everybody knows that there are times when one's colleagues are difficult to understand or get on with. This is an exercise designed to help you pin-point some of the areas where you and your colleagues may need to improve your understanding of each other. You can do it alone, or you can do it as part of a team-building exercise.

How to do it

To begin, you need some 3 x 5 inch cards or pieces of paper — one for each of your colleagues and one for yourself. Write the names of each colleague, one per card, and your own name on the last card.

Have in front of you a record sheet such as that shown in Fig. 16.8. Along the top write the names you have on the cards. (Fig. 16.8 is part-completed to help you).

Now take the first three cards. Think about the people they represent. Can you think of something that two of these people have in common that makes them different from the third, in terms of the way they behave at work? Write the description of the pair on the left-hand side of the first line on the record sheet, and the description of the odd one out on the right-hand side of the same line.

You may be able to think of more than one way in which the pair of people are like each other and different from the third. If you can, write the new distinction on a fresh line. Or you may be able to see different pairs within the same triad. If you can, write the distinctions down as before.

Write down as many distinctions as you can think of, from the viewpoint of how these people behave at work.

When you have finished the first group of three, select another triad and do the same. You may find that some of the distinctions are the same as before; in this case do not bother to write them again, but think of new ones instead.

Carry on until you have run out of ideas, or until you have between 20 to 30 distinctions.

The next step is to turn each of these distinctions into a scale. Think of the extreme left-hand end of your first distinction as 1, and the extreme right-hand end

1	John	Joe	Bill	Pat	Helen	Derek								5
see difficulty first	1	1	5	3	4	2								see potential first
proactive	1	5	1	4	1	3								reactive
mean with resources	2	4	1	5	2	4								extravagant with resources

Figure 16.8

as 5. Rate each of the people whose names are across the top of the form on this scale from 1 to 5. If the scale does not apply to a particular person, write 0. Be careful not to get confused — ask yourself whether each person is more like the left-hand description or the right-hand; if it is more like the left-hand, is it 1 or 2? if more like the right-hand, is it 4 or 5?

The next step is to think harder about the words you have used to describe each person. Take each person on the record form in turn; look first at person 1, consider how you have described him on each of the ratings, and ask the question: 'If I were showing a complete stranger this person at work with me, what would I show him to justify my rating of this person on this scale?' Think hard about this — it may lead you to examining some stereotypes and unquestioned judgements. Change the ratings, or the descriptions, if you want to.

Now in the far right-hand column, imagine and describe your ideal colleague, just by folding the paper and bringing the real one next to the ideal one. Look for areas where there are differences of 3 or more — these are areas where this colleague is very different from your ideal. About each of these areas, ask yourself:

1. Does is matter?
2. Can it be altered?
3. Who can alter it?
4. How can I make it easy for him/her to do what I want, in areas where I believe he/she is seriously impacting my effectiveness?
5. How will I know when things have changed?

You may find this a useful exercise to do with your colleagues. Work individually at first. Then share your ratings, either all at once or piece by piece. Look to see if you describe one another in the same terms. Where your colleague and you yourself use different terms in your descriptions, see if you can do the rating using each other's terms — do you use the terms in the same way? This may help you get greater insight into past misunderstandings, and new ideas about one another's skills.

Bibliography

Most books on Repertory Grid technique are written for the clinician or the professional psychologist. The industrial user is likely to find therefore that although the technique remains the same, the problems it is applied to differ from the ones discussed in this book. We give below a brief summary of the major books available on Grid technique, with a commentary for the industrial user.

KELLY, G. A., *The Psychology of Personal Constructs*, (2 volumes), Norton, New York, 1955.

The original work; probably not the book for the complete newcomer, but worth buying if you are going to use Grid seriously for counselling etc.

KELLY, G. A., *A Theory of Personality*, Norton, New York, 1963.

A condensed version of the earlier work, and a better place for the newcomer to start.

BANNISTER, D. and F. FRANSELLA. *Inquiring Man: the Theory of Personal Constructs*, Penguin, London, 1971.

Probably the best introduction to PCT and Grid technique, by two of the acknowledged experts in the theory and practice of Grid.

FRANSELLA, F. and D. BANNISTER, *A Manual for Repertory Grid Technique*, Academic Press, London, 1977.

An outline of Grid practice and analysis, full of useful ideas, and deliberately removed from PCT and the clinical world. In writing it, the authors recognise the demand for a book on Grid practice unrelated to theory, and satisfy the demand without prostituting the theory.

BANNISTER, D. and J. M. M. MAIR. *The Evaluation of Personal Constructs*, Academic Press, London, 1968.

An outline of some basic issues about Grid's method of measuring — reliability, validity, etc. — and how Grid techniques relate to other ways of measuring attitudes and perceptions.

ADAMS-WEBBER, J. R., *Personal Construct Theory: Concepts and Applications*, John Wiley & Sons, London, 1979.

Another good review of the technique and its applications; this book is stronger on non-clinical applications than many of the others.

BANNISTER, D. (ed.), *Perspectives in Personal Construct Theory*, Academic Press, London, 1970.

BANNISTER, D. (ed.), *New Perspectives in Personal Construct Theory*, Academic Press, London, 1977.

FRANSELLA, F. (ed.), *Personal Construct Psychology 1977*, Academic Press, London, 1978.

Three books containing papers from conferences of Grid practitioners; the quality is better than one often finds in collections of conference papers, and the Grid practitioner with some experience will find them well worth dipping into or studying in depth.

SLATER, P. (ed.), 'Explorations of Interpersonal Space', Volume 1 of a series *'The Measurement of Intrapersonal Space by Grid Technique'*, John Wiley & Sons, London, 1976.

SLATER, P. (ed.), 'Dimensions of Intrapersonal Space', Volume 2 of a series *'The Measurement of Intrapersonal Space by Grid Technique'*, John Wiley & Sons, London, 1977.

The first volume in the series contains examples of the application of Grid technique to a variety of problems, and the second treats the issues involved in analysing a Grid by principal-components and related methods. The first volume is likely to be more useful to the industrial user than the second.

FRANSELLA, F., *Personal Change and Reconstruction*, Academic Press, London, 1972.

An account of how Grid technique was used in the diagnosis and treatment of stuttering.

DUCK, S., *Personal Relationships and Personal Constructs*, John Wiley & Sons, London, 1973.

An account of how Grid technique was used to predict and measure the development of friendships.

RYLE, A., *Frames and Cages*, Sussex University Press, Brighton, 1973.

Using Grid to identify and treat the problems of university students.

HARBISON, J. and J. HARBISON. *A Society Under Stress: Children and Young People in Northern Ireland*, Open Books, Shepton Mallet (UK), 1980.

Contains examples of Grid used to demonstrate people's perceptions of the problems they face.

STEWART, A. and V. STEWART, *Tomorrow's Managers Today*, 2nd edn, Institute of Personnel Management, London, 1981.

Contains an account of the use of Grid techniques in the diagnostic stage of developing a management assessment centre.

All the previous five books are examples of Grid technique being applied to specific problems and are likely to be of interest to the general reader with a basic understanding of Grid and personal construct theory.

Index